# HEROES EVERY CHILD SHOULD KNOW

# HEROES EVERY CHILD SHOULD KNOW

EDITED BY

## H. W. MABIE

## YESTERDAY'S CLASSICS

### CHAPEL HILL, NORTH CAROLINA

This edition, first published in 2006 by Yesterday's Classics, is an unabridged republication of the work originally published by Doubleday, Page & Co. in 1906. For a listing of books published by Yesterday's Classics, please visit www.yesterdaysclassics.com. Yesterday's Classics is the publishing arm of the Baldwin Project which presents the complete text of dozens of classic books for children at www.mainlesson.com under the editorship of Lisa M. Ripperton and T. A. Roth.

ISBN-10:  1-59915-097-2
ISBN-13:  978-1-59915-097-0

Yesterday's Classics
PO Box 3418
Chapel Hill, NC 27515

# INTRODUCTORY NOTE

## TO

## "HEROES EVERY CHILD SHOULD KNOW"

THE endeavour has been made in this volume to bring together the heroic men of different races, periods and types; and in the selection of material the most attractive, intelligent and authoritative literature has been drawn upon. In cases in which the material selected belongs distinctively to the best literature, no changes have been made, although narratives have been abbreviated; in cases in which the material has a historical rather than a distinctively literary quality, the text has been treated for "substance of doctrine," and omissions have been freely made, and connecting words, phrases and even sentences have been introduced to give the narrative clear connection and completeness. In the preparation of the material for the volume the intelligence and skill of Miss Kate Stephens have been so freely used that she is entitled to the fullest recognition as associate editor.

H. W. M.

# ACKNOWLEDGMENTS

## TO

## "HEROES EVERY CHILD SHOULD KNOW"

The editor and publishers wish to extend their thanks and acknowledgment to the firms who have kindly permitted the use of material in this volume:

To The Macmillan Co. for selections from "Heroes of Chivalry and Romance," "Stories of Charlemagne and the Peers of France," "Old English History," "The Crusaders," "Father Damien: A Journey from Cashmere to His Home in Hawaii"; to Thomas Nelson & Son for material from "Martyrs and Saints of the First Twelve Centuries"; to J. M. Dent & Co. for selections from "Stories from Le Morte d'Arthur and The Mabinogion" in the Temple Classics for Young People; to E. P. Dutton & Co. for material from "Chronicle of the Cid"; to Longmans, Green & Co. for material from "The Book of Romance"; to John C. Winston Co. for material from "Stories from History"; to Lothrop, Lee & Shepard for material from "The True Story of Abraham Lincoln."

# CONTENTS

# CONTENTS

# PERSEUS

ONCE upon a time there were two princes who were twins. Their names were Acrisius and Prœtus, and they lived in the pleasant vale of Argos, far away in Hellas. They had fruitful meadows and vineyards, sheep and oxen, great herds of horses feeding down in Lerna Fen, and all that men could need to make them blest: and yet they were wretched, because they were jealous of each other. From the moment they were born they began to quarrel; and when they grew up each tried to take away the other's share of the kingdom, and keep all for himself.

But there came a prophet to Acrisius and prophesied against him, and said, "Because you have risen up against your own blood, your own blood shall rise up against you; because you have sinned against your kindred, by your kindred you shall be punished. Your daughter Danae shall have a son, and by that son's hands you shall die. So the gods have ordained, and it will surely come to pass."

And at that Acrisius was very much afraid; but he did not mend his ways. He had been cruel to his own family, and, instead of repenting and being kind to them, he went on to be more cruel than ever: for he shut up his fair daughter Danae in a cavern underground, lined with brass, that no one might come near her. So he fancied himself more cunning than the gods: but you will see presently whether he was able to escape them.

Now it came to pass that in time a son came to Danae: so beautiful a babe that any but King Acrisius would have had pity on it. But he had no pity; for he took Danae and her babe down to the seashore, and put them into a great chest and thrust them out to sea, for the winds and the waves to carry them whithersoever they would.

The northwest wind blew freshly out of the blue mountains, and down the pleasant vale of Argos, and away and out to sea. And away and out to sea before it floated the mother and her babe, while all who watched them wept, save that cruel father, King Acrisius.

So they floated on and on, and the chest danced up and down upon the billows, and the baby slept upon its mother's breast: but the poor mother could not sleep, but watched and wept, and she sang to her baby as they floated; and the song which she sang you shall learn yourselves some day.

And now they are past the last blue headland, and in the open sea; and there is nothing round them but the waves, and the sky, and the wind. But the waves are gentle, and the sky is clear, and the breeze is tender and low.

So a night passed, and a day, and a long day it was for Danae; and another night and day beside, till

Danae was faint with hunger and weeping, and yet no land appeared. And all the while the babe slept quietly; and at last poor Danae drooped her head and fell asleep likewise with her cheek against the babe's.

After a while she was awakened suddenly; for the chest was jarring and grinding, and the air was full of sound. She looked up, and over her head were mighty cliffs, all red in the setting sun, and around her rocks and breakers, and flying flakes of foam. She clasped her hands together, and shrieked aloud for help. And when she cried, help met her: for now there came over the rocks a tall and stately man, and looked down wonderingly upon poor Danae tossing about in the chest among the waves.

He wore a rough cloak of frieze, and on his head a broad hat to shade his face; in his hand he carried a trident for spearing fish, and over his shoulder was a casting-net; but Danae could see that he was no common man by his stature, and his walk, and his flowing golden hair and beard; and by the two servants who came behind him, carrying baskets for his fish. But she had hardly time to look at him before he had laid aside his trident and leapt down the rocks, and thrown his casting-net so surely over Danae and the chest, that he drew it, and her, and the baby, safe upon a ledge of rock.

Then the fisherman took Danae by the hand, and lifted her out of the chest, and said:

"O beautiful damsel, what strange chance has brought you to this island in so frail a ship? Who are you, and whence? Surely you are some King's daughter and this boy somewhat more than mortal."

And as he spoke he pointed to the babe; for its face shone like the morning star.

But Danae only held down her head, and sobbed out:

"Tell me to what land I have come, unhappy that I am; and among what men I have fallen!"

And he said, "This isle is called Seriphos, and I am a Hellen, and dwell in it. I am the brother of Polydectes the King; and men call me Dictys the netter, because I catch the fish of the shore."

Then Danae fell down at his feet, and embraced his knees and cried:

"Oh, sir, have pity upon a stranger, whom a cruel doom has driven to your land; and let me live in your house as a servant; but treat me honourably, for I was once a king's daughter, and this my boy (as you have truly said) is of no common race. I will not be a charge to you, or eat the bread of idleness; for I am more skilful in weaving and embroidery than all the maidens of my land."

And she was going on; but Dictys stopped her, and raised her up, and said:

"My daughter, I am old, and my hairs are growing grey; while I have no children to make my home cheerful. Come with me then, and you shall be a daughter to me and to my wife, and this babe shall be our grandchild. For I fear the gods, and show

4

hospitality to all strangers; knowing that good deeds, like evil ones, always return to those who do them."

So Danae was comforted, and went home with Dictys the good fisherman, and was a daughter to him and to his wife.

Fifteen years were passed and gone and the babe was now grown to a tall lad and a sailor, and went many voyages after merchandise to the islands round. His mother called him Perseus, but all the people in Seriphos said that he was not the son of mortal man, and called him Zeus, the son of the king of the Immortals. For though he was but fifteen, he was taller by a head than any man in the island; and he was the most skilful of all in running and wrestling and boxing, and in throwing the quoit and the javelin, and in rowing with the oar, and in playing on the harp, and in all which befits a man. And he was brave and truthful, gentle and courteous, for good old Dictys had trained him well; and well it was for Perseus that he had done so.

Now one day at Samos, while the ship was lading, Perseus wandered into a pleasant wood to get out of the sun, and sat down on the turf and fell asleep. And as he slept a strange dream came to him—the strangest dream which he had ever had in his life.

There came a lady to him through the wood, taller than he, or any mortal man; but beautiful exceedingly, with grey eyes, clear and piercing, but strangely soft and mild. On her head was a helmet, and in her hand a spear. And over her shoulder, above her long blue robes, hung a goat-skin, which bore up a mighty shield of brass, polished like a mirror. She stood and looked at him with her clear grey eyes; and Perseus saw that her eyelids never moved, nor her eyeballs, but looked straight through and through him, and into his very heart, as if she could see all the secrets of his soul, and knew all that he had ever thought or longed for since the day that he was born. And Perseus dropped his eyes, trembling and blushing, as the wonderful lady spoke.

"Perseus, you must do an errand for me."

"Who are you, lady? And how do you know my name?"

"I am Pallas Athené; and I know the thoughts of all men's hearts, and discern their manhood or their baseness. And from the souls of clay I turn away, and they are blest, but not by me. They fatten at ease, like sheep in the pasture, and eat what they did not sow, like oxen in the stall. They grow and spread, like the gourd along the ground; but, like the gourd, they give no shade to the traveller, and when they are ripe death gathers them, and they go down unloved into hell, and their name vanishes out of the land.

"But to the souls of fire I give more fire, and to those who are manful I give a might more than man's. These are the heroes, the sons of the Immortals who are blest, but not like the souls of clay. For I drive them forth by strange paths, Perseus, that they may fight the Titans and the monsters, the enemies of gods and men. Through

6

doubt and need, danger and battle, I drive them; and some of them are slain in the flower of youth, no man knows when or where; and some of them win noble names, and a fair and green old age; but what will be their latter end I know not, and none, save Zeus, the father of gods and men. Tell me now, Perseus, which of these two sorts of men seem to you more blest?"

Then Perseus answered boldly: "Better to die in the flower of youth, on the chance of winning a noble name, than to live at ease like the sheep, and die unloved and unrenowned."

Then that strange lady laughed, and held up her brazen shield, and cried: "See here, Perseus; dare you face such a monster as this, and slay it, that I may place its head upon this shield?"

And in the mirror of the shield there appeared a face and as Perseus looked on it his blood ran cold. It was the face of a beautiful woman; but her cheeks were pale as death, and her brows were knit with everlasting pain, and her lips were thin and bitter like a snake's; and, instead of hair, vipers wreathed about her temples, and shot out their forked tongues; while round her head were folded wings like an eagle's, and upon her bosom claws of brass.

And Perseus looked awhile, and then said: "If there is anything so fierce and foul on earth, it were a noble deed to kill it. Where can I find the monster?"

Then the strange lady smiled again, and said: "Not yet; you are too young, and too unskilled; for this is Medusa the Gorgon, the mother of a monstrous brood."

And Perseus said, "Try me; for since you spoke to me a new soul has come into my breast, and I should be ashamed not to dare anything which I can do. Show me, then, how I can do this!"

"Perseus," said Athené, "think well before you attempt; for this deed requires a seven years' journey, in which you cannot repent or turn back nor escape; but if your heart fails you, you must die in the Unshapen Land, where no man will ever find your bones."

"Better so than live despised," said Perseus. "Tell me, then, oh tell me, fair and wise Goddess, how I can do but this one thing, and then, if need be, die!"

Then Athené smiled and said:

"Be patient, and listen; for if you forget my words, you will indeed die. You must go northward to the country of the Hyperboreans, who live beyond the pole, at the sources of the cold north wind, till you find the three Grey Sisters, who have but one eye and one tooth between them. You must ask them the way to the Nymphs, the daughters of the Evening Star, who dance about the golden tree, in the Atlantic island of the west. They will tell you the way to the Gorgon, that you may slay her, my enemy, the mother of monstrous beasts. Once she was a maiden as beautiful as morn, till in her pride she sinned a sin at which the sun hid his face; and from that day her hair was turned to vipers, and her hands to eagle's claws; and her heart was filled with shame and rage, and her lips with bitter venom; and her eyes became so terrible that whosover looks on them is turned to stone; and her children are the winged horse and the giant of the golden sword; and her grandchildren are Echidna the witch-adder, and Geryon the three-headed tyrant, who feeds his herds beside the herds of hell. So she became the sister of the Gorgons, the daughters of the Queen of the Sea. Touch them not, for they are immortal; but bring me only Medusa's head."

"And I will bring it!" said Perseus; "but how am I to escape her eyes? Will she not freeze me too into stone?"

"You shall take this polished shield," said Athené, "and when you come near her look not at her yourself, but at her image in the brass; so you may strike her safely. And when you have struck off her head, wrap it, with your face turned away, in the folds of the goat-skin on which the shield hangs. So you will bring it safely back to me, and win to yourself renown, and a place among the heroes who feast with the Immortals upon the peak where no winds blow."

Then Perseus said, "I will go, though I die in going. But how shall I cross the seas without a ship? And who will show me my way? And when I find her, how shall I slay her, if her scales be iron and brass?"

Now beside Athené appeared a young man more light-limbed than the stag, whose eyes were like sparks of fire. By his side was a scimitar of diamond, all of one clear precious stone, and on his feet were golden sandals, from the heels of which grew living wings.

Then the young man spoke: "These sandals of mine will bear you across the seas, and over hill and dale like a bird, as they bear me all day long; for I am Hermes, the far-famed Argus-slayer, the messenger of the Immortals who dwell on Olympus."

Then Perseus fell down and worshipped, while the young man spoke again:

"The sandals themselves will guide you on the road, for they are divine and cannot stray; and this sword itself the Argus-slayer, will kill her, for it is divine, and needs no second stroke. Arise, and gird them on, and go forth."

So Perseus arose, and girded on the sandals and the sword.

And Athené cried, "Now leap from the cliff and be gone."

But Perseus lingered.

"May I not bid farewell to my mother and to Dictys? And may I not offer burnt offerings to you, and to Hermes the far-famed Argus-slayer, and to Father Zeus above?"

"You shall not bid farewell to your mother, lest your heart relent at her weeping. I will comfort her and Dictys until you return in peace. Nor shall you offer burnt offerings to the Olympians; for your offering shall be Medusa's head. Leap, and trust in the armour of the Immortals."

Then Perseus looked down the cliff and shuddered; but he was ashamed to show his dread. Then he thought of Medusa and the renown before him, and he leapt into the empty air.

And behold, instead of falling he floated, and stood, and ran along the sky. He looked back, but Athené had vanished, and Hermes; and the sandals led him on northward ever, like a crane who follows the spring toward the Ister fens.

So Perseus started on his journey, going dry-shod over land and sea; and his heart was high and joyful, for the winged sandals bore him each day a seven days' journey. And he turned neither to the right hand nor the left, till he came to the Unshapen Land, and the place which has no name.

And seven days he walked through it on a path which few can tell, till he came to the edge of the everlasting night, where the air was full of feathers, and the soil was hard with ice; and there at last he found the three Grey Sisters, by the shore of the freezing sea, nodding upon a white log of driftwood, beneath the cold white winter moon; and they chanted a low song together, "Why the old times were better than the new."

There was no living thing around them, not a fly, not a moss upon the rocks. Neither seal nor sea gull dare come near, lest the ice should clutch them in its claws. The surge broke up in foam, but it fell again in flakes of snow; and it frosted the hair of the three Grey Sisters, and the bones in the ice cliff above their heads. They passed the eye from one to the other, but for all that they could not see; and they passed the tooth from one to the other, but for all that they could not eat; and they sat in the full glare of the moon, but they were none the warmer for her beams. And Perseus pitied the three Grey Sisters; but they did not pity themselves.

So he said, "Oh, venerable mothers, wisdom is the daughter of old age. You therefore should know many things. Tell me, if you can, the path to the Gorgon."

Then one cried, "Who is this who reproaches us with old age?" And another, "This is the voice of one of the children of men."

Then one cried, "Give me the eye, that I may see him"; and another, "Give me the tooth, that I may bite him." But Perseus, when he saw that they were foolish and proud, and did not love the children of men, left off pitying them. Then he stepped close to them, and watched till they passed the eye from hand to hand. And as they groped about between themselves, he held out his own hand gently, till one of them put the eye into it, fancying that it was the hand of her sister. Then he sprang back, and laughed, and cried:

"Cruel and proud old women, I have your eye; and I will throw it into the sea, unless you tell me the path to the Gorgon, and swear to me that you tell me right."

Then they wept, and chattered, and scolded; but in vain. They were forced to tell the truth, though, when they told it, Perseus could hardly make out the road.

"You must go," they said, "foolish boy, to the southward, into the ugly glare of the sun, till you come to Atlas the Giant, who holds the heaven and the earth apart. And you must ask his daughters, the Hesperides, who are young and foolish like yourself. And now give us back our eye, for we have forgotten all the rest."

So Perseus gave them back their eye. And he leaped away to the southward, leaving the snow and the ice behind. And the terns and the sea gulls swept laughing round his head, and called to him to stop and play, and the dolphins gambolled up as he passed, and offered to carry him on their back. And all night long the sea nymphs sang sweetly. Day by day the sun rose higher and leaped more swiftly into the sea at night, and more swiftly out of the sea at dawn; while Perseus skimmed over the billows like a sea gull, and his feet were never wetted; and leapt on from wave to wave, and his limbs were never weary, till he saw far away a mighty mountain, all rose-red in the setting sun. Perseus knew that it was Atlas, who holds the heavens and the earth apart.

He leapt on shore, and wandered upward, among pleasant valleys and waterfalls. At last he heard sweet voices singing; and he guessed that he was come to the garden of the Nymphs, the daughters of the Evening Star. They sang like nightingales among the thickets, and Perseus stopped to hear their song; but the words which they spoke he could not understand. So he stepped forward and saw them dancing, hand in hand around the charmed tree, which bent under its golden fruit; and round the tree foot was coiled the dragon, old Ladon the sleepless snake, who lies there for ever, listening to the song of the maidens, blinking and watching with dry bright eyes.

Then Perseus stopped, not because he feared the dragon, but because he was bashful before those fair maids; but when they saw him, they too stopped, and called to him with trembling voices:

"Who are you, fair boy? Come dance with us around the tree in the garden which knows no winter, the home of the south wind and the sun. Come hither and play with us awhile; we have danced alone here for a thousand years, and our hearts are weary with longing for a playfellow."

"I cannot dance with you, fair maidens; for I must do the errand of the Immortals. So tell me the way to the Gorgon, lest I wander and perish in the waves."

Then they sighed and wept; and answered:

"The Gorgon! she will freeze you into stone."

"It is better to die like a hero than to live like an ox in a stall. The Immortals have lent me weapons, and they will give me wit to use them."

Then they sighed again and answered: "Fair boy, if you are bent on your own ruin, be it so. We

14

know not the way to the Gorgon; but we will ask the giant Atlas above upon the mountain peak." So they went up the mountain to Atlas their uncle, and Perseus went up with them. And they found the giant kneeling, as he held the heavens and the earth apart.

They asked him, and he answered mildly, pointing to the sea board with his mighty hand, "I can see the Gorgons lying on an island far away, but this youth can never come near them, unless he has the hat of darkness, which whosoever wears cannot be seen."

Then cried Perseus, "Where is that hat, that I may find it?"

But the giant smiled. "No living mortal can find that hat, for it lies in the depths of Hades, in the regions of the dead. But my nieces are immortal, and they shall fetch it for you, if you will promise me one thing and keep your faith."

Then Perseus promised; and the giant said, "When you come back with the head of Medusa, you shall show me the beautiful horror, that I may lose my feeling and my breathing, and become a stone for ever; for it is weary labour for me to hold the heavens and the earth apart."

Then Perseus promised, and the eldest of the Nymphs went down, and into a dark cavern among the cliffs, out of which came smoke and thunder, for it was one of the mouths of hell.

15

And Perseus and the Nymphs sat down seven days, and waited trembling, till the Nymph came up again; and her face was pale, and her eyes dazzled with the light for she had been long in the dreary darkness; but in her hand was the magic hat.

Then all the Nymphs kissed Perseus, and wept over him a long while; but he was only impatient to be gone. And at last they put the hat upon his head, and he vanished out of their sight.

But Perseus went on boldly, past many an ugly sight, far away into the heart of the Unshapen Land, till he heard the rustle of the Gorgons' wings and saw the glitter of their brazen talons; and then he knew that it was time to halt, lest Medusa should freeze him into stone.

He thought awhile with himself, and remembered Athené's words. He arose aloft into the air, and held the mirror of the shield above his head, and looked up into it that he might see all that was below him.

And he saw the three Gorgons sleeping. He knew that they could not see him, because the hat of darkness hid him; and yet he trembled as he sank down near them, so terrible were those brazen claws.

Two of the Gorgons were foul as swine, and lay sleeping heavily, with their mighty wings outspread; but Medusa tossed to and fro restlessly, and as she tossed Perseus pitied her. But as he looked, from among her tresses the vipers' heads awoke, and peeped up with their bright dry eyes, and showed their fangs, and hissed; and Medusa, as she

16

tossed, threw back her wings and showed her brazen claws.

Then Perseus came down and stepped to her boldly, and looked steadfastly on his mirror, and struck with Herpé stoutly once; and he did not need to strike again.

Then he wrapped the head in the goat-skin, turning away his eyes, and sprang into the air aloft, faster than he ever sprang before.

For Medusa's wings and talons rattled as she sank dead upon the rocks; and her two foul sisters woke, and saw her lying dead.

Into the air they sprang yelling, and looked for him who had done the deed. They rushed, sweeping and flapping, like eagles after a hare; and Perseus's blood ran cold as he saw them come howling on his track; and he cried, "Bear me well now, brave sandals, for the hounds of Death are at my heels!"

And well the brave sandals bore him, aloft through cloud and sunshine, across the shoreless sea; and fast followed the hounds of Death. But the sandals were too swift, even for Gorgons, and by nightfall they were far behind, two black specks in the southern sky, till the sun sank and he saw them no more.

Then he came again to Atlas, and the garden of the Nymphs; and when the giant heard him coming he groaned, and said, "Fulfil thy promise to me." Then Perseus held up to him the Gorgon's head, and he had rest from all his toil; for he became a crag of stone, which sleeps forever far above the clouds.

Perseus thanked the Nymphs, and asked them, "By what road shall I go homeward again, for I have wandered far in coming hither?"

And they wept and cried, "Go home no more, but stay and play with us, the lonely maidens, who dwell for ever far away from gods and men."

But he refused, and they told him his road. And he leapt down the mountain, and went on, lessening and lessening like a sea gull, away and out to sea.

So Perseus flitted onward to the northeast, over many a league of sea, till he came to the rolling sand hills and the dreary Lybian shore.

And he flitted on across the desert: over rock ledges, and banks of shingle, and level wastes of sand, and shell drifts bleaching in the sunshine, and the skeletons of great sea monsters, and dead bones of ancient giants, strewn up and down upon the old sea floor. And as he went the blood drops fell to the earth from the Gorgon's head, and became poisonous asps and adders, which breed in the desert to this day.

Over the sands he went, till he saw the Dwarfs who fought with cranes. Their spears were of reeds and rushes, and their houses of the eggshells of the cranes; and Perseus laughed, and went his way to the northeast, hoping all day long to see the blue

Mediterranean sparkling, that he might fly across it to his home.

But now came down a mighty wind, and swept him back southward toward the desert. All day long he strove against it; but even the winged sandals could not prevail. So he was forced to float down the wind all night; and when the morning dawned there was nothing but the blinding sun in the blinding blue; and round him there was nothing but the blinding sand.

And Perseus said, "Surely I am not here without the will of the Immortals, for Athené will not lie. Were not these sandals to lead me in the right road? Then the road in which I have tried to go must be a wrong road."

Then suddenly his ears were opened, and he heard the sound of running water. And at that his heart was lifted up, though he scarcely dare believe his ears; and within a bowshot of him was a glen in the sand, and marble rocks, and date trees, and a lawn of gay green grass. And through the lawn a streamlet sparkled and wandered out beyond the trees, and vanished in the sand. And Perseus laughed for joy, and leapt down the cliff and drank of the cool water, and ate of the dates, and slept upon the turf, and leapt up and went forward.

Then he towered in the air like an eagle, for his limbs were strong again; and he flew all night across the mountain till the day began to dawn, and rosy-fingered Eos came blushing up the sky. And then, behold, beneath him was the long green garden of Egypt and the shining stream of Nile.

And he saw cities walled up to heaven, and temples, and obelisks, and pyramids, and giant gods of stone. And he came down amid fields of barley and flax, and millet, and clambering gourds; and saw the people coming out of the gates of a great city, and setting to work, each in his place, among the water courses, parting the streams among the plants cunningly with their feet, according to the wisdom of the Egyptians. But when they saw him they all stopped their work, and gathered round him, and cried:

"Who art thou, fair youth? and what bearest thou beneath thy goat-skin there? Surely thou art one of the Immortals; for thy skin is white like ivory, and ours is red like clay. Thy hair is like threads of gold, and ours is black and curled. Surely thou art one of the Immortals"; and they would have worshipped him then and there; but Perseus said:

"I am not one of the Immortals; but I am a hero of the Hellens. And I have slain the Gorgon in the wilderness, and bear her head with me. Give me food, therefore, that I may go forward and finish my work."

Then they gave him food, and fruit, but they would not let him go. And when the news came into the city that the Gorgon was slain, the priests came out to meet him, and the maidens, with songs and dances, and timbrels and harps; and they would have brought him to their temple and to their King; but

Perseus put on the hat of darkness, and vanished away out of their sight.

And Perseus flew along the shore above the sea; and he went on all the day; and he went on all the night.

And at the dawn of day he looked toward the cliffs; and at the water's edge, under a black rock, he saw a white image stand.

"This," thought he, "must surely be the statue of some sea god; I will go near and see what kind of gods these barbarians worship."

But when he came near, it was no statue, but a maiden of flesh and blood; for he could see her tresses streaming in the breeze; and as he came closer still, he could see how she shrank and shivered when the waves sprinkled her with cold salt spray. Her arms were spread above her head, and fastened to the rock with chains of brass; and her head drooped on her bosom, either with sleep, or weariness, or grief. But now and then she looked up and wailed, and called her mother; yet she did not see Perseus, for the cap of darkness was on his head.

Full of pity and indignation, Perseus drew near and looked upon the maid. And, lifting the hat from his head, he flashed into her sight. She shrieked with terror, and tried to hide her face with her hair, for she could not with her hands; but Perseus cried:

"Do not fear me, fair one; I am a Hellen, and no barbarian. What cruel men have bound you? But first I will set you free."

And he tore at the fetters, but they were too strong for him; while the maiden cried:

"Touch me not; I am accursed, devoted as a victim to the sea gods. They will slay you, if you dare to set me free."

"Let them try," said Perseus; and drawing Herpé from his thigh, he cut through the brass as if it had been flax.

"Now," he said, "you belong to me, and not to these sea gods, whosoever they may be!" But she only called the more on her mother.

"Why call on your mother? She can be no mother to have left you here."

And she answered, weeping:

"I am the daughter of Cepheus, King of Iopa, and my mother is Cassiopœia of the beautiful tresses, and they called me Andromeda, as long as life was mine. And I stand bound here, hapless that I am, for the sea monster's food, to atone for my mother's sin. For she boasted of me once that I was fairer than the Queen of the Fishes; so she in her wrath sent the sea floods, and her brother the Fire King sent the earthquakes, and wasted all the land, and after the floods a monster bred of the slime who devours all living things. And now he must devour me, guiltless though I am—me who never harmed a living thing, nor saw a fish upon the shore but I gave it life, and threw it back into the sea; for in our land we eat no fish, for fear of their queen. Yet the priests say that nothing but my blood can atone for a sin which I never committed."

But Perseus laughed, and said, "A sea monster? I have fought with worse than him: I would have faced Immortals for your sake: how much more a beast of the sea?"

Then Andromeda looked up at him, and new hope was kindled in her breast, so proud and fair did he stand with one hand round her, and in the other the glittering sword. But she only sighed, and wept the more, and cried:

"Why will you die, young as you are? Is there not death and sorrow enough in the world already? It is noble for me to die, that I may save the lives of a whole people; but you, better than them all, why should I slay you too? Go you your way; I must go mine." And then, suddenly looking up, she pointed to the sea, and shrieked:

"There he comes, with the sunrise, as they promised. I must die now. How shall I endure it? Oh, go! Is it not dreadful enough to be torn piecemeal, without having you to look on?" And she tried to thrust him away.

But he said: "I go; yet promise me one thing ere I go: that if I slay this beast you will be my wife, and come back with me to my kingdom in fruitful Argos. Promise me, and seal it with a kiss."

Then she lifted up her face, and kissed him; and Perseus laughed for joy, and flew upward, while Andromeda crouched trembling on the rock.

On came the great sea monster, coasting along like a huge black galley. His great sides were fringed with clustering shells and seaweeds, and the water gurgled in and out of his wide jaws.

At last he saw Andromeda, and shot forward to take his prey, while the waves foamed white behind him, and before him the fish fled leaping.

Then down from the height of the air fell Perseus like a shooting star; down to the crests of the waves, while Andromeda hid her face as he shouted; and then there was silence for a while.

At last she looked up trembling, and saw Perseus springing toward her; and instead of the monster a long black rock, with the sea rippling quietly round it.

Who then so proud as Perseus, as he leapt back to the rock, and lifted his fair Andromeda in his arms, and flew with her to the cliff top, as a falcon carries a dove?

Who so proud as Perseus, and who so joyful as all the Æthiop people? For they had stood watching the monster from the cliffs, wailing for the maiden's fate. And already a messenger had gone to Cepheus and Cassiopœia, where they sat in sackcloth and ashes on the ground, in the innermost palace chambers, awaiting their daughter's end. And they came, and all the city with them, to see the wonder, with songs and with dances, with cymbals and harps, and received their daughter back again, as one alive from the dead.

Then Cepheus said, "Hero of the Hellens, stay here with me and be my son-in-law, and I will give you the half of my kingdom."

"I will be your son-in-law," said Perseus. "but of your kingdom I will have none, for I long after the pleasant land of Greece, and my mother who waits for me at home."

Then Cepheus said, "You must not take my daughter away at once, for she is to us like one alive from the dead. Stay with us here a year, and after that you shall return with honour." And Perseus consented. So they went up to the palace; and when they came in, there stood in the hall Phineus, the brother of Cepheus, chafing like a bear robbed of her whelps, and with him his sons, and his servants, and many an armed man, and he cried to Cepheus:

"You shall not marry your daughter to this stranger of whom no one knows even the name. Was not Andromeda betrothed to my son? And now she is safe again, has he not a right to claim her?"

But Perseus laughed, and answered: "If your son is in want of a bride, let him save a maiden for himself."

Then he unveiled the Gorgon's head, and said, "This has delivered my bride from one wild beast; it shall deliver her from many." And as he spoke Phineus and all his men-at-arms stopped short, and stiffened each man as he stood; and before Perseus had drawn the goat-skin over the face again, they were all turned into stone. Then Perseus bade the people bring levers and roll them out.

So they made a great wedding feast, which lasted seven whole days, and who so happy as Perseus and Andromeda?

And when a year was ended Perseus hired Phœnicians from Tyre, and cut down cedars, and built himself a noble galley; and painted its cheeks with vermilion and pitched its sides with pitch; and in it he put Andromeda, and all her dowry of jewels, and rich shawls, and spices from the East; and great was the weeping when they rowed away. But the remembrance of his brave deed was left behind; and Andromeda's rock was shown at Iopa in Palestine till more than a thousand years were past.

So Perseus and the Phœnicians rowed to the westward, across the sea, till they came to the pleasant Isles of Hellas, and Seriphos, his ancient home.

Then he left his galley on the beach, and went up as of old; and he embraced his mother, and Dictys his good foster-father, and they wept over each other a long while, for it was seven years and more since they had met.

Then he went home to Argos, and reigned there well with fair Andromeda. But the will of the gods was accomplished towards Acrisius, his grandfather, for he died from the falling of a quoit which Perseus had thrown in a game.

Perseus and Andromeda had four sons and three daughters, and died in a good old age. And when they died, the ancients say, Athené took them up into the sky, with Cepheus and Cassiopœia. And there on starlight nights you may see them shining still; Cepheus with his kingly crown, and Cassiopœia in her ivory chair, plaiting her star-spangled tresses, and Perseus with the Gorgon's head, and fair Andromeda beside him, spreading her long white arms across the heavens, as she stood when chained to the stone for the monster. All night long they shine, for a beacon to wandering sailors; but all day they feast with the gods, on the still blue peaks of Olympus.

# HERCULES

MANY, many years ago in the far-off land of Hellas, which we call Greece, lived a happy young couple whose names were Alcmene and Amphitryon. Now Amphitryon, the husband, owned many herds of cattle. So also the father of Alcmene, who was King of Mycenae, owned many.

All these cattle grazing together and watering at the same springs became united in one herd. And this was the cause of much trouble, for Amphitryon fell to quarreling with the father of his wife about his portion of the herd. At last he slew his father-in-law, and from that day he fled his old home at Mycenae.

Alcmene went with her husband and the young couple settled at Thebes, where were born to them two boys—twins—which were later named Hercules and Iphicles.

From the child's very birth Zeus, the King of all heaven that is the air and clouds, and the father of gods and men—from the boy's very birth Zeus loved Hercules. But when Hera, wife of Zeus, who shared his honours, saw this love she was angry. Especially she was angry because Zeus foretold that Hercules should become the greatest of men.

Therefore one night, when the two babies were but eight months old, Hera sent two huge serpents to destroy them. The children were asleep in the great shield of brass which Amphitryon carried in battle for his defence. It was a good bed, for it was round and curved toward the centre, and filled with soft blankets which Alcmene and the maids of the house had woven at their looms. Forward toward this shield the huge snakes were creeping, and just as they lifted their open mouths above the rim, and were making ready to seize them, the twins opened their eyes. Iphicles screamed with fright. His cries wakened their mother, Alcmene, who called in a loud voice for help. But before Amphitryon and the men of the household could draw their swords and rush to the rescue, the baby Hercules, sitting up in the shield unterrified and seizing a serpent in each hand, had choked and strangled them till they died.

From his early years Hercules was instructed in the learning of his time. Castor, the most experienced charioteer of his day, taught him, Eurytus also, how to shoot with a bow and arrows; Linus how to play upon the lyre; and Eumolpus, grandson of the North Wind, drilled him in singing. Thus time passed to his eighteenth year when, so great already had become his strength and knowledge, he killed a fierce lion which had preyed upon the flocks of Amphitryon while they were grazing on Mount Cithaeron, and which had in fact laid waste many a fat farm of the surrounding country.

But the anger of Hera still followed Hercules, and the goddess sent upon him a madness. In this craze the hero did many unhappy deeds. For punishment and in expiation he condemned himself to exile, and at last he went to the great shrine of the god Apollo at Delphi to ask whither he should go and where settle. The Pythia, or priestess in the temple, desired him to settle at Tiryns, to serve as bondman to Eurystheus, who ruled at Mycenae as King, and to perform the great labours which Eurystheus should impose upon him. When these tasks were all accomplished, the inspired priestess added, Hercules should be numbered among the immortal gods.

## THE FIRST LABOUR—WRESTLING WITH THE NEMEAN LION

The first task which Eurystheus required of Hercules was to bring him the skin of a lion which no arrow nor other weapon could wound, and which had long been a terror to the good people who lived in Nemea. Hercules set forth armed with bow and quiver, but paused in the outer wood of Nemea long enough to cut himself his famous club. There too he fell in with an honest countryman who pledged him to make a sacrifice to Zeus, the saviour, if he, Hercules, should return victorious; but if he were slain by the monstrous lion, then the countryman should make the sacrifice a funeral offering to himself as a hero.

So Hercules proceeded, far into a dense wood, deserted because all people feared the fierce beast it protected. On he went till after many days he sighted the lion at rest near the cave which was its den. Standing behind a tree of great girth, Hercules fitted and let fly an arrow. It struck and glanced, leaving the animal unharmed. Then he tried another shot, aiming at the heart. Again the arrow failed. But the lion was by this time roused, and his eyes shot fiery glances, and the heavy roar from his throat made the woods most horribly resound. Then the devoted Hercules seized his heavy wooden club, and rushing forward drove the lion by the suddenness and fierceness of his assault into his den. But the den had two entrances. Against one Hercules rolled huge stones, and entering the cave by the other he grasped the lion's throat with both hands, and thus held him struggling and gasping for breath till he lay at his feet dead.

Hercules swung the mighty bulk upon his shoulders and proceeded to seek the countryman with whom his pledge stood. So great had been his journey, and so hard his search, that he did not find the good man till the last of the thirty days. There he stood just on the point of offering a sheep to Hercules, supposing him dead. Together they sacrificed the sheep to Zeus instead, and Hercules, vigorous and victorious, bore the mighty lion's body to Eurystheus at Mycenae.

Entering the place and throwing the carcass down before the king, Hercules so terrified Eurystheus by this token of his wonderful strength that the King forbade him ever again to enter the city. Indeed some say that the terror of Eurystheus was so great that he had a jar or vessel of brass secretly constructed underground which he might use as a safe retreat in case of danger. This "jar" was probably a chamber and its walls covered within with plates of brass. For now in our own day is seen there at Mycenae a room under the earth, and the nails which fastened the brass plates to the wall still remain. Ever after the conquest of this lion Hercules clothed himself with the skin.

## THE SECOND LABOUR—DESTROYING THE LERNEAN HYDRA

The second task of Hercules was to destroy a hydra or water snake which dwelt in the marsh of Lerna, a small lake near Mycenae. The body of this snake was large and from its body sprang nine heads. Eight of these heads were mortal, but the ninth head was undying.

Hercules stepped into his chariot and his dear nephew Iolaus, who was permitted by the Delphic priestess to drive for him, took up the reins. The way to Lerna was pleasant. In spring-time crocuses and hyacinths sprang by the roadside, and in early summer the nightingales sang in the olive groves, vineyard and forest. That so great and horrible a monster could be near!

When Hercules and Iolaus came to Lerna they drew close to ground rising near a spring, and

Hercules dismounting and searching found the very hole into which the hydra had retired. Into this he shot fiery arrows. The arrows discomforting the snake it crawled forth and, darting at him furiously, endeavoured to twine itself about his legs. The hero began then to wield his mighty club. He crushed head after head upon the snake's body, but for every one crushed two sprang in its place.

At length the hydra had coiled so firmly round one leg, that Hercules could not move an inch from the spot. And now an enormous crab came from the water out of friendship for the hydra, and that too crept up to Hercules and, seizing his foot, painfully wounded him.

Swinging his club with heroic vigor Hercules beat the crab to death. Then he called to Iolaus to fire a little grove of trees near by. Iolaus at once set the fire, and when the saplings were well aflame he seized them and, standing by the hero, as fast as Hercules cut off a head of the hydra he seared the neck with a flaming brand. The searing prevented the heads from growing again. When all the eight mortal heads had thus been dispatched Hercules struck off the one said to be immortal and buried it in the roadway, setting a heavy stone above. The body of the hydra he cut up and dipped his arrows in the gall, which was so full of poison that the least scratch from such an arrow would bring certain death.

Eurystheus received the news of the destruction of the water snake with bad grace. He claimed that Hercules had not destroyed the monster alone, but only with the assistance of Iolaus. All the people, however, rejoiced greatly, and they hastened to drain the marsh where the hydra had dwelt so that never again could such an enemy abide upon their lands.

## THE THIRD LABOUR—CAPTURING THE ARCADIAN HIND

In the days in which Hercules lived, Arcadia was a beautiful country of cool, sweet-scented woods, clear mountain streams, and sloping meadow-sides from which rose every now and then the roof of a hunter's cottage or a shepherd's hutch. It was a country also peculiarly pleasing to Artemis, the goddess of the chase, and peculiarly also it was the haunt of all animals especially dear to the goddess.

A hind was there of such loveliness and grace that Artemis had marked her for her own, and given her a pair of golden horns so that she might be known from all other deer and her life thus preserved. For no good Hellen, or Greek, would slay for food any animal sacred to a god. This beautiful golden-horned hind Eurystheus ordered Hercules to bring to him alive, for the irreverence of the King did not go so far as to demand her dead.

So Hercules went forth for the hunting and, not wishing to wound the hind, pursued her for one entire year. Up hill he went, down many a mountain dale, across many a gleaming river, through deep forest and open field, and always dancing before him were the golden tips of horns of the hind—near enough to be seen, too far to be seized. At last tired with the pursuit the lovely beast one day took refuge upon a mountain side, and there as she sought the water of a river, Hercules struck her with an arrow. The wound was slight, but it helped the hero to catch the creature, and to lift her to his shoulders. Thereupon, he started for the court of Eurystheus.

But the way was long, and it lay through a part of Arcadia where the bush was heavy, and forests were deep, and mountains were high, and while Hercules was pursuing his way and bearing his meek-eyed burden, he one day met the fair goddess to whom the hind was sacred. Her brother, the beautiful god Apollo, was with her.

Artemis seeing her captured deer cried to the hero, "Mortal, oho! thus wilt thou violate a creature set aside by the gods?" "Mighty Artemis and huntress," answered Hercules, "this hind I know is thine. A twelve-month have I chased and at last caught her. But the god Necessity forced me! Oh, immortal one, I am not impious. Eurystheus commanded me to catch the hind and the priestess of Apollo enjoined me to observe the King's command."

When Artemis understood how Hercules was bondman she dismissed her anger, and sent him forward with kind words, and thus he brought the golden-horned hind to Mycenae and sent it in to the King.

## THE FOURTH LABOUR—CAPTURING THE BOAR OF ERYMANTHUS

In the northwestern part of the famed Arcadia where the golden-horned hind roamed was a range of mountains called Erymanthus. Over the high tops of this range wandered also a wild beast, but unlike the lovely hind he was fierce and terrible of aspect and deadly in encounter. He was known as the boar of Erymanthus. This tusked and terrible being the King of Mycenae, Eurystheus, commanded the mighty Hercules, his bondman, to bring alive to him.

Again Hercules set out, and again he fared over hill and across bright waters, and as he went the birds sang spring songs to him from vine and tree shade, and yellow crocuses carpeted the earth. In his journey he came one day to the home of Pholus, a centaur, who dwelt with other centaurs upon the side of a mountain. Now the centaurs were, of all the dwellers of that distant land, most unlike us modern folks. For report has it that they were half that noble creature man, and half that noble creature horse: that is to say, they were men as far as the waist, and then came the body of the horse with its swift four feet. There are those, indeed, who claim that the centaurs were men and rode their mountain ponies so deftly that man and horse seemed one whole creature. Be that as it may, upon this mountain side the centaur

Pholus dwelt with others of his kind, and there to visit with him came Hercules.

The centaur with his hospitable heart and own hands prepared a dinner of roast meat for the hungry traveller, and as they sat at the board in genial converse they had much enjoyment. But Hercules was also thirsty, and the sparkling water from the mountain spring seemed not to satisfy him. He asked the centaur for wine. "Ah, wine, my guest-friend Hercules," answered Pholus, "I have none of my own. Yonder is a jar of old vintage, but it belongs to all the centaurs of our mountain and I cannot open it." "But friend Pholus," said Hercules pressingly, "I would I had a little for my stomach's sake."

Now the centaur had a kind heart as we have said, and he rejoiced that Hercules had come, and to give the hero his desires he opened the jar. The wine was made from grapes that grew under the fair skies of Arcadia and its fragrance was like a scent of lilies or of roses, and when the soft winds entered the door, near which Hercules sat drinking, it seized the perfume and bore it over the mountain side. Now hear of all the mischief a little wine may make.

The fragrance in the air told the centaurs, wherever each happened to be, that their wine jar had been opened, and they rushed to its resting place perhaps to defend it from any wayfaring thief, perhaps to help drink it, we do not know. But each came angrily to the mouth of the cave of Pholus and all were armed with stones and staves which they had seized as they hastened onward. When they first entered with raging cries and threatening gesture Hercules grasped the brands burning on the hospitable hearth and drove them back. As others pressed behind them the hero drew forth his arrows poisoned with the gall of the Lernean hydra, and sent among them many a shaft. Thus they fought retreating and, they fleeing and Hercules pursuing, came finally to the dwelling of Chiron, most famed of all the centaurs and a teacher of Hercules in his youth, teacher of his great art of surgery.

The wine raging in the veins of Hercules made him for the moment forgetful of all the good Chiron had bestowed upon him, and still letting fly his poisonous arrows he, aiming at another, hit the noblest of the centaurs. Grief seized Hercules when he saw what he had done and he ran and drew out the arrow and applied a soft ointment which Chiron himself had taught him to make. But it was in vain, for the centaur, inspiring teacher and famed for his love of justice as he was, soon gave up the ghost.

Saddened at his own madness Hercules now returned to the cave of his guest-friend Pholus. There among others his host lay, and stark dead. He had drawn an arrow from the body of one who had died from its wound, and, while examining it and wondering how so slight a shaft could be so fatal, had accidentally dropped it out of his hand. It struck his foot and he expired that very moment.

Hercules paid all funeral honour to his friends and afterward departing from the unhappy neighbourhood took up his search of the boar.

Heavy snows were lying on the crests of Erymanthus when Hercules came upon the tracks of the wild creature, and following patiently finally reached his lair. There the boar stood, his tusks pointed outward ready for attack, his eyes snapping vindictively. He was indeed a terrible thing to see.

Hercules, instead of shooting at the animal, began to call, and shouting with loud cries he so confused the boar that he ran into the vast snowdrift standing near by. Thereupon the hero seized and bound him with a wild grapevine he had brought for the purpose. And so swinging him over his shoulder he took his way toward Mycenae.

The King Eurystheus was terribly frightened at the very prospect of having the boar to keep, and when he heard Hercules was coming to town with the animal on his shoulders he took to the brazen underground chamber, which he had built, when Hercules came in with the body of the Nemean lion. There he stayed for several days, according to a good old historian, Diodorus, who in writing of the King told that he was so great a coward.

## THE FIFTH LABOUR—CLEANSING THE STABLES OF AUGEAS

Although Eurystheus was seized with tremor at the coming of Hercules with the Erymanthian boar, still he continued relentless, and demanded the performance of the next task, which was nothing less than the cleaning out in one day of stables where numerous cattle had been confined for many years. These noisome stalls belonged to Augeas, a King of Elis and a man rich in herds—so rich indeed that as the years passed and his cattle increased he could not find men enough to care for his kine and their house. Thus the animals had continued, and had so littered their abiding place that it had become well nigh intolerable and a source of disease and even of pestilence to the people.

When Hercules came to King Augeas he said nothing to him of the command Eurystheus had laid upon him, but looking through the stables which covered a space of many meadows he spoke of the cattle and the evil condition of their housing. "The moon-eyed kine will do better in clean stables," said the wise Hercules, "and if thou wilt pledge me a tenth of thy herds I will clean out thy stalls in a day." To this Augeas delightedly agreed and, speaking as they were in the presence of the young son of the King, Hercules called upon the prince to witness the pact.

Now Hercules in going about the great stables had noticed that at the upper end of their building flowed a swift river, and at the lower end was a second swift stream. When therefore Augeas had pledged himself to the work, Hercules, beginning early next day, took down the walls at the upper end of the stalls and the walls at the lower end. Then with his own mighty hands he dug channels and canals and led the waters of the upper swift-flowing river into the heavily littered floor of the stalls. And the waters rose and pushed the litter before them and made one channel into the lower river, and then another and another and so, working through the hours of the day, the upper river scoured the stables clean and carried the refuse to the lower river. And the lower river took the burden and carried it out to the salt sea, which is ever and always cleaning and purifying whatever comes to its waters. And when night fell there stood the hero Hercules looking at his work—the filthy stables of Augeas cleaned.

When next day Hercules asked for the tenth of the herds which the King had pledged, Augeas refused to stand by his agreement. He had learned that this labour of cleaning his stables had been imposed upon Hercules, and he claimed he should pay nothing for it; in fact, he denied he had promised anything, and offered to lay the matter before judges. The cause therefore was tried, and at the trial the young son of the King, who had witnessed the pact, testified to the truth of Hercules' claim. This so enraged his father that in most high-handed manner he banished both his son and the hero from Elis without waiting for the judgment of the court. Hercules returned to Mycenae. But again the cowardly and contemptible Eurystheus refused to count this labour, saying Hercules had done it for hire.

## THE SIXTH LABOUR—SHOOTING THE STYMPHALIAN BIRDS

Far in the famed land of Arcadia is a beautiful lake known so many years ago, as in the time of Hercules, and even by us in our day, as Lake Stymphalus. It is a lake of pure sweet water and it lies, as such waters lie in our own country, high up in mountains and amid hillsides covered with firs and poplars and clinging vines and wild blossoms.

In our day the lake is a resort for gentle singing birds, but in the time of Hercules other birds were there also. The other birds were water fowls, and they had gathered at Lake Stymphalus because they had been driven out of their old home by wolves, who alone were hungrier and more destructive than they. These fowls had claws of iron, and every feather of theirs was sharper than a barbed arrow, and so strong and fierce and ravenous they were that they would dart from the air and attack hunters, yea, and pecking them down would tear and strip their flesh till but a bony skeleton remained of that which a few minutes before had been a strong, active, buoyant man seeking in the chase food for his hearthside.

To make way with this horrid tribe of the air was the sixth command Eurystheus laid upon Hercules. Toward Lake Stymphalus therefore turned our hero. Again he walked Arcadian waysides, and again as he fared the spring sun shone above, and the birds sang welcome, and the narcissus lifted its golden cup, and as he went his heart rejoiced in his life, whatever the difficulty of his labour, and in the beauty of the world before his eyes. And as he walked also he thought of how he should accomplish the great undertaking upon which he was bent.

While thus deliberating the grey-eyed goddess of wisdom, Athené, came to him—just as this goddess even in our day comes to those who think—and she suggested to his mind that he should scare the fowl from their retreat by brazen rattles. The goddess did even more than put the notion of using a rattle in the mind of Hercules. It is said she actually brought him one, a huge, bronze clapper made for him by the forger of the gods, limping Hephæstus.

Hercules took this rattle and mounting a neighbouring height shook it in his great hands till every hill echoed and the very trees quivered with the horrid sound. And the man-eating birds? Not one remained hidden. Each and every one rose terrified in the air, croaking and working its steely talons and sharp-pointed feathers in dire fear.

Now from his quiver the hero fast picked his barbed arrows, and fast he shot and every shot brought to his feet one of the terrible man-eaters, till at last he had slain every one. Or, if indeed, any of the tribe had escaped, they had flown far away, for never after, in all the long history of Lake Stymphalus, have such creatures appeared again above its fair waters.

So ended the sixth labour of Hercules.

## THE SEVENTH LABOUR—CAPTURING THE CRETAN BULL

Just as Zeus who, as we said in the beginning, was King of all heaven that is the air and clouds, so Posidon was King of the sea. With his queen, Amphitrite, he lived far down underneath the waves, and dwelt in a palace splendid with all the beautiful things of the deep.

In the midst of the blue waters of the Mediterranean where Posidon had his home, lies an island called Crete, and long ago in the days when Hercules laboured, a King, whose name was Minos, ruled over this land. The island is long and narrow and has much sea coast, and because of this fact King Minos stood in intimate relations with the god of the sea.

Now one day in an especial burst of friendliness, Minos vowed to sacrifice to Posidon whatever should come out of the salt waters. The god in pleasure at the vow, and to test mayhap the devotion of Minos, sent at once a beautiful bull leaping and swimming through the waves. When the creature had come to the rocky coast and made land, its side shone with such beauty, and its ivory-white horns garlanded with lilies set so like a crown above its graceful head that Minos and all the people who saw it marvelled that anywhere could have grown such a bull. And a sort of greed and deceit seized Minos as he gazed, and for his sacrifice to Posidon he resolved to use another bull. And so he ordered his herdsman to take this fair creature that had come from the sea and to put it among his herd, and also to bring forth another for the offering.

Because of this avarice of Minos the god below the waves was angry and he made the bull wild and furious, so that no herdsman dared approach to feed or care for it. For his seventh task Eurystheus commanded Hercules to fetch him this mad bull of Crete.

Hercules accordingly boarded one of the ships that plied in that far-off day, as well as in this time of ours, between the rocky coast of Crete and the fair land of Hellas, and in due time the hero came to Minos' court. "I have come, sire," said Hercules, "for the mad bull that terrifies thy herdsmen and is rumoured beyond capture." "Ay, young man," cried the king, "thou hast come for my bull and my bull shalt thou have. When thou hast taken it, it is thine," and the King laughed grimly, for the strength and fury of the creature he deemed beyond any man's control.

Hercules sought the grove where Posidon's gift had strayed from its fellows, and there deftly seizing it by the horns, he bound its feet with stout straps of bull's hide and its horns he padded with moss of the sea from which it came, and so having made it powerless he lifted it to his shoulders and carried it to the shore. A swift black ship was just spreading sail from Crete, and entering upon it the hero soon ended his journey and laid his capture before Eurystheus.

A day or two later Hercules loosed the bull, which, after wandering through the woodlands of Arcadia, crossed the isthmus and came to the plains of Marathon, whence, after doing much damage, it swam off to sea and was never heard of after.

So far we have told how Hercules accomplished seven of the tasks laid upon him. Space does not permit us to recount in detail the other five. The eighth task was to bring to Eurystheus the man-eating mares of the King of Windy Thrace. The ninth task was to fetch a girdle which Ares, god of war, had given the Queen of the Amazons—an exceedingly difficult labour, for the Amazons were a nation of women-warriors renowned for valour. For the tenth task Eurystheus demanded the purple oxen of a famous giant who dwelt on an island far out in the ocean. The eleventh task was to bring apples from the garden of the Hesperides—golden apples guarded by a dragon with a hundred heads, no one of which ever closed its eyes in sleep. And the twelfth and last task, which was to free the mighty Hercules from his bondage to cowardly Eurystheus, was to fetch Cerberus, the three-headed dog, who guarded the entrance to Hades, the unseen abode of departed spirits.

Each and every one of these labours the strong hero accomplished. Having won his freedom and gained the honours promised by the priestess at Delphi many years before, Hercules worked many a noble deed and finally in reward for his much enduring and his aid to mortals, he was carried upon a thunder cloud to the upper air, and entered into the very gates of heaven.

# DANIEL

IT PLEASED Darius to set over the kingdom an hundred and twenty princes, which should be over the whole kingdom.

And over these three presidents; of whom Daniel was first: that the princes might give accounts unto them, and the King should have no damage.

Then this Daniel was preferred above the presidents and princes, because an excellent spirit was in him; and the King thought to set him over the whole realm.

Then the presidents and princes sought to find occasion against Daniel concerning the kingdom; but they could find none occasion nor fault; forasmuch as he was faithful, neither was there any error or fault found in him.

Then said these men, We shall not find any occasion against this Daniel, except we find it against him concerning the law of his God.

Then these presidents and princes assembled together to the King, and said thus unto him, King Darius, live for ever.

All the presidents of the kingdom, the governors, and the princes, the counsellors, and the captains, have consulted together to establish a royal statute, and to make a firm decree, that whosoever shall ask a petition of any god or man for thirty days, save of thee, O King, he shall be cast into the den of lions.

Now, O King, establish the decree, and sign the writing, that it be not changed, according to the law of the Medes and Persians, which altereth not.

Wherefore King Darius signed the writing and the decree.

Now when Daniel knew that the writing was signed, he went into his house; and his windows being open in his chamber toward Jerusalem, he kneeled upon his knees three times a day, and prayed, and gave thanks before his God, as he did aforetime.

Then these men assembled, and found Daniel praying and making supplication before his God.

Then they came near, and spake before the King concerning the King's decree; Hast thou not signed a decree, that every man that shall ask a petition of any god or man within thirty days, save of thee, O King, shall be cast into the den of lions? The King answered and said, The thing is true, according to the law of the Medes and Persians, which altereth not.

Then answered they and said before the King, That Daniel, which is of the children of the captivity of Judah, regardeth not thee, O King, nor the decree that thou hast signed, but maketh his petition three times a day.

Then the King, when he heard these words, was sore displeased with himself, and set his heart on Daniel to deliver him: and he laboured till the going down of the sun to deliver him.

Then these men assembled unto the King, and said unto the King, Know, O King, that the law of the Medes and Persians is, That no decree nor statute which the King establisheth may be changed.

Then the King commanded, and they brought Daniel, and cast him into the den of lions. Now the King spake and said unto Daniel, Thy God whom thou servest continually, he will deliver thee.

And a stone was brought, and laid upon the mouth of the den; and the King sealed it with his own signet, and with the signet of his lords; that the purpose might not be changed concerning Daniel.

Then the King went to his palace, and passed the night fasting: neither were instruments of music brought before him: and his sleep went from him.

Then the King arose very early in the morning, and went in haste unto the den of lions.

And when he came to the den, he cried with a lamentable voice unto Daniel: and the King spake and said to Daniel, O Daniel, servant of the living God, is thy God, whom thou servest continually, able to deliver thee from the lions?

Then said Daniel unto the King, O King, live for ever.

My God hath sent his angel, and hath shut the lions' mouths, that they have not hurt me: forasmuch as before him innocency was found in me: and also before thee, O King, have I done no hurt.

Then was the King exceeding glad for him, and commanded that they should take Daniel up out of the den. So Daniel was taken up out of the den, and no manner of hurt was found upon him, because he believed in his God.

# DAVID

NOW the Philistines gathered together their armies to battle, and were gathered together at Shochoh, which belongeth to Judah, and pitched between Shochoh and Azekah, in Ephes-dammim.

And Saul and the men of Israel were gathered together, and pitched by the valley of Elah, and set the battle in array against the Philistines.

And the Philistines stood on a mountain on the one side, and Israel stood on a mountain on the other side; and there was a valley between them.

And there went out a champion out of the camp of the Philistines, named Goliath, of Gath, whose height was six cubits and a span.

And he had an helmet of brass upon his head, and he was armed with a coat of mail; and the weight of the coat was five thousand shekels of brass.

And he had greaves of brass upon his legs, and a target of brass between his shoulders.

And the staff of his spear was like a weaver's beam; and his spear's head weighed six hundred shekels of iron; and one bearing a shield went before him.

And he stood and cried unto the armies of Israel, and said unto them, Why are ye come out to set your battle in array? am not I a Philistine, and ye servants to Saul? choose you a man for you, and let him come down to me.

If he be able to fight with me, and to kill me, then will we be your servants: but if I prevail against him, and kill him, then shall ye be our servants, and serve us.

And the Philistine said, I defy the armies of Israel this day; give me a man, that we may fight together.

When Saul and all Israel heard those words of the Philistine, they were dismayed, and greatly afraid.

Now David was the son of that Ephrathite of Bethlehem-judah, whose name was Jesse; and he had eight sons: and the man went among men for an old man in the days of Saul.

And the three eldest sons of Jesse went and followed Saul to the battle: and the names of his three sons that went to the battle were Eliab the firstborn, and next unto him Abinadab, and the third Shammah.

And David was the youngest: and the three eldest followed Saul.

But David went and returned from Saul to feed his father's sheep at Bethlehem.

And the Philistine drew near morning and evening, and presented himself forty days.

And Jesse said unto David his son, Take now for thy brethren an ephah of this parched corn, and these ten loaves, and run to the camp to thy brethren;

And carry these ten cheeses unto the captain of their thousand, and look how thy brethren fare, and take their pledge.

Now Saul, and they, and all the men of Israel, were in the valley of Elah, fighting with the Philistines.

And David rose up early in the morning, and left the sheep with a keeper, and took, and went, as Jesse had commanded him; and he came to the trench, as the host was going forth to the fight, and shouted for the battle.

For Israel and the Philistines had put the battle in array army against army.

And David left his carriage in the hand of the keeper of the carriage, and ran into the army, and came and saluted his brethren.

And as he talked with them, behold, there came up the champion, the Philistine of Gam, Goliath by name, out of the armies of the Philistines, and spake according to the same words; and David heard them.

And all the men of Israel, when they saw the man, fled from him, and were sore afraid.

And the men of Israel said, Have ye seen this man that is come up? surely to defy Israel is he come up; and it shall be, that the man who killeth him, the

King will enrich him with great riches, and will give him his daughter, and make his father's house free in Israel.

And David spake to the men that stood by him, saying, What shall be done to the man that killeth this Philistine, and taketh away the reproach from Israel? for who is this uncircumcised Philistine, that he should defy the armies of the living God?

And the people answered him after this manner, saying, So shall it be done to the man that killeth him.

And Eliab his eldest brother heard when he spake unto the men; and Eliab's anger was kindled against David, and he said, Why camest thou down hither? and with whom hast thou left those few sheep in the wilderness? I know thy pride, and the naughtiness of thine heart; for thou art come down that thou mightest see the battle.

And David said, What have I now done? Is there not a cause?

And he turned from him toward another, and spake after the same manner: and the people answered him again after the former manner.

And when the words were heard which David spake, they rehearsed them before Saul: and he sent for him.

And David said to Saul, Let no man's heart fail because of him; thy servant will go and fight with this Philistine.

And Saul said to David, Thou art not able to go against this Philistine to fight with him: for thou art but a youth, and he a man of war from his youth.

And David said unto Saul, Thy servant kept his father's sheep, and there came a lion, and a bear, and took a lamb out of the flock:

And I went out after him, and smote him, and delivered it out of his mouth: and when he arose against me, I caught him by his beard, and smote him, and slew him.

Thy servant slew both the lion and the bear: and this uncircumcised Philistine shall be as one of them, seeing he hath defied the armies of the living God.

David said moreover, The Lord that delivered me out of the paw of the lion, and out of the paw of the bear, he will deliver me out of the hand of this Philistine. And Saul said unto David, Go, and the Lord be with thee.

And Saul armed David with his armour, and he put an helmet of brass upon his head; also he armed him with a coat of mail.

And David girded his sword upon his armour, and he essayed to go; for he had not proved it. And David said unto Saul, I cannot go with these; for I have not proved them. And David put them off him.

And he took his staff in his hand, and chose him five smooth stones out of the brook, and put them in a shepherd's bag which he had, even in a scrip; and his sling was in his hand: and he drew near to the Philistine.

And the Philistine came on and drew near unto David; and the man that bore the shield went before him.

And when the Philistine looked about, and saw David, he disdained him: for he was but a youth, and ruddy, and of a fair countenance.

And the Philistine said unto David, Am I a dog, that thou comest to me with staves? And the Philistine cursed David by his gods.

And the Philistine said to David, Come to me, and I will give thy flesh unto the fowls of the air, and to the beasts of the field.

Then said David to the Philistine, Thou comest to me with a sword, and with a spear, and with a shield: but I come to thee in the name of the Lord of hosts, the God of the armies of Israel, whom thou hast defied.

This day will the Lord deliver thee into mine hand; and I will smite thee, and take thine head from thee; and I will give the carcasses of the host of the Philistines this day unto the fowls of the air, and to the wild beasts of the earth; that all the earth may know that there is a God in Israel.

And all this assembly shall know that the Lord saveth not with sword and spear: for the battle is the Lord's and He will give you into our hands.

And it came to pass, when the Philistine arose, and came and drew nigh to meet David, that

David hasted, and ran toward the army to meet the Philistine.

And David put his hand to his bag, and took thence a stone, and slang it, and smote the Philistine in his forehead, that the stone sunk into his forehead; and he fell upon his face to the earth.

So David prevailed over the Philistine with a sling and with a stone, and smote the Philistine, and slew him; but there was no sword in the hand of David.

Therefore David ran, and stood upon the Philistine, and took his sword, and drew it out of the sheath thereof, and slew him, and cut off his head therewith. And when the Philistines saw their champion was dead, they fled.

And the men of Israel and of Judah arose, and shouted, and pursued the Philistines, until thou comest to the valley, and to the gates of Ekron. And the wounded of the Philistines fell down by the way to Shaaraim, even unto Gath, and unto Ekron.

And the children of Irsael returned from chasing after the Philistines, and they spoiled their tents.

And David took the head of the Philistine, and brought it to Jerusalem; but he put his armour in his tent.

And when Saul saw David go forth against the Philistine, he said unto Abner, the captain of the host, Abner, whose son is this youth? And Abner said, As thy soul liveth, O King, I cannot tell.

And the King said, Enquire thou whose son the stripling is.

And as David returned from the slaughter of the Philistine, Abner took him, and brought him before Saul with the head of the Philistine in his hand.

And Saul said to him, Whose son art thou, thou young man? And David answered, I am the son of thy servant Jesse the Bethlehemite.

# ST. GEORGE

IN THE year 280, in a town in Cappadocia, was born that great soldier and champion of the oppressed whom we call St. George. His parents were Christians, and by them, and especially by his mother, he was most carefully instructed and trained.

When the youth came to the age of seventeen years he took up the profession of arms, and since he was gifted with beauty of person, intelligence, and an exquisite courtesy, he rose rapidly to a considerable military rank. Especially he pleased his imperial master, Diocletian.

One day while the Emperor, who was devoted to the worship of Apollo, was consulting at a shrine of that god upon an affair of much importance, from the dark depths of the cavern came forth a voice saying, "The just who are on the earth keep me from telling the truth. By them the inspiration of the Sacred Tripod is made a lie." At once the Emperor was stricken with consternation and asked who these just people were. "Master," answered one of the priests of Apollo, "they are the Christians." This answer so enraged Diocletian that he rekindled his persecutions.

Now from the first the young soldier George had burned with indignation because of the unspeakable cruelties put upon Christians, and he had spoken out boldly in defence of his brethren. His friends had counselled silence and prudence. But George would have none. He knew, however, that he might be called upon to suffer at any time, and he hoped to do better work for the world and to die after braver effort. He therefore distributed his money and his fine apparel among the poor and needy, set free all the slaves he possessed, and went forth upon knightly travel.

While pricking one day through the plains of Libya he came to a certain city called Silene, the people of which were bewailing a dire misfortune that had come upon them. An enormous dragon had issued from a marsh neighbouring the town and had devoured all their flocks and herds. Already the monster had taken dwelling near the city walls, and at such distance the people had been able to keep him only by granting him two sheep every day for his food and drink. If they had failed in this he would have come within their walls and poisoned every man, woman, and child with his plague-like breath.

But now already all the flocks and herds had been eaten. Nothing remained to fill the insatiable maw of the dragon but the little people of the homes and hearths of all the town. Every day two children were now given him. Each child taken was under the age of fifteen, and was chosen by lot. Thus it happened that every house and every street and all the public squares echoed with the wailing of unhappy parents and the cries of the innocents who were soon to be offered.

Now it chanced that the King of the city had one daughter, an exceeding fair girl both in mind and body, and after many days of the choosing of lots for the sacrifice, and after many a blooming girl and boy had met an unhappy death, the lot fell to this maiden, Cleodolinda. When her father, the King, heard his misfortune, in his despair he offered all the gold in the state treasury and even half his kingdom, to redeem the maiden. But at this many fathers and mothers who had lost their children murmured greatly and said, "O King, art thou just? By thy edict thou hast made us desolate. And now behold thou wouldst withhold thine own child!"

Thus the people spake, and speaking they waxed wroth greatly, and so joining together they marched threatening to burn the King in his palace unless he delivered the maiden to fulfil her lot. To such demands the King perforce submitted, and at last he asked only a delay of eight days which he might spend with the lovely girl and bewail her fate. This the people granted.

At the end of the time agreed to the fair victim was led forth. She fell at her father's feet asking his blessing and protesting she was ready to die for her people. Then amid tears and lamentations she was led to the walls and put without. The gates were shut and barred against her.

She walked towards the dwelling of the dragon, slowly and painfully, for the road was strewn with the bones of her playmates, and she wept as she went on her way.

It was this very morning that George, courageously seeking to help the weak, and strong to serve the truth, was passing by in his knightly journeying. He saw stretched before him the noisome path, and, moved to see so beautiful a maiden in tears, he checked his charger and asked her why she wept. The whole pitiful story she recounted, to which the valiant one answered, "Fear not; I will deliver you."

"Oh noble youth," cried the fair victim, "tarry not here lest you perish with me. Fly, I beseech you."

"God forbid that I should fly," said George in answer; "I will lift my hand against this loathly thing, and I will deliver you through the power that lives in all true followers of Christ."

At that moment the dragon was seen coming forth from his lair half flying and half crawling towards them. "Fly, I beseech you, brave knight," cried the fair girl trembling, "Leave me here to die."

But George answered not. Rather he put spurs to his horse and, calling upon his Lord, rushed towards the monster, and, after a terrible and prolonged combat, pinned the mighty hulk to the earth with his lance. Then he called to the maiden to bring him her girdle. With this he bound the dragon fast, and gave the end of the girdle into her hand,

and the subdued monster crawled after them like a dog.

Walking in this way they approached the city. All the onlooking people were stricken with terror, but George called out to them saying, "Fear nothing. Only believe in Christ, through whose help I have conquered this adversary, and live in accord with His teachings, and I will destroy him before your eyes."

So the King and the people believed and such a life they endeavoured to live.

Then St. George slew the dragon and cut off his head, and the King gave great treasure to the knight. But all the rewards George distributed among the sick and necessitous and kept nothing for himself, and then he went further on his way of helpfulness.

About this time the Emperor Diocletian issued an edict which was published the length and breadth of his empire. This edict was nailed to the doors of temples, upon the walls of public markets, in all places people frequented, and those who read it read it with terror and hid their faces in despair. For it condemned all Christians. But St. George when he saw the writing was filled with indignation. That spirit and courage which comes to all of us from communion with the eternal powers heartened and strengthened him, and he tore down the unhappy utterance and trampled it under foot.

Thus prepared for death George approached the Emperor. "What wouldst thou?" cried Diocletian angrily, having heard from his proconsul

Dacian that this young man deserved torture. "Liberty, sir, for the innocent Christians," answered the martyr. "At the least liberty, since their liberty can hurt no one."

"Young man," returned Diocletian with threatening looks, "think of thine own liberty and thy future."

Before George could make answer the ill-will of the tyrant waxed to ardent hatred and he summoned guards to take the martyr to prison. Once within the dungeon the keepers threw him to the ground, put his feet in stocks and placed a stone of great weight upon his chest. But even so, in the midst of torture, the blessed one ceased not to give thanks to God for this opportunity to bear witness to Christ's teachings.

The next day they stretched the martyr on a wheel full of sharp spokes. But a voice from heaven came to comfort him and said, "George, fear not; so it is with those who witness to the truth." And there appeared to him an angel brighter than the sun, clothed in a white robe, who stretched out a hand to embrace and encourage him in his pain. Two of the officers of the prison who saw this beautiful vision became Christians and from that day endeavoured to live after the teachings of Christ.

There is still another tale that after George had been comforted by the angel who descended from heaven, his tormentors flung him into a cauldron of boiling lead, and when they believed they had subdued him by the force of his agonies, they brought him to a temple to assist in their worship, and the people ran in crowds to behold his humiliation, and the priests mocked him.

The Emperor, seeing the constancy of George, once more sought to move him by entreaties. But the great soldier refused to be judged by words, only by deeds. He even demanded to go to see the gods Diocletian himself worshipped.

The Emperor, believing that at length George was coming to his right mind, and was about to yield, ordered the Roman Senate and people to assemble in order that all might be witnesses of George's acknowledgement of his own, Diocletian's, gods.

When they were thus gathered together in the Emperor's temple, and the eyes of all the people were fixed upon the weak and tortured saint to see what he would do, he drew near a statue of the sun-god Apollo, and stretching out his hand toward the image he said slowly, "Wouldst thou that I should offer thee sacrifices as to a god?" The demon who was in the statue made answer, "I am not God. There is but one God and Christ is his greatest prophet." At that very hour were heard horrible wailing sounds coming from the mouths of idols the world over, and the statues of the old gods either all fell over or crumbled to dust. One account says that St. George knelt down and prayed, and thunder and lightning from heaven fell upon the idols and destroyed them.

Angry at the breaking of their power, the priests of the gods cried to the Emperor that he must rid himself of so potent a magician and cut off his head. The priests also incited the people to lay hands on the martyr.

So it was commanded that George, the Christian knight, should be beheaded. He was dragged to the place of execution, and there, bending his neck to the sword of the executioner and absorbed in prayer, he received bravely and thankfully the stroke of death in April, 303.

So stands St. George ever before the youth of the world, one of the champions of Christendom, a model of courage, a brave interceder for the oppressed, an example of pure, firm and enduring doing for others, a true soldier of Christ.

# KING ARTHUR

LONG years ago, there ruled over Britain a King called Uther Pendragon. A mighty prince was he, and feared by all men; yet, when he sought the love of the fair Igraine of Cornwall, she would have naught to do with him, so that, from grief and disappointment, Uther fell sick, and at last seemed like to die.

Now in those days, there lived a famous magician named Merlin, so powerful that he could change his form at will, or even make himself invisible; nor was there any place so remote but that he could reach it at once, merely by wishing himself there. One day, suddenly he stood at Uther's bedside, and said: "Sir King, I know thy grief, and am ready to help thee. Only promise to give me, at his birth, the son that shall be born to thee, and thou shalt have thy heart's desire." To this the King agreed joyfully, and Merlin kept his word: for he gave Uther the form of one whom Igraine had loved dearly, and so she took him willingly for her husband.

When the time had come that a child should be born to the King and Queen, Merlin appeared before Uther to remind him of his promise; and Uther swore it should be as he had said. Three days later, a prince was born and, with pomp and ceremony, was christened by the name of Arthur; but immediately thereafter, the King commanded that the child should be carried to the postern-gate, there to be given to the old man who would be found waiting without.

Not long after, Uther fell sick, and he knew that his end was come; so, by Merlin's advice; he called together his knights and barons, and said to them: "My death draws near. I charge you, therefore, that ye obey my son even as ye have obeyed me; and my curse upon him if he claim not the crown when he is a man grown." Then the King turned his face to the wall and died.

Scarcely was Uther laid in his grave before disputes arose. Few of the nobles had seen Arthur or even heard of him, and not one of them would have been willing to be ruled by a child; rather, each thought himself fitted to be King, and, strengthening his own castle, made war on his neighbours until confusion alone was supreme and the poor groaned because there was none to help them.

Now when Merlin carried away Arthur—for Merlin was the old man who had stood at the postern-gate—he had known all that would happen, and had taken the child to keep him safe from the fierce barons until he should be of age to rule wisely and well, and perform all the wonders prophesied of him. He gave the child to the care of the good knight

Sir Ector to bring up with his son Kay, but revealed not to him that it was the son of Uther Pendragon that was given into his charge.

At last, when years had passed and Arthur was grown a tall youth well skilled in knightly exercises, Merlin went to the Archbishop of Canterbury and advised him that he should call together at Christmas-time all the chief men of the realm to the great cathedral in London; "For," said Merlin, "there shall be seen a great marvel by which it shall be made clear to all men who is the lawful King of this land." The Archbishop did as Merlin counselled. Under pain of a fearful curse, he bade barons and knights come to London to keep the feast, and to pray heaven to send peace to the realm.

The people hastened to obey the Archbishop's commands, and, from all sides, barons and knights came riding in to keep the birth-feast of our Lord. And when they had prayed, and were coming forth from the cathedral, they saw a strange sight. There, in the open space before the church, stood, on a great stone, an anvil thrust through with a sword; and on the stone were written these words: "Whoso can draw forth this sword, is rightful King of Britain born."

At once there were fierce quarrels, each man clamouring to be the first to try his fortune, none doubting his own success. Then the Archbishop decreed that each should make the venture in turn, from the greatest baron to the least knight, and each in turn, having put forth his utmost strength, failed to move the sword one inch, and drew back ashamed. So the Archbishop dismissed the company, and having appointed guards to watch over the stone, sent messengers through all the land to give word of great jousts to be held in London at Easter, when each knight could give proof of his skill and courage, and try whether the adventure of the sword was for him.

Among those who rode to London at Easter was the good Sir Ector, and with him his son, Sir Kay, newly made a knight, and the young Arthur. When the morning came that the jousts should begin, Sir Kay and Arthur mounted their horses and set out for the lists; but before they reached the field, Kay looked and saw that he had left his sword behind. Immediately Arthur turned back to fetch it for him, only to find the house fast shut, for all were gone to view the tournament. Sore vexed was Arthur, fearing lest his brother Kay should lose his chance of gaining glory, till, of a sudden, he bethought him of the sword in the great anvil before the cathedral. Thither he rode with all speed, and the guards having deserted their post to view the tournament, there was none to forbid him the adventure. He leapt from his horse, seized the hilt, and instantly drew forth the sword as easily as from a scabbard; then, mounting his horse and thinking no marvel of what he had done, he rode after his brother and handed him the weapon.

When Kay looked at it, he saw at once that it was the wondrous sword from the stone. In great joy he sought his father, and showing it to him, said:

"Then must I be King of Britain." But Sir Ector bade him say how he came by the sword, and when Sir Kay told how Arthur had brought it to him, Sir Ector bent his knee to the boy, and said: "Sir, I perceive that ye are my King, and here I tender you my homage"; and Kay did as his father. Then the three sought the Archbishop, to whom they related all that had happened; and he, much marvelling, called the people together to the great stone, and bade Arthur thrust back the sword and draw it forth again in the presence of all, which he did with ease. But an angry murmur arose from the barons, who cried that what a boy could do, a man could do; so, at the Archbishop's word, the sword was put back, and each man, whether baron or knight, tried in his turn to draw it forth, and failed. Then, for the third time, Arthur drew forth the sword. Immediately there arose from the people a great shout: "Arthur is King! Arthur is King! We will have no King but Arthur"; and, though the great barons scowled and threatened, they fell on their knees before him while the Archbishop placed the crown upon his head, and swore to obey him faithfully as their lord and sovereign.

Thus Arthur was made King; and to all he did justice, righting wrongs and giving to all their dues. Nor was he forgetful of those that had been his friends; for Kay, whom he loved as a brother, he made Seneschal and chief of his household, and to Sir Ector, his foster father, he gave broad lands.

Thus Arthur was made King, but he had to fight for his own; for eleven great Kings drew together and refused to acknowledge him as their lord, and chief amongst the rebels was King Lot of Orkney who had married Arthur's sister, Bellicent.

By Merlin's advice, Arthur sent for help overseas, to Ban and Bors, the two great Kings who ruled in Gaul. With their aid, he overthrew his foes in a great battle near the river Trent; and then he passed with them into their own lands and helped them drive out their enemies. So there was ever great friendship between Arthur and the Kings Ban and Bors, and all their kindred; and afterward some of the most famous Knights of the Round Table were of that kin.

Then King Arthur set himself to restore order throughout his kingdom. To all who would submit and amend their evil ways, he showed kindness; but those who persisted in oppression and wrong he removed, putting in their places others who would deal justly with the people. And because the land had become overrun with forest during the days of misrule, he cut roads through the thickets, that no longer wild beasts and men, fiercer than the beasts, should lurk in their gloom, to the harm of the weak and defenceless. Thus it came to pass that soon the peasant ploughed his fields in safety, and where had been wastes, men dwelt again in peace and prosperity.

Amongst the lesser Kings whom Arthur helped to rebuild their towns and restore order, was King Leodegrance of Cameliard. Now Leodegrance had one fair child, his daughter Guenevere; and from the time that first he saw her, Arthur gave her all his love. So he sought counsel of Merlin, his chief adviser. Merlin heard the King sorrowfully, and he said: "Sir King, when a man's heart is set, he may not change. Yet had it been well if ye had loved another."

So the King sent his knights to Leodegrance, to ask of him his daughter; and Leodegrance consented, rejoicing to wed her to so good and knightly a King. With great pomp, the princess was conducted to Canterbury, and there the King met her, and they two were wed by the Archbishop in the great Cathedral, amid the rejoicings of the people.

On that same day did Arthur found his Order of the Round Table, the fame of which was to spread throughout Christendom and endure through all time. Now the Round Table had been made for King Uther Pendragon by Merlin, who had meant thereby to set forth plainly to all men the roundness of the earth. After Uther died, King Leodegrance had possessed it; but when Arthur was wed, he sent it to him as a gift, and great was the King's joy at receiving it. One hundred and fifty knights might take their places about it, and for them Merlin made sieges, or seats. One hundred and twenty-eight did Arthur knight at that great feast; thereafter, if any sieges were empty, at the high festival of Pentecost new knights were ordained to fill them, and by magic was the name of each knight found inscribed, in letters of gold, in his proper siege. One seat only long remained unoccupied, and that was the Siege

Perilous. No knight might occupy it until the coming of Sir Galahad; for, without danger to his life, none might sit there who was not free from all stain of sin.

With pomp and ceremony did each knight take upon him the vows of true knighthood: to obey the King; to show mercy to all who asked it; to defend the weak; and for no worldly gain to fight in a wrongful cause: and all the knights rejoiced together, doing honour to Arthur and to his Queen. Then they rode forth to right the wrong and help the oppressed, and by their aid the King held his realm in peace, doing justice to all.

Now, as time passed, King Arthur gathered into his Order of the Round Table knights whose peers shall never be found in any age; and foremost amongst them all was Sir Launcelot du Lac. Such was his strength that none against whom he laid lance in rest could keep the saddle, and no shield was proof against his sword dint; but for his courtesy even more than for his courage and strength, Sir Launcelot was famed far and near. Gentle he was and ever the first to rejoice in the renown of another; and in the jousts, he would avoid encounter with the young and untried knight, letting him pass to gain glory if he might.

It would take a great book to record all the famous deeds of Sir Launcelot, and all his adventures. He was of Gaul, for his father, King Ban, ruled over Benwick; he was named Launcelot du Lac by the Lady of the Lake who reared him when his mother died. Early he won renown; then, when there was peace in his own land, he passed into Britain, to Arthur's Court, where the King received him gladly, and made him Knight of the Round Table and took him for his trustiest friend. And so it was that, when Guenevere was to be brought to Canterbury, to be married to the King, Launcelot was chief of the knights sent to wait upon her, and of this came the sorrow of later days. For, from the moment he saw her, Sir Launcelot loved Guenevere, for her sake remaining wifeless all his days, and in all things being her faithful knight. But busy-bodies and mischief-makers spoke evil of Sir Launcelot and the Queen, and from their talk came the undoing of the King and the downfall of his great work. But that was after long years, and after many true knights had lived their lives, honouring the King and Queen, and doing great deeds.

Before Merlin passed from the world of men, he had uttered many marvellous prophesies, and one that boded ill to King Arthur; for he foretold that, in the days to come, a son of Arthur's sister should stir up bitter war against the King, and at last a great battle should be fought, when many a brave knight should find his doom.

Now, among the nephews of Arthur, was one most dishonourable; his name was Mordred. No knightly deed had he ever done, and he hated to hear the good report of others because he himself was a coward and envious. But of all the Round Table there was none that Mordred hated more than Sir Launcelot du Lac, whom all true knights held in most honour; and not the less did Mordred hate

Launcelot that he was the knight whom Queen Guenevere had in most esteem. So, at last, his jealous rage passing all bounds, he spoke evil of the Queen and of Launcelot, saying that they were traitors to the King. Now Sir Gawain and Sir Gareth, Mordred's brothers, refused to give ear to these slanders, holding that Sir Launcelot, in his knightly service of the Queen, did honour to King Arthur also; but by ill-fortune another brother, Sir Agravaine, had ill-will to the Queen, and professed to believe Mordred's evil tales. So the two went to King Arthur with their ill stories.

Now when Arthur had heard them, he was wroth; for never would he lightly believe evil of any, and Sir Launcelot was the knight whom he loved above all others. Sternly then he bade them begone and come no more to him with unproven tales against any, and, least of all, against Sir Launcelot and their lady, the Queen.

The two departed, but in their hearts was hatred against Launcelot and the Queen, more bitter than ever for the rebuke they had called down upon themselves.

Great was the King's grief. Despite all that Mordred could say, he was slow to doubt Sir Launcelot, whom he loved, but his mind was filled with forebodings; and well he knew that their kin would seek vengeance on Sir Launcelot, and the noble fellowship of the Round Table be utterly destroyed.

All too soon it proved even as the King had feared. Many were found to hold with Sir Mordred; some from envy of the honour and worship of the noble Sir Launcelot; and among them even were those who dared to raise their voice against the Queen herself, calling for judgment upon her as leagued with a traitor against the King, and as having caused the death of so many good knights. Now in those days the law was that if any one were accused of treason by witnesses, or taken in the act, that one should die the death by burning, be it man or woman, knight or churl. So then the murmurs grew to a loud clamour that the law should have its course, and that King Arthur should pass sentence on the Queen. Then was the King's woe doubled; "For," said he, "I sit as King to be a rightful judge and keep all the law; wherefore I may not do battle for my own Queen, and now there is none other to help her." So a decree was issued that Queen Guenevere should be burnt at the stake outside the walls of Carlisle.

Forthwith, King Arthur sent for his nephew, Sir Gawain, and said to him: "Fair nephew, I give it in charge to you to see that all is done as has been decreed." But Sir Gawain answered boldly: "Sir King, never will I be present to see my lady the Queen die. It is of ill counsel that ye have consented to her death." Then the King bade Gawain send his two young brothers, Sir Gareth and Sir Gaheris, to receive his commands, and these he desired to attend the Queen to the place of execution. So Gareth made answer for both: "My Lord the King,

78

we owe you obedience in all things, but know that it is sore against our wills that we obey you in this; nor will we appear in arms in the place where that noble lady shall die"; then sorrowfully they mounted their horses and rode to Carlisle.

When the day appointed had come, the Queen was led forth to a place without the walls of Carlisle, and there she was bound to the stake to be burnt to death. Loud were her ladies' lamentations, and many a lord was found to weep at that grievous sight of a Queen brought so low; yet was there none who dared come forward as her champion, lest he should be suspected of treason. As for Gareth and Gaheris, they could not bear the sight and stood with their faces covered in their mantles. Then, just as the torch was to be applied to the faggots, there was a sound as of many horses galloping, and the next instant a band of knights rushed upon the astonished throng, their leader cutting down all who crossed his path until he had reached the Queen, whom he lifted to his saddle and bore from the press. Then all men knew that it was Sir Launcelot, come knightly to rescue the Queen, and in their hearts they rejoiced. So with little hindrance they rode away, Sir Launcelot and all his kin with the Queen in their midst, till they came to the castle of the Joyous Garde where they held the Queen in safety and all reverence.

At last Sir Launcelot desired of King Arthur assurance of liberty for the Queen, as also safe conduct for himself and his knights, that he might bring Dame Guenevere, with due honour, to the

King at Carlisle; and thereto the King pledged his word.

So Launcelot set forth with the Queen, and behind them rode a hundred knights arrayed in green velvet, the housings of the horses of the same all studded with precious stones; thus they passed through the city of Carlisle, openly, in the sight of all, and there were many who rejoiced that the Queen was come again and Sir Launcelot with her, though they of Gawain's party scowled upon him.

When they were come into the great hall where Arthur sat, with Sir Gawain and other great lords about him, Sir Launcelot led Guenevere to the throne and both knelt before the King; then, rising, Sir Launcelot lifted the Queen to her feet, and thus he spoke to King Arthur, boldly and well before the whole court: "My lord, Sir Arthur, I bring you here your Queen, than whom no truer nor nobler lady ever lived; and here stand I, Sir Launcelot du Lac, ready to do battle with any that dare gainsay it"; and with these words Sir Launcelot turned and looked upon the lords and knights present in their places, but none would challenge him in that cause, not even Sir Gawain, for he had ever affirmed that Dame Guenevere was a true and honourable lady.

Then Sir Launcelot spoke again; "Now, my Lord Arthur, in my own defence it behooves me to say that never in aught have I been false to you."

"Peace," said the King to Sir Launcelot: "We give you fifteen days in which to leave this kingdom." Then Sir Launcelot sighed heavily and said: "Full well I see that nothing availeth me." Then he went to the Queen where she sat, and said: "Madam, the time is come when I must leave this fair realm that I have loved. Think well of me, I pray you, and send for me if ever there be aught in which a true knight may serve lady." Therewith he turned him about and, without greeting to any, passed through the hall, and with his faithful knights rode to the Joyous Garde, though ever thereafter, in memory of that sad day, he called it the Dolorous Garde.

In after times when the King had passed overseas to France, leaving Sir Mordred to rule Britain in his stead, there came messengers from Britain bearing letters for King Arthur; and more evil news than they brought might not well be, for they told how Sir Mordred had usurped his uncle's realm. First, he had caused it to be noised abroad that King Arthur was slain in battle with Sir Launcelot, and, since there be many ever ready to believe any idle rumour and eager for any change, it had been no hard task for Sir Mordred to call the lords to a Parliament and persuade them to make him King. But the Queen could not be brought to believe that her lord was dead, so she took refuge in the Tower of London from Sir Mordred's violence, nor was she to be induced to leave her strong refuge for aught that Mordred could promise or threaten.

Forthwith, King Arthur bade his host make ready to move, and when they had reached the coast, they embarked and made sail to reach Britain with all possible speed.

Sir Mordred, on his part, had heard of their sailing, and hasted to get together a great army. It was grievous to see how many a stout knight held by Mordred, ay, even many whom Arthur himself had raised to honour and fortune; for it is the nature of men to be fickle. Thus it was that, when Arthur drew near to Dover, he found Mordred with a mighty host, waiting to oppose his landing. Then there was a great sea-fight, those of Mordred's party going out in boats, to board King Arthur's ships and slay him and his men or ever they should come to land. Right valiantly did King Arthur bear him, as was his wont, and boldly his followers fought in his cause, so that at last they drove off their enemies and landed at Dover in spite of Mordred and his array.

Now, by this time, many that Mordred had cheated by his lying reports, had drawn unto King Arthur, to whom at heart they had ever been loyal, knowing him for a true and noble King and hating themselves for having been deceived by such a false usurper as Sir Mordred.

One night, as King Arthur slept, he thought that Sir Gawain stood before him, looking just as he did in life, and said to him: "My uncle and my King, God in his great love has suffered me to come unto you, to warn you that in no wise ye fight on the morrow; for if ye do, ye shall be slain, and with you the most part of the people on both sides. Make ye, therefore, a treaty." Immediately, the King awoke and called to him the best and wisest of his knights. Then all were agreed that, on any terms whatsoever, a treaty should be made with Sir Mordred, even as

Sir Gawain had said; and, with the dawn, messengers went to the camp of the enemy, to call Sir Mordred to a conference. So it was determined that the meeting should take place in the sight of both armies, in an open space between the two camps, and that King Arthur and Mordred should each be accompanied by fourteen knights. Little enough faith had either in the other, so when they set forth to the meeting, they bade their hosts join battle if ever they saw a sword drawn.

Now as they talked, it befell that an adder, coming out of a bush hard by, stung a knight in the foot; and he, seeing the snake, drew his sword to kill it and thought no harm thereby. But on the instant that the sword flashed, the trumpets blared on both sides and the two hosts rushed to battle. Never was there fought a fight of such enmity; for brother fought with brother, and comrade with comrade, and fiercely they cut and thrust, with many a bitter word between; while King Arthur himself, his heart hot within him, rode through and through the battle, seeking the traitor Mordred. So they fought all day, till at last the evening fell. Then Arthur, looking round him, saw of his valiant knights but two left, Sir Lucan and Sir Bedivere, and these sore wounded; and there, over against him, by a great heap of the dead, stood Sir Mordred, the cause of all this ruin. Thereupon the King, his heart nigh broken with grief for the loss of his true knights, cried with a loud voice, "Traitor! now is thy doom upon thee!" and with his spear gripped in both hands, he rushed upon Sir Mordred and smote him that the weapon stood out a fathom behind. And Sir Mordred knew that he had his death wound. With all the might that he had, he thrust him up the spear to the haft and, with his sword, struck King Arthur upon the head, that the steel pierced the helmet and bit into the head; then Mordred fell back, stark and dead.

Sir Lucan and Sir Bedivere went to the King where he lay, swooning from the blow, and bore him to a little chapel on the seashore. As they laid him on the ground, Sir Lucan fell dead beside the King, and Arthur, coming to himself, found but Sir Bedivere alive beside him.

So King Arthur lay wounded to the death, grieving, not that his end was come, but for the desolation of his kingdom and the loss of his good knights. And looking upon the body of Sir Lucan, he sighed and said: "Alas! true knight, dead for my sake! If I lived, I should ever grieve for thy death, but now mine own end draws nigh." Then, turning to Sir Bedivere, who stood sorrowing beside him, he said: "Leave weeping now, for the time is short and much to do. Hereafter shalt thou weep if thou wilt. But take now my sword Excalibur, hasten to the water side, and fling it into the deep. Then, watch what happens and bring me word thereof." "My Lord," said Sir Bedivere, "your command shall be obeyed"; and, taking the sword, he departed. But as he went on his way, he looked on the sword, how wondrously it was formed and the hilt all studded with precious stones; and, as he looked, he called to mind the marvel by which it had come into the King's keeping. For on a certain day, as Arthur walked on the shore of a great lake, there had appeared above the surface of the water a hand brandishing a sword. On the instant, the King had leaped into a boat, and, rowing into the lake, had got the sword and brought it back to land. Then he had seen how, on one side the blade, was written, "Keep me," but on the other, "Throw me away," and, sore perplexed, he had shown it to Merlin, the great wizard, who said: "Keep it now. The time for casting away has not yet come." Thinking on this, it seemed to Bedivere that no good, but harm, must come of obeying the King's word; so hiding the sword under a tree, he hastened back to the little chapel. Then said the King: "What saw'st thou?" "Sir," answered Bedivere, "I saw naught but the waves, heard naught but the wind." "That is untrue," said King Arthur; "I charge thee, as thou art true knight, go again and spare not to throw away the sword."

Sir Bedivere departed a second time, and his mind was to obey his lord; but when he took the sword in his hand, he thought: "Sin it is and shameful, to throw away so glorious a sword." Then, hiding it again, he hastened back to the King. "What saw'st thou?" said Sir Arthur. "Sir, I saw the water lap on the crags." Then spoke the King in great wrath: "Traitor and unkind! Twice hast thou betrayed me! Art dazzled by the splendour of the jewels, thou that, till now, hast ever been dear and true to me? Go yet again, but if thou fail me this time, I will arise and, with mine own hands, slay thee."

Then Sir Bedivere left the King and, that time, he took the sword quickly from the place where he had hidden it and, forbearing even to look upon it, he twisted the belt about it and flung it with all his force into the water. A wondrous sight he saw for, as the sword touched the water, a hand rose from out the deep, caught it, brandished it thrice, and drew it beneath the surface.

Sir Bedivere hastened back to the King and told him what he had seen. "It is well," said Arthur; "now, bear me to the water's edge; and hasten, I pray thee, for I have tarried overlong and my wound has taken cold." So Sir Bedivere raised the King on his back and bore him tenderly to the lonely shore, where the lapping waves floated many an empty helmet and the fitful moonlight fell on the upturned faces of the dead. Scarce had they reached the shore when there hove in sight a barge, and on its deck stood three tall women, robed all in black and wearing crowns on their heads. "Place me in the barge," said the King, and softly Sir Bedivere lifted the King into it. And these three Queens wept sore over Arthur, and one took his head in her lap and chafed his hands, crying: "Alas! my brother, thou hast been overlong in coming and, I fear me, thy wound has taken cold." Then the barge began to move slowly from the land. When Sir Bedivere saw this, he lifted up his voice and cried with a bitter cry: "Ah! my Lord Arthur, thou art taken from me! And I, whither shall I go?" "Comfort thyself," said the King, "for in me is no comfort more. I pass to the

Valley of Avilion, to heal me of my grievous wound. If thou seest me never again, pray for me."

So the barge floated away out of sight, and Sir Bedivere stood straining his eyes after it till it had vanished utterly. Then he turned him about and journeyed through the forest until, at daybreak, he reached a hermitage. Entering it, he prayed the holy hermit that he might abide with him, and there he spent the rest of his life in prayer and holy exercise.

But of King Arthur is no more known. Some men, indeed, say that he is not dead, but abides in the happy Valley of Avilion until such time as his country's need is sorest, when he shall come again and deliver it. Others say that, of a truth, he is dead, and that, in the far West, his tomb may be seen, and written on it these words:

"Here lies Arthur, once King
and King to be."

# SIR GALAHAD

MANY times had the Feast of Pentecost come round, and many were the knights that Arthur had made after he founded the Order of the Round Table; yet no knight had appeared who dared claim the seat named by Merlin the Siege Perilous. At last, one vigil of the great feast, a lady came to Arthur's court at Camelot and asked Sir Launcelot to ride with her into the forest hard by, for a purpose not then to be revealed. Launcelot consenting, they rode together until they came to a nunnery hidden deep in the forest; and there the lady bade Launcelot dismount, and led him into a great and stately room. Presently there entered twelve nuns and with them a youth, the fairest that Launcelot had ever seen. "Sir," said the nuns, "we have brought up this child in our midst, and now that he is grown to manhood, we pray you make him knight, for of none worthier could he receive the honour." "Is this thy own desire?" asked Launcelot of the young squire; and when he said that so it was, Launcelot promised to make him knight after the great festival had been celebrated in the church next day.

So on the morrow, after they had worshipped, Launcelot knighted Galahad—for that was the youth's name—and asked him if he would ride at once with him to the King's court; but the young knight excusing himself, Sir Launcelot rode back alone to Camelot, where all rejoiced that he was returned in time to keep the feast with the whole Order of the Round Table.

Now, according to his custom, King Arthur was waiting for some marvel to befall before he and his knights sat down to the banquet. Presently a squire entered the hall and said: "Sir King, a great wonder has appeared. There floats on the river a mighty stone, as it were a block of red marble, and it is thrust through by a sword, the hilt of which is set thick with precious stones." On hearing this, the King and all his knights went forth to view the stone and found it as the squire had said; moreover, looking closer, they read these words: "None shall draw me hence, but only he by whose side I must hang; and he shall be the best knight in all the world." Immediately, all bade Launcelot draw forth the sword, but he refused, saying that the sword was not for him. Then, at the King's command, Sir Gawain made the attempt and failed, as did Sir Percivale after him. So the knights knew the adventure was not for them, and returning to the hall, took their places about the Round Table.

No sooner were they seated than an aged man, clothed all in white, entered the hall, followed by a young knight in red armour, by whose side hung an empty scabbard. The old man approached King Arthur and bowing low before him, said: "Sir, I bring you a young knight of the house and lineage of

Joseph of Arimathea, and through him shall great glory be won for all the land of Britain." Greatly did King Arthur rejoice to hear this, and welcomed the two right royally. Then when the young knight had saluted the King, the old man led him to the Siege Perilous and drew off its silken cover; and all the knights were amazed, for they saw that where had been engraved the words, "The Siege Perilous," was written now in shining gold: "This is the Siege of the noble prince, Sir Galahad." Straightway the young man seated himself there where none other had ever sat without danger to his life; and all who saw it said, one to another: "Surely this is he that shall achieve the Holy Grail." Now the Holy Grail was the blessed dish from which our Lord had eaten the Last Supper, and it had been brought to the land of Britain by Joseph of Arimathea; but because of men's sinfulness, it had been withdrawn from human sight, only that, from time to to time, it appeared to the pure in heart.

When all had partaken of the royal banquet, King Arthur bade Sir Galahad come with him to the river's brink; and showing him the floating stone with the sword thrust through it, told him how his knights had failed to draw forth the sword. "Sir," said Galahad, "it is no marvel that they failed, for the adventure was meant for me, as my empty scabbard shows." So saying, lightly he drew the sword from the heart of the stone, and lightly he slid it into the scabbard at his side. While all yet wondered at this adventure of the sword, there came riding to them a lady on a white palfrey who, saluting King Arthur, said: "Sir King, Nacien the hermit sends thee word that this day shall great honour be shown to thee and all thine house; for the Holy Grail shall appear in thy hall, and thou and all thy fellowship shall be fed therefrom." And so to Launcelot she said: "Sir Knight, thou hast ever been the best knight of all the world; but another has come to whom thou must yield precedence." Then Launcelot answered humbly: "I know well I was never the best." "Ay, of a truth thou wast and art still, of sinful men," said she, and rode away before any could question her further.

So, that evening, when all were gathered about the Round Table, each knight in his own siege, suddenly there was heard a crash of thunder, so mighty that the hall trembled, and there flashed into the hall a sunbeam, brighter far than any that had ever before been seen; and then, draped all in white samite, there glided through the air what none might see, yet what all knew to be the Holy Grail. And all the air was filled with sweet odours, and on every one was shed a light in which he looked fairer and nobler than ever before. So they sat in an amazed silence, till presently King Arthur rose and gave thanks to God for the grace given to him and to his court. Then up sprang Sir Gawain and made his avow to follow for a year and a day the Quest of the Holy Grail, if perchance he might be granted the vision of it. Immediately other of the knights followed his example, binding themselves to the Quest of the Holy Grail until, in all, one hundred and fifty had vowed themselves to the adventure.

Then was King Arthur grieved, for he foresaw the ruin of his noble Order. And turning to Sir Gawain, he said: "Nephew, ye have done ill, for through you I am bereft of the noblest company of knights that ever brought honour to any realm in Christendom. Well I know that never again shall all of you gather in this hall, and it grieves me to lose men I have loved as my life and through whom I have won peace and righteousness for all my realm." So the King mourned and his knights with him, but their oaths they could not recall.

Great woe was there in Camelot next day when, after worship in the cathedral, the knights who had vowed themselves to the Quest of the Holy Grail got to horse and rode away. A goodly company it was that passed through the streets, the townfolk weeping to see them go; Sir Launcelot du Lac and his kin, Sir Galahad of whom all expected great deeds, Sir Bors and Sir Percivale, and many another scarcely less famed than they. So they rode together that day to the Castle of Vagon, where they were entertained right hospitably, and the next day they separated, each to ride his own way and see what adventures should befall him.

So it came to pass that, after four days' ride, Sir Galahad reached an abbey. Now Sir Galahad was still clothed in red armour as when he came to the King's court, and by his side hung the wondrous sword; but he was without a shield. They of the abbey received him right heartily, as also did the brave King Bagdemagus, Knight of the Round Table, who was resting there. When they greeted each other, Sir Galahad asked King Bagdemagus what adventure had brought him there. "Sir," said Bagdemagus, "I was told that in this abbey was preserved a wondrous shield which none but the best knight in the world might bear without grievous harm to himself. And though I know well that there are better knights than I, to-morrow I purpose to make the attempt. But, I pray you, bide at this monastery a while until you hear from me; and if I fail, do ye take the adventure upon you." "So be it," said Sir Galahad.

The next day, at their request, Sir Galahad and King Bagdemagus were led into the church by a monk and shown where, behind the altar, hung the wondrous shield, whiter than snow save for the blood-red cross in its midst. Then the monk warned them of the danger to any who, being unworthy, should dare to bear the shield. But King Bagdemagus made answer: "I know well that I am not the best knight in the world, yet will I try if I may bear it." So he hung it about his neck, and, bidding farewell, rode away with his squire.

The two had not journeyed far before they saw a knight approach, armed all in white mail and mounted upon a white horse. Immediately he laid his spear in rest and, charging King Bagdemagus, pierced him through the shoulder and bore him from his horse; and standing over the wounded knight, he said: "Knight, thou hast shown great folly, for none shall bear this shield save the peerless knight, Sir Galahad." Then, taking the shield, he gave it to the squire and said: "Bear this shield to the

good Knight Galahad and greet him well from me."
"What is your name?" asked the squire. "That is not
for thee or any other to know." "One thing, I pray
you," said the squire; "why may this shield be borne
by none but Sir Galahad without danger?" "Because
it belongs to him only," answered the stranger
knight, and vanished.

Then the squire took the shield and setting
King Bagdemagus on his horse, bore him back to
the abbey where he lay long, sick unto death. To
Galahad the squire gave the shield and told him all
that had befallen. So Galahad hung the shield about
his neck and rode the way that Bagdemagus had
gone the day before; and presently he met the White
Knight, whom he greeted courteously, begging that
he would make known to him the marvels of the
red-cross shield. "That will I gladly," answered the
White Knight. "Ye must know, Sir Knight, that this
shield was made and given by Joseph of Arimathea
to the good King Evelake of Sarras, that, in the
might of the holy symbol, he should overthrow the
heathen who threatened his kingdom. But
afterwards, King Evelake followed Joseph to this
land of Britain where they taught the true faith unto
the people who before were heathen. Then when
Joseph lay dying, he bade King Evelake set the shield
in the monastery where ye lay last night, and foretold
that none should wear it without loss until that day
when it should be taken by the knight, ninth and last
in descent from him, who should come to that place
the fifteenth day after receiving the degree of
knighthood. Even so has it been with you, Sir

Knight." So saying, the unknown knight disappeared and Sir Galahad rode on his way.

After Sir Launcelot had parted from his fellows at the Castle of Vagon, he rode many days through the forest without adventure, till he chanced upon a knight close by a little hermitage in the wood. Immediately, as was the wont of errant knights, they prepared to joust, and Launcelot, whom none before had overthrown, was borne down, man and horse, by the stranger knight. Thereupon a nun, who dwelt in the hermitage, cried: "God be with thee, best knight in all this world," for she knew the victor for Sir Galahad. But Galahad, not wishing to be known, rode swiftly away; and presently Sir Launcelot got to horse again and rode slowly on his way, shamed and doubting sorely in his heart whether this quest were meant for him.

Afterward Sir Galahad rescued Sir Percivale from twenty knights who beset him, and rode on his way till night-fall, when he sought shelter at a little hermitage. Thither there came in the night a damsel who desired to speak with Sir Galahad; so he arose and went to her. "Galahad," said she, "arm you and mount your horse and follow me, for I am come to guide you in your quest." So they rode together until they had come to the seashore and there the damsel showed Galahad a great ship into which he must enter. Then she bade him farewell, and he, going on to the ship, found there already the good knights Sir Bors and Sir Percivale, who made much joy of the meeting. They abode in that ship until they had come to the castle of King Pelles, who welcomed them right gladly. Then, as they all sat at supper that night, suddenly the hall was filled with a great light, and the holy vessel appeared in their midst, covered all in white samite. While they all rejoiced, there came a voice, saying: "My Knights whom I have chosen, ye have seen the holy vessel dimly. Continue your journey to the city of Sarras and there the perfect vision shall be yours."

Now in the city of Sarras had dwelt a long time Joseph of Arimathea, teaching its people the true faith, before ever he came into the land of Britain; but when Sir Galahad and his fellows came there after long voyage, they found it ruled by a heathen King named Estorause, who cast them into a deep dungeon. There they were kept a year, but at the end of that time, the tyrant died. Then the great men of the land gathered together to consider who should be their King; and, while they were in council, came a voice bidding them take as their King the youngest of the three knights whom Estorause had thrown into prison. So in fear and wonder they hastened to the prison, and, releasing the three knights, made Galahad King as the voice had bidden them.

Thus Sir Galahad became King of the famous city of Sarras, in far Babylon. He had reigned a year when, one morning early, he and the other two knights, his fellows, went into the chapel, and there they saw, kneeling in prayer, an aged man, robed as a bishop, and round him hovered many angels. The knights fell on their knees in awe and reverence, whereupon he that seemed a bishop turned to them and said: "I am Joseph of Arimathea, and I am come to show you the perfect vision of the Holy Grail." On the instant there appeared before them, without veil or cover, the holy vessel, in a radiance of light such as almost blinded them. Sir Bors and Sir Percivale, when at length they were recovered from the brightness of that glory, looked up to find that the holy Joseph and the wondrous vessel had passed from their sight. Then they went to Sir Galahad where he still knelt as in prayer, and behold, he was dead; for it had been with him even as he had prayed; in the moment when he had seen the vision, his soul had gone back to God.

So the two knights buried him in that far city, themselves mourning and all the people with them. And immediately after, Sir Percivale put off his arms and took the habit of a monk, living a devout and holy life until, a year and two months later, he also died and was buried near Sir Galahad. Then Sir Bors armed him, and bidding farewell to the city, sailed away until, after many weeks, he came again to the land of Britain. There he took horse, and stayed not till he had come to Camelot. Great was the rejoicing of Arthur and all his knights when Sir Bors was once more among them. When he had told all the adventures which had befallen him and the good knights, his companions, all who heard were filled with amaze. But the King he caused the wisest clerks in the land to write in great books of the Holy Grail, that the fame of it should endure unto all time.

# SIR GALAHAD

## BY ALFRED LORD TENNYSON

My tough lance thrusteth sure,
My strength is as the strength of ten,
   Because my heart is pure.
The shattering trumpet shrilleth high,
   The hard brands shiver on the steel,
The splinter'd spear-shafts crack and fly,
   The horse and rider reel:
They reel, they roll in clanging lists,
   And when the tide of combat stands,
Perfume and flowers fall in showers
   That lightly rain from ladies' hands.

How sweet are looks that ladies bend
   On whom their favours fall!
For them I battle till the end,
   To save from shame and thrall:
But all my heart is drawn above,
   My knees are bow'd in crypt and shrine:
I never felt the kiss of love,
   Nor maiden's hand in mine.
More bounteous aspects on me beam,
   Me mightier transports move and thrill;
So keep I fair thro' faith and prayer
   A virgin heart in work and will.

When down the stormy crescent goes,
   A light before me swims,
Between dark stems the forest glows,
   I hear a noise of hymns:
   I hear a voice, but none are there;
The stalls are void, the doors are wide,
   The tapers burning fair.

Fair gleams the snowy altar-cloth,
    The silver vessels sparkle clean,
The shrill bell rings, the censer swings,
    And solemn chaunts resound between.

Sometimes on lonely mountain-meres
    I find a magic bark;
I leap on board: no helmsman steers:
    I float till all is dark.
A gentle sound, an awful light!
    Three angels bear the Holy Grail:
With folded feet, in stoles of white,
    On sleeping wings they sail.
Ah, blessed vision! blood of God!
    My spirit beats her mortal bars,
As down dark tides the glory slides,
    And star-like mingles with the stars.

When on my goodly charger borne
    Thro' dreaming towns I go,
The cock crows ere the Christmas morn,
    The streets are dumb with snow.
The tempest crackles on the leads,
    And, ringing, spins from brand and mail;
But o'er the dark a glory spreads,
    And gilds the driving hail.
I leave the plain, I climb the height;
    No branchy thicket shelter yields;
    Fly o'er waste fens and windy fields.
A maiden knight—to me is given
    Such hope, I know not fear,
I yearn to breathe the airs of heaven
    That often meet me here.
I muse on joy that will not cease,
    Pure spaces clothed in living beams,
Pure lilies of eternal peace,
    Whose odours haunt my dreams;

And, stricken by an angel's hand,
  This mortal armour that I wear,
This weight and size, this heart and eyes,
  Are touch'd, are turn'd to finest air.

The clouds are broken in the sky,
  And thro' the mountain-walls
A rolling organ-harmony
  Swells up, and shakes and falls.
Then move the trees, the copses nod,
  Wings flutter, voices hover clear:
"O just and faithful knight of God!
  Ride on! the prize is near."
So pass I hostel, hall, and grange;
  By bridge and ford, by park and pale,
All-arm'd I ride, whate'er betide,
  Until I find the Holy Grail.

# SIEGFRIED

NOW there dwelt in a castle in the Netherland a certain King, Siegmund by name, who had to wife a fair lady Sieglind. These two had a son whom they called Siegfried, a very gallant prince. Very carefully did they train and teach him, but the root of the matter was in the lad himself, for he had an honest and good heart, and was in all things a very perfect knight. This Siegfried being come to man's estate, and being well practised in arms, and having also as much of wealth as he needed, turned his thoughts to marriage, desiring to win a fair bride for himself.

It came to Prince Siegfried's ears that there was a very fair maiden in the Rhineland, and that many noble knights had come from far and wide to make their suits to her, but that she would have none of them. Never yet had she seen the man whom she would take for her husband. All this the Prince heard, and he said, "This Kriemhild will I have for my wife." But King Siegmund, when he heard of his son's purpose, was not a little troubled thereat; and Queen Sieglind wept, for she knew the brother of Kriemhild, and she was aware of the strength and valour of his warriors. So they said to the Prince, "Son, this is not a wise wooing." But

Siegfried made answer, "My father, I will have none of wedlock, if I may not marry where I love." Thereupon the King said: "If thou canst not forego this maiden, then thou shalt have all the help that I can give."

Queen Sieglind said: "If you are still minded to go, then I will prepare for you and your companions the best raiment that ever warrior wore."

Siegfried bowed low to his mother, saying: "So be it; only remember that twelve comrades only will I take with me."

So the Queen and her ladies sat stitching night and day, taking no rest till the raiment was ready. King Siegmund the while commanded that the men should polish their war-gear, coats of mail, and helmets, and shields.

The thirteen comrades departed and, on the seventh day, they rode into the town of Worms in Rhineland, a gallant company, bravely arrayed, for their garments flashed with gold, and their war-gear, over their coats of mail and their helmets, were newly polished. Their long swords hung down by their sides, even to their spurs, and sharp were the javelins which they held in their hands. The javelin of Siegfried was two spans broad in the blade, and had a double edge. Terrible were the wounds that it made. Their bridles were gilded, and their horse-girths of silk. A comely sight they were to see, and the people came from all round to gaze upon them.

Tidings had been brought to King Gunther that certain warriors were come, very gallant to look upon and richly clad, but that no one knew who they were, and whence they came. "Now," said the King, "this troubles me much that no one can tell whence these warriors come." To him Ortwein, the High Server, made answer, "Seeing, sire, that no man knows aught about these strangers, let some one fetch Hagen, my uncle; he knows all the kingdoms of the world, and the dwellers therein."

So Hagen went to the window and looked at the men. Well pleased was he with their clothing and their gear of war; but he had never seen their like in the Rhineland. So he said: "Whencesoever these men have come, my lord, that they are princes or of a prince's company is clear. But stay; Siegfried, the famous hero, I have never seen with my eyes, but I verily believe that is he. If it indeed be, there is no warrior in this land, that is his match for strength and valour.

"Once upon a time riding alone, with none to help him, he came upon the treasure of the Nibelungs. It had been newly taken out of the hollow of a mountain, and the Nibelungs were making ready to share it. And when they saw him, one cried aloud, 'Here comes Siegfried, the great champion from the Netherland!' So the two princes of the Nibelungs bade him welcome, and would have him divide the treasure among them. A mighty store it was, of jewels such plenty that scarce five-score wagons could carry them away, and of red gold yet more. All this they would have Siegfried divide among them. And for his wages they gave him the Nibelungs' sword. But little did they know what should befall at his hand. For lo! ere he had ended his dividing, they stirred up strife against him. Twelve stout comrades had the princes, and with these the princes thought to have slain Siegfried. But they availed nought; with the very sword which they had given him for his reward—Balmung was its name—he slew them all. The giants he slew, and the Kings also, and when Albrich the dwarf would have avenged his lords—for he was the keeper of the treasure—Siegfried overcame him also, and wrested from him the Hood of Darkness, which whoso dons, straightway he vanishes from the sight of all men.

"But the treasure he would not take for himself. 'Carry it back,' said he to Albrich the dwarf, 'to the hole whence it was taken, and keep it for me. And you shall swear a great oath to do me any service that I shall ask of you, whensoever and wheresoever may seem good to me.'

"Another story have I heard tell of Siegfried, how he slew a dragon with his own hand and sword, and how he bathed him in the dragon's blood, and made his skin so hard and horny that no sword may pierce it. Let us therefore receive him with all courtesy; for verily he is a right strong and valiant knight, and 'tis better, I ween, to be his friend than his enemy."

"Methinks thou art right," said King Gunther. "Let us go down and greet him courteously."

Never were guests more honoured as, of a surety, never guests had bolder mien. And as the days went by the Kings and their guests gave themselves to sport and pastime; but whatever they did, Siegfried was ever the first; none could put the stone so far, or cast the spear with so sure an aim. Sometimes the fair ladies of the court looked on, and not a few looked on the young Prince from the Netherland with favour. But he had ever one only in his heart, ever the fair Kriemhild.

King Gunther purposed in his heart to marry a wife. No daughter of his own land would he woo, though there were many fair maidens in the Rhineland. But there came to him tidings of a Queen that dwelt beyond the sea; not to be matched was she for beauty, nor had she any peer for strength. Her love she proffered to any warrior who could vanquish her at three games, hurling of the spear, and putting the stone, and leaping. But if the suitor himself should be vanquished, then must he lose his head. Such were the conditions of her wooing, and many brave warriors had died for her.

On a certain day King Gunther and his chiefs sat in council, and the matter was this—where shall the King seek a wife who shall both be for a comfort to him and for a glory to the land? Then spake the King, "I will seek Queen Brunhild and no other. For her will I hazard my life; nor do I care to live if I may not win her for my wife." To him spake Siegfried, "I would have you give up this purpose. He who woos Brunhild plays for too high a stake. Take my counsel, sire, and go not on such a journey." "I should think it scorn," said he, "to fear a woman, were she ever so bold and strong." "Ah, sire," Siegfried made answer, "you know not how strong she is. Were you four men and not one only, you could not prevail over her."

But King Gunther would not yield. "How strong soever she be, and whatever the chances that befall me, I will woo this fair Brunhild," he said. Then said Hagen, the King's uncle, "Since you are resolved to take in hand this enterprise, ask Prince Siegfried to help you." Then said King Gunther to Siegfried, "Will you help me to win this Brunhild for my wife? Do this, and ask of me what you will." Siegfried made answer, "Give me your sister: I ask no other reward but that I may have the fair Kriemhild to wife." "That I promise," said the King. "Of a surety, so soon as I shall have brought the fair Brunhild to this realm, then will I give you my sister to wife; and I pray from my heart that you may live long and happily together." Then the two sware to each other.

"Tell me now," said Gunther, "how shall we travel to this land where Brunhild dwells? Shall we go in such state as befits a King? If you think fit, I could well bring together thirty thousand warriors." "Thirty thousand would avail nothing," answered Siegfried, "so strong she is and savage. We will take no army, but go as simple knights, taking two companions with us, and the two shall be Sir Hagen and Sir Dankwart." "And wherewithal shall we be clothed?" said King Gunther. "As richly as maybe," answered Siegfried. "My mother has a great store of goodly raiment," said the King. Then spake Hagen, "Nay, sire, go not to the Queen, but rather to your sister. She will provide all things that you need."

So they went to the Lady Kriemhild and told her all their purpose, and how they should need goodly raiment, three changes for the day, and that for four days. With good will did the fair Kriemhild receive them, and promised that she would give them what they needed. As she promised, so she did; for she and her ladies, thirty maids skilful in the work of the needle, laboured night and day to furnish a rich store of apparel. The fair Kriemhild planned them and cut them to just measure with her own hand and her ladies sewed them. Silks there were, some from Arabia, white as snow, and from the Lesser Asia others, green as grass, and strange skins of fishes from distant seas, and fur of the ermine, with black spots on snowy white, and precious stones and gold of Arabia. In seven weeks all was prepared, both apparel and also arms and armour; and there was nothing that was either over-long or over-short, or that could be surpassed for comeliness. Great thanks did the warriors give to each fair seamstress, and to Kriemhild the beautiful the greatest thanks of all.

So the four companions embarked on their ship, with Siegfried for their helmsman, for he knew all the tides and currents of Rhine. Well furnished were they with food and wine and all things that they needed; and prosperous was their voyage, both while they sailed down the river and while they crossed the sea.

On the twelfth morning they came to the land of Queen Brunhild. And when King Gunther saw how the coast stretched far away, and how on every height there stood a fair castle, he said to Siegfried, "Tell me, Siegfried, if you can, whose are those castles, and this fair land. Never in all my life, I assure you, have I seen castles so fairly planned and built so well." Siegfried made answer, "These castles and this fair land are Queen Brunhild's and this strong fortress that you see is Isenstein. And now, my comrades, I have a counsel for your ears. To-day we shall stand in Queen Brunhild's court, and we must be wise and wary when we stand before her. Let therefore one and the same story be found in the mouth of all—that Gunther is my master, and that I am Gunther's man. If we would win our purpose there is no surer plan than this." So spake Siegfried to his comrades. And to the King he said, "Mark, I pray you, what I do for the love of your fair sister."

While they talked one to the other the bark drifted so near to the shore that they could see the maidens standing at the castle windows. "Who are these?" said King Gunther to Siegfried. Said Siegfried, "Look with all your eyes at these fair ladies, and tell me which of them pleases you best, and which, could you win her, you would choose for your wife." Gunther made answer, "One that I see at yonder window in a snow-white vest is surely the loveliest of all. She, if I can win her, shall surely be my wife." "You have chosen well," said Siegfried; "that maiden in the snow-white vest is Brunhild, the fairest and fiercest of women."

Meanwhile the Queen had bidden her maidens depart from the windows. " 'Tis a shame," said she, "that you should make yourselves a sight for strangers."

And now came the four comrades from their bark to the castle. Siegfried led a noble charger by the bridle, and stood by the stirrup till King Gunther had mounted, serving him as a vassal serves his lord. This Brunhild marked from where she stood. "A noble lord," thought she in her heart, "whom such a vassal serves." Then Siegfried mounted his own steed, and Hagen and Dankwart did the like. A fairer company never was seen. The King and Siegfried were clothed in white, and white were their horses, and their shields flashed far as they moved. So, in lordly fashion, they rode to the hall of Queen Brunhild, and the bells of gold that hung from their saddles tinkled as they went. Hagen and Dankwart, on the other hand, wore black apparel, and their chargers were black.

Meanwhile the fair Brunhild inquired of her nobles who these strangers might be that had come across the sea, and on what errand they had come. One of them answered, "Fair lady, I have never seen these stout warriors, save one only, who is greatly like to the noble Siegfried. If this be he, I would have you give him a hearty welcome. Next to him is a man of right royal mien, a King, I trow, who rules with his sceptre mighty lands and herd. The third has a lowering brow, but is a stout warrior withal; the fourth is young and modest of look, but for all his gentle bearing, we should all rue it, I trow, if wrong were done to him."

Then spake Queen Brunhild, "Bring me now my royal vesture; if Siegfried seeks to woo me for his wife, he must risk his life on the cast; I fear him not so much as to yield to him without a struggle." So the Queen arrayed her in her royal robes, and went to the hall of audience, and a hundred maidens and more followed her, fair of face and in fair array. And after the maidens came five hundred warriors and more, each bearing his sword in his hand, the very flower of Isenland.

Said Queen Brunhild to Siegfried, "You are welcome, good Sir Siegfried. Show me, if you will, for what cause you have come hither." "I thank you a thousand times," answered Siegfried, "that you have greeted me so courteously, but know that I must give place to this noble hero. He is my lord and master; I am his vassal. Let your favour be for him. His kingdom is by the Rhine side, and we have sailed all this way from thence that he may woo you for his bride. That is his fixed intent, nor will he yield whatever may befall. Gunther is his name; a great King is he, and nothing will content him but to carry you back with him to the Rhine."

Queen Brunhild answered, "If he is the master and you the man, then let him know that he must match me in my games and conquer me. If he prevail, then will I be his wedded wife; but if I prevail, then must he die, he and you and all his comrades." Then spake Sir Hagen, "Lady, tell us

110

now the games at which my master must contend; and know that you must strive full hard, if you would conquer him, for he has a full trust that he will win you for his bride." The Queen answered, "He must cast the stone further than I, and also leap behind it further than I leap; and also he must cast the spear with me. It seems to me that you are over-hasty; let him count the cost, ere he lose both fame and life." Then Siegfried whispered to the King, "Have no fear for what shall be, and cast away all your care. Let the fair Brunhild do what she will, I will bear you harmless." So the King spake aloud, "Fairest of the fair, tell me your pleasure; were it a greater task willingly would I undertake it, for if I win you not for my bride, willingly will I lose my head."

Then the fair Brunhild called for her battle gear, her arms, and her breastplate of gold and her mighty shield; and over all she drew a surcoat of silk, marvellously made. Fierce and angry was her countenance as she looked at the strangers, and Hagen and Dankwart were troubled to see her, for they doubted how it might go with their master. " 'Tis a fatal journey," said they, "and will bring us to trouble."

Meanwhile Siegfried hied him with nimble foot to the bark, and there he took, from the secret corner where he kept it, the Hood of Darkness, by which, at his will, he could make himself invisible. Quickly did he go, and quickly returned, and now no one could see him, for he wore the hood. Through the crowd he went at his pleasure, seeing all but seen of none.

Meanwhile men had marked out the ring for the fray, and chiefs had been chosen as umpires, seven hundred men in armour who should judge betwixt the combatants. First of the two came the fair Brunhild. So mighty was her presence, a man had thought her ready to match herself in battle with all the Kings in the world. And there was carried before her a mighty shield of ruddy gold, very thick and broad and heavy, overlaid with studs of steel. Four chamberlains could scarce bear the weight. Sir Hagen, when he saw it, said, "How now, my lord King? this fair one whom you would woo must surely be the devil's wife. "Next came three men who scarce could carry the Queen's javelin, with its mighty spear-head, heavy and great as though three had been melted into one. And when King Gunther saw it, he said to himself, "This is a danger from which the devil himself can scarce escape. I would that I were once more by the banks of Rhine; he that would might woo and win this fair maiden for me." After this there was brought the mighty stone which Brunhild was to hurl. Twelve knights could scarce support it, so big it was.

And now the Queen addressed her to the contest, rolling her sleeves about her arms, and fitting her buckler, and poising her mighty spear in her hand. And the strangers, when they saw it, were sore afraid for all their courage.

But now came Siegfried to King Gunther's side and touched his hand. Greatly amazed was the King for he did not understand his champion's device. "Who was it that touched me?" he said, and looked round, but saw no one. " 'Tis I," answered the Prince, "your trusty friend, Siegfried. Have no fear of the maiden. Let me carry the buckler; you shall seem to do each deed, but I will do it in truth. But be careful to hide the device. Should the maiden discover it, she will not spare to bring it to nought." Right glad was Gunther to know that his strong ally was at hand.

And now the Queen threw the spear with all her might against the shield Siegfried bore upon his arm. New was the shield and stout of make, but the spear-head passed clean through it, and rang on the hero's coat of mail, dealing him so sore a blow that the blood gushed forth from his mouth. Of a truth, but for the Hood of Darkness, that hour both the champions had died. Then Siegfried caught the great spear in his hand, and tore it from the shield, and hurled it back. "She is too fair to slay." said he to himself, and he turned the spear point behind him, and smote the maiden with the shaft on the silken vest that she wore. Loud rang the blow, and the fire-sparks leapt from her armour. Never could Gunther, for all his strength, have dealt such a blow, for it felled the strong Brunhild to the ground. Lightly did she leap up again, crying, "King Gunther, I thank you for the blow; 'twas shrewdly given," for she thought that the King had dealt it.

But great was the wrath in her heart to find that her spear had sped in vain. And now she turned to the great stone where it lay, and poised it in her hand, and hurled it with all her might. And having hurled it, she herself leapt after it. Twelve full arms' length hurtled the great stone through the air, so mighty was the maiden, and she herself overpassed it by a pace. Then came Gunther to the place, with Siegfried unseen by his side. And Siegfried caught the stone and poised it—but it seemed to all as if Gunther did it—and threw it yet another arm's length beyond the cast of the maid, and passed the stone himself, aye, and carried King Gunther along with him, so mighty was he!

But when the Queen saw that she was vanquished, she flushed with shame and wrath, and turning to her lords, she spake aloud, "Come hither, my kinsmen and lieges. You must now be thralls of King Gunther of Burgundy."

So the chiefs of Isenland laid their swords at Gunther's feet and did him homage, for they thought that he had vanquished by his own strength; and he, for he was a very gentle, courteous knight, greeted the maid right pleasantly, and she, for her part, took him by the hand and said, "Henceforth, Sir King, all the rule and power that I have held is yours."

There is no need to tell how Gunther and Brunhild and all their company travelled to Rhineland with great joy, and how Queen Uté and her sons and the fair Kriemhild, and all the people of the land, gave them a hearty welcome and how in due time King Gunther was married to the fair Brunhild. Nor is there need of many words to relate how Siegfried also took to wife the beautiful Kriemhild, as it had been promised him. Nor were there any to gainsay save Brunhild only, for she grudged that her husband's sister should be given to a vassal, for such in truth she deemed him to be. Very ill content she was, though the King would fain have satisfied her, saying that he was a very noble knight, and was lord of many woodlands, and had great store of gold and treasure.

So Siegfried wedded the fair Kriemhild and took her with him to his own land. A goodly welcome did the Netherlands give her. And Siegmund gave up his kingdom to his son, and the two lived in much peace and love together, and when in the tenth year a son was born to them, they called him by the name of his uncle Gunther.

Also Gunther and Brunhild lived together in much happiness. They also had a son, and they called him by the name of Siegfried.

But Brunhild was ill content that Siegfried being, for so she deemed, her husband's vassal, should pay no homage to his lord and do no service for his fee. And she was very urgent with her husband that he should suffer this no longer. But the King was fain to put her off. "Nay," said he, "the journey is too long. Their land is far from ours; why should we trouble him to come? Also he is a great prince and a powerful." "Be he as great as he will," she answered, " 'tis a vassal's duty to pay homage to his lord." But Gunther laughed to himself. Little thought had he of homage from Siegfried. Then the Queen changed her voice. "Dear lord," she said, "how gladly would I see Siegfried and your dear sister once more. Well do I remember how fair she was and how kind, how gracious of speech when we sat together, brides both of us." With such words she persuaded her husband. "There are no guests that would be more welcome," said he; "I will find messengers who shall bid them come to the Rhineland."

Great was the joy in Rhineland when the messengers returned and told how they had been welcomed and royally entertained and loaded with gifts, and how that Siegfried and his Queen Kriemhild and a company of gallant knights were coming to the festival. Great was the joy and manifold the preparations.

No sooner did the King hear the news than he sought out Queen Brunhild where she sat in her chamber. "Bear you in mind," said he, "how Kriemhild my sister welcomed you when you came hither from your own land. Do you, therefore, dear wife, welcome her with the like affection." "So shall it be," answered the Queen.

And indeed, when the guests came, right royal was the welcome that they had. For Gunther and Brunhild rode forth from the city to meet them, and greeted them most heartily. All was mirth and jollity. By the day there were tilts and tournaments and sports of every kind, and at night there was feasting in the hall. And so they did for twelve days.

But Brunhild ever cherished a thought of mischief in her heart. "Why," she said to herself, "why has Siegfried stayed so long to do homage for that which he holds of us in fee? I shall not be content till Kriemhild answer me in this."

It fell out on a certain day, while sundry knights were in the castle court, that the two Queens sat together. The fair Kriemhild then began, "My husband is so mighty a man that he should rule these kingdoms of right." "Nay," answered Brunhild, "that might be were you and your husband only alive, and all others dead, but so long as Gunther lives he must needs be King." Then said fair Kriemhild, "See how he shines among the knights, a very moon among the stars." Brunhild answered, "However brave and strong he may be, and stately to look upon, Gunther, your brother, is better than he." "Nay," said Kriemhild, "better he is not, nay, nor even his peer." "How say you?" answered Brunhild in wrath; "I spake not without cause. When I saw the two for the first time, then I heard with my own ears how Siegfried confessed that he was Gunther's man. Yea, I heard him say it, and I hold him to be such." "This is folly," said Kriemhild; "think you that my brothers could have given me to be bride to a vassal? Away, Brunhild, with such idle talk, if we would still be friends." "I will not away with it," Brunhild made answer. "Shall I renounce the service which he and all the vassals are bound to render to their lord?" "Renounce it you must," cried Kriemhild in great wrath. "The service of a vassal he will never do; he is of higher degree than Gunther my brother, though Gunther is a noble King." "You bear yourself far too proudly," answered Brunhild.

But the deadliest cause of quarrel was yet to come. Said Queen Kriemhild to Queen Brunhild when next she saw her: "Think you that when you were vanquished in your own land it was Gunther, my brother, that vanquished you?" "Yea," answered the Queen, "did I not see it with my own eyes?" "Nay," said Kriemhild, "it was not so. See you this ring?" And she took a ring that she had upon her finger and held it forth. "Do you know it?" And Brunhild looked and knew it for her own. "That," said Kriemhild, "Siegfried, my husband, took from you when you were smitten by his spear and knew not what had befallen you, so sore was the blow. You saw him not, for he had the Hood of Darkness on him and was invisible. But it was he that smote you with the spear, and put the stone further than you, and passed you in the leap. And this ring he gave me for a token, if ever you should boast yourself against me. Talk, therefore, no more of lords and vassals. My husband feigned this vassalage that he might deceive you the more readily."

But Brunhild held her peace, for the ring was a proof which she could not gainsay. She held her peace, but she cherished her rage, keeping it in the depths of her heart, and sware that she would be avenged on the man that had so deceived her.

When Hagen saw that Queen Brunhild was in continual trouble and sadness he would fain know the cause. " 'Tis of Siegfried's doing," she answered. "He has wronged me beyond pardon." And she besought him that he would avenge her and King Gunther upon him.

So Hagan plotted evil, saying enemies were coming against Gunther, and Siegfried and his knights made them ready to go forth to the King's defence. And of the chiefs of Rhineland not a few offered themselves as comrades, knowing nothing of the treachery that Hagen and his fellows were preparing against him.

But before they departed Hagen went to bid farewell to Queen Kriemhild. Said she, "I have good comfort in my heart to think how valiant a husband I have, and how zealous he is to help his friends, for I have loved my kinsmen always, nor ever wished them ill." "Tell me, dear lady," said Hagen, "what service I can do to your husband, for there is no one whom I love better than him." The Queen made answer, "I have no fear that my lord will fall in battle by any man's sword, save only that he is too ready to follow even to rashness his own warlike spirit." "Dear lady," said Hagen, "if there is any danger which you hold in special fear, tell me that I may defend him against it." Then Kriemhild, in the simpleness of her heart, told him the secret. "In years gone by," said she, "my husband slew a dragon among the mountains, and when he had slain the monster, he bathed himself in its blood. So mighty was the charm, that thenceforth no steel had power to wound him. And yet, for all this, I am ever in fear lest by some mischance a weapon should pierce him. Hearken now, my cousin, for you are of my kindred, hearken, and see how I put my trust in your honour. While Siegfried washed his limbs in the blood of the dragon, there fell a leaf from a linden tree between his shoulders. There and there only can steel harm him." " 'Tis easy," said the false Hagen, "for me to defend so small a spot. Only do you sew a little token on his cloak, that I may the better know the spot that most needs protection when we stand together in the fight." "I will do so," said the Queen; "I will sew a little cross with threads of silk on his cloak, and you will guard him when he fights in the throng of his foes." "That will I do, dear lady," said the traitor.

Hagen went straightway to King Gunther and said, "I have learnt that which I needed to know; put off this march; let us go on a hunt. So that which we would do will be easier done." "I will order that," answered the King.

Siegfried, before he set out for the hunting, bade farewell to his wife: "God grant," said he, "that we may soon meet happily again; meanwhile be merry among your kinsfolk here." But Kriemhild thought of how she had discovered the secret to Hagen, and was sore afraid, yet dared not tell the truth. Only she said to her husband, "I pray you to leave this hunting. Only this night past I had an evil dream. I saw two wild boars pursuing you over the heath, and the flowers were red as with blood. Greatly I fear some treason, my Siegfried." "Nay," said he, "there is not one in Rhineland here that bears me ill-will. Whom have I wronged?" "I know not," answered the Queen, "but yet my heart bodes evil. For I had yet another dream. I seemed to see two mountains fall with a terrible noise on your head. If you go, you will break my heart." But he laughed at her fears, and kissed her, and so departed.

Then Siegfried went on the hunting, and Gunther and Hagen went with him, and a company of hunters and hounds. When they came to the forest Siegfried said, "Now who shall begin the hunting?" Hagen made answer, "Let us divide into two companies ere we begin, and each shall beat the coverts as he will; so shall we see who is the more skilful in the chase." "I need no pack," said Siegfried; "give me one well-trained hound that can track the game through the coverts. That will suffice for me." So a lime-hound was given to him. All that the good hound started did Siegfried slay; no beast could outrun him or escape him. A wild boar first he slew, and next to the boar a lion; he shot an arrow through the beast from side to side. After the lion he slew a buffalo and four elks, and a great store of game besides, so that the huntsmen said, "Leave us something in our woods, Sir Siegfried."

King Gunther bade blow the horn for breakfast. When Siegfried's huntsman heard the blast he said: "Our hunting-time is over; we must back to our comrades." So they went with all speed to the trysting-place.

The whole company sat down to their meal. There was plenty of every kind, but wine was wanting. "How is this?" said Siegfried: "the kitchen is plentiful; but where is the wine?" Said Gunther the King, " 'Tis Hagen's fault, who makes us all go dry." "True, Sir King," said Hagen, "my fault it is. But I know of a runnel, cold and clear, that is hard by. Let us go thither and quench our thirst." Then Siegfried rose from his place, for his thirst was sore, and would have sought the place. Said Hagen, when he saw him rise, "I have heard say that there is no man in all the land so fleet of foot as Siegfried. Will he deign to let us see his speed?" "With all my heart," cried the hero. "Let us race from hence to the runnel." " 'Tis agreed," said Hagen the traitor. "Furthermore," said Siegfried, "I will carry all the equipment that I bare in the chase." So Gunther and Hagen stripped them to their shirts, but Siegfried carried sword and spear, all his hunting-gear, and yet was far before the two at the runnel.

Yet, such was his courtesy, that he would not drink before the King had quenched his thirst. He was ill repaid, I trow, for his grace. For when the King had drunk, as Siegfried knelt plunging his head into the stream, Sir Hagen took his spear and smote him on the little crosslet mark that was worked on his cloak between his shoulders. And when he had struck the blow he fled in mortal fear. When Siegfried felt that he was wounded, he rose with a great bound from his knees and sought for his weapons. But these the false Hagen had taken and laid far away. Only the shield was left. This he took in his hand and hurled at Hagen with such might that it felled the traitor to the ground, and was itself broken to pieces. If the hero had but had his good sword Balmung in his hand, the murderer had not escaped with his life that day.

Then all the Rhineland warriors gathered about him. Among them was King Gunther, making pretence to lament. To him said Siegfried, "Little it profits to bewail the man whose murder you have plotted. Did I not save you from shame and defeat? Is this the recompense that you pay? And yet even of you I would ask one favour. Have some kindness for my wife. She is your sister; if you have any knightly faith and honour remaining, guard her well." Then there came upon him the anguish of death. Yet one more word he spake, "Be sure that in slaying me you have slain yourselves." And when he had so spoken he died.

Then they laid his body on a shield and carried it back, having agreed among themselves to tell this tale, that Sir Siegfried having chosen to hunt by himself was slain by robbers in the wood.

# ROLAND

THE trumpets sounded and the army went on its way to France. The next day King Charles called his lords together. "You see," said he, "these narrow passes. Whom shall I place to command the rearguard? Choose you a man yourselves." Said Ganelon, "Whom should we choose but my son-in-law, Count Roland? You have no man in your host so valiant. Of a truth he will be the salvation of France." The King said when he heard these words, "What ails you, Ganelon? You look like to one possessed."

When Count Roland knew what was proposed concerning him, he spake out as a true knight should speak: "I am right thankful to you, my father-in-law, that you have caused me to be put in this place. Of a truth the King of France shall lose nothing by my means, neither charger, nor mule, nor packhorse, nor beast of burden."

Then Roland turned to the King and said, "Give me twenty thousand only, so they be men of valour, and I will keep the passes in all safety. So long as I shall live, you need fear no man."

Then Roland mounted his horse. With him were Oliver his comrade, and Otho and Berenger, and Gerard of Roussillon, an aged warrior, and others, men of renown. And Turpin the Archbishop cried, "By my head, I will go also." So they chose twenty thousand warriors with whom to keep the passes.

Meanwhile King Charles had entered the valley of Roncesvalles. High were the mountains on either side of the way, and the valleys were gloomy and dark. But when the army had passed through the valley, they saw the fair land of Gascony, and as they saw it they thought of their homes and their wives and daughters. There was not one of them but wept for very tenderness of heart. But of all that company there was none sadder than the King himself, when he thought how he had left his nephew Count Roland behind him in the passes of Spain.

And now the Saracen King Marsilas began to gather his army. He laid a strict command on all his nobles and chiefs that they should bring with them to Saragossa as many men as they could gather together. And when they were come to the city, it being the third day from the issuing of the King's command, they saluted the great image of Mahomet, the false prophet, that stood on the topmost tower. This done they went forth from the city gates. They made all haste, marching across the mountains and valleys of Spain till they came in sight of the standard of France, where Roland and Oliver and the Twelve Peers were ranged in battle array.

The Saracen champions donned their coats of mail, of double substance most of them, and they set upon their heads helmets of Saragossa of well-tempered metal, and they girded themselves with swords of Vienna. Fair were their shields to view, their lances were from Valentia, their standards were of white, blue, and red. Their mules they left with the servants, and, mounting their chargers, so moved forwards. Fair was the day and bright the sun, as their armour flashed in the light and the drums were beaten so loudly that the Frenchmen heard the sound.

Said Oliver to Roland, "Comrade, methinks we shall soon do battle with the Saracens." "God grant it," answered Roland. " 'Tis our duty to hold the place for the King, and we will do it, come what may. As for me, I will not set an ill example."

Oliver climbed to the top of a hill, and saw from thence the whole army of the heathen. He cried to Roland his companion, "I see the flashing of arms. We men of France shall have no small trouble therefrom. This is the doing of Ganelon the traitor."

"Be silent," answered Roland, "till you shall know; say no more about him."

Oliver looked again from the hilltop, and saw how the Saracens came on. So many there were that he could not count their battalions. He descended to the plain with all speed, and came to the array of the French, and said, "I have seen more heathen than man ever yet saw together upon the earth. There are a hundred thousand at the least. We shall have such a battle with them as has never before been fought. My brethren of France, quit you like men, be strong; stand firm that you be not conquered." And all the army shouted with one voice, "Cursed be he that shall fly."

Then Oliver turned to Roland, and said, "Sound your horn; my friend, Charles will hear it, and will return." "I were a fool," answered Roland, "so to do. Not so; but I will deal these heathen some mighty blows with Durendal my sword. They have been ill-advised to venture into these passes. I swear that they are condemned to death, one and all."

After a while, Oliver said again, "Friend Roland, sound your horn of ivory. Then will the King returns and bring his army with him, to our help." But Roland answered again, "I will not do dishonour to my kinsmen, or to the fair land of France. I have my sword; that shall suffice for me. These evil-minded heathen are gathered together against us to their own hurt. Surely not one of them shall escape from death." "As for me," said Oliver, "I see not where the dishonour would be. I saw the valleys and the mountains covered with the great multitude of Saracens. Theirs is, in truth, a mighty array, and we are but few." "So much the better," answered Roland. "It makes my courage grow. 'Tis better to die than to be disgraced. And remember, the harder our blows the more the King will love us."

Roland was brave, but Oliver was wise. "Consider," he said, "comrade. These enemies are over-near to us, and the King over-far. Were he here, we should not be in danger; but there are some here to-day who will never fight in another battle."

Then Turpin the Archbishop struck spurs into his horse, and rode to a hilltop. Then he turned to the men of France, and spake: "Lords of France, King Charles has left us here; our King he is, and it is our duty to die for him. To-day our Christian Faith is in peril: do ye fight for it. Fight ye must; be sure of that, for there under your eyes are the Saracens. Confess, therefore, your sins, and pray to God that He have mercy upon you. And now for your soul's health I will give you all absolution. If you die, you will be God's martyrs, every one of you, and your places are ready for you in His Paradise."

Thereupon the men of France dismounted, and knelt upon the ground, and the Archbishop blessed them in God's name. "But look," said he, "I set you a penance—smite these pagans." Then the men of France rose to their feet. They had received absolution, and were set free from all their sins, and the Archbishop had blessed them in the name of God. After this they mounted their swift steeds, and clad themselves in armour, and made themselves ready for the battle.

Said Roland to Oliver, "Brother, you know that it is Ganelon who has betrayed us. Good store he has had of gold and silver as a reward; 'tis the King Marsilas that has made merchandise of us, but verily it is with our swords that he shall be paid." So saying, he rode on to the pass, mounted on his good steed Veillantif. His spear he held with the point to the sky; a white flag it bore with fringes of gold which fell down to his hands. A stalwart man was he, and his countenance was fair and smiling. Behind him followed Oliver, his friend; and the men of France pointed to him, saying, "See our champion!" Pride was in his eye when he looked towards the Saracens; but to the men of France his regard was all sweetness and humility. Full courteously he spake to them: "Ride not so fast, my lords," he said; "verily these heathen are come hither, seeking martyrdom. 'Tis a fair spoil that we shall gather from them to-day. Never has King of France gained any so rich." And as he spake, the two hosts came together.

Said Oliver, "You did not deem it fit, my lord, to sound your horn. Therefore you lack the help which the King would have sent. Not his the blame, for he knows nothing of what has chanced. But do you, lords of France, charge as fiercely as you may, and yield not one whit to the enemy. Think upon these two things only—how to deal a straight blow and to take it. And let us not forget King Charles's cry of battle." Then all the men of France with one voice cried out, "Mountjoy!" He that heard them so cry had never doubted that they were men of valour. Proud was their array as they rode on to battle, spurring their horses that they might speed the more. And the Saracens, on their part, came forward with a good heart. Thus did the Frenchmen and the heathen meet in the shock of battle.

Full many of the heathen warriors fell that day. Not one of the Twelve Peers of France but slew his man. But of all none bare himself so valiantly as Roland. Many a blow did he deal to the enemy with his mighty spear, and when the spear was shivered in his hand, fifteen warriors having fallen before it, then he seized his good sword Durendal, and smote man after man to the ground. Red was he with the blood of his enemies, red was his hauberk, red his arms, red his shoulders, aye, and the neck of his horse. Not one of the Twelve lingered in the rear, or was slow to strike, but Count Roland was the bravest of the brave. "Well done, Sons of France!" cried Turpin the Archbishop, when he saw them lay on in such sort.

Next to Roland for valour and hardihood came Oliver, his companion. Many a heathen warrior did he slay, till at last his spear was shivered in his hand. "What are you doing, comrade?" cried Roland, when he was aware of the mishap. "A man wants no staff in such a battle as this. 'Tis the steel and nothing else that he must have. Where is your sword Hautclere, with its hilt of gold and its pommel of crystal?" "On my word," said Oliver, "I have not had time to draw it; I was so busy with striking." But as he spake he drew the good sword from its scabbard, and smote a heathen knight, Justin of the Iron Valley. A mighty blow it was, cleaving the man in twain down to his saddle—aye, and the saddle itself with its adorning of gold and jewels, and the very backbone also of the steed whereon he rode, so that horse and man fell dead together on the plains. "Well done!" cried Roland; "you are a true brother of mine. 'Tis such strokes as this that make the King love us."

Nevertheless, for all the valour of Roland and his fellows the battle went hard with the men of France. Many lances were shivered, many flags torn, and many gallant youths cut off in their prime. Never more would they see mother and wife. It was an ill deed that the traitor Ganelon wrought when he sold his fellows to King Marsilas!

And now there befell a new trouble. King Almaris, with a great host of heathen, coming by an unknown way, fell upon the rear of the host where there was another pass. Fiercely did the noble Walter that kept the same charge the newcomers, but they overpowered him and his followers. He was wounded with four several lances, and four times did he swoon, so that at the last he was constrained to leave the field of battle, that he might call the Count Roland to his aid. But small was the aid which Roland could give him or any one. Valiantly he held up the battle, and with him Oliver, and Turpin the Archbishop, and others also; but the lines of the men of France were broken, and their armour thrust through, and their spears shivered, and their flags trodden in the dust. For all this they made such slaughter among the heathen that King Almaris, who led the armies of the enemy, scarcely could win back his way to his own people, wounded in four places and sorely spent. A right good warrior was he; had he but been a Christian but few had matched him in battle.

Count Roland saw how grievously his people had suffered and spake thus to Oliver his comrade: "Dear comrade, you see how many brave men lie dead upon the ground. Well may we mourn for fair France, widowed as she is of so many valiant champions. But why is our King not here? O Oliver, my brother, what shall we do to send him tidings of our state?" "I know not," answered Oliver. "Only this I know—that death is to be chosen rather than dishonour."

After a while Roland said again, "I shall blow my horn; King Charles will hear it, where he has encamped beyond the passes, and he and his host will come back." "That would be ill done," answered Oliver, "and shame both you and your race. When I gave you this counsel you would have none of it. Now I like it not. 'Tis not for a brave man to sound the horn and cry for help now that we are in such case." "The battle is too hard for us," said Roland again, "and I shall sound my horn, that the King may hear." And Oliver answered again, "When I gave you this counsel, you scorned it. Now I myself like it not. 'Tis true that had the King been here, we had not suffered this loss. But the blame is not his. 'Tis your folly, Count Roland, that has done to death all these men of France. But for that we should have conquered in this battle, and have taken and slain King Marsilas. But now we can do nothing for France and the King. We can but die. Woe is me for our country, aye, and for our friendship, which will come to a grievous end this day."

The Archbishop perceived that the two friends were at variance, and spurred his horse till he came where they stood. "Listen to me," he said, "Sir Roland and Sir Oliver. I implore you not to fall out with each other in this fashion. We, sons of France, that are in this place, are of a truth condemned to death, neither will the sounding of your horn save us, for the King is far away, and cannot come in time. Nevertheless, I hold it to be well that you should sound it. When the King and his army shall come, they will find us dead—that I know full well. But they will avenge us, so that our enemies shall not go away rejoicing. And they will also recover our bodies, and will carry them away for burial in holy places, so that the dogs and wolves shall not devour them."

"You say well," cried Roland, and he put his horn to his lips, and gave so mighty a blast upon it, that the sound was heard thirty leagues away. King Charles and his men heard it, and the King said, "Our countrymen are fighting with the enemy." But Ganelon answered, "Sire, had any but you so spoken, I had said that he spoke falsely."

Then Roland blew his horn a second time; with great pain and anguish of body he blew it, and the red blood gushed from his lips; but the sound was heard yet further than at first. Again the King heard it, and all his nobles, and all his men. "That," said he, "is Roland's horn; he never had sounded it were he not in battle with the enemy." But Ganelon answered again: "Believe me, Sire, there is no battle. You are an old man, and you have the fancies of a child. You know what a mighty man of valour is this Roland. Think you that any one would dare to attack him? No one, of a truth. Ride on, Sire, why halt you here? The fair land of France is yet far away."

Roland blew his horn a third time, and when the King heard it he said, "He that blew that horn drew a deep breath." And Duke Naymes cried out, "Roland is in trouble; on my conscience he is fighting with the enemy. Some one has betrayed him; 'tis he, I doubt not, that would deceive you now. To arms, Sire! utter your war-cry, and help your own house and your country. You have heard the cry of the noble Roland."

Then King Charles bade all the trumpets sound, and forthwith all the men of France armed themselves, with helmets, and hauberks, and swords with pummels of gold. Mighty were their shields, and their lances strong, and the flags that they carried were white and red and blue. And when they made an end of their arming they rode back with all haste. There was not one of them but said to his comrade, "If we find Roland yet alive, what mighty strokes will we strike for him!"

But Ganelon the King handed over to the knaves of his kitchen. "Take this traitor," said he, "who has sold his country." Ill did Ganelon fare among them. They pulled out his hair and his beard and smote him with their staves; then they put a great chain, such as that with which a bear is bound, about his neck, and made him fast to a pack-horse.

This done, the King and his army hastened with all speed to the help of Roland. In the van and the rear sounded the trumpets as though they would answer Roland's horn. Full of wrath was King Charles as he rode; full of wrath were all the men of France. There was not one among them but wept and sobbed; there was not one but prayed, "Now, may God keep Roland alive till we come to the battlefield, so that we may strike a blow for him." Alas! it was all in vain; they could not come in time for all their speed.

Count Roland looked round on the mountain-sides and on the plains. Alas! how many noble sons of France he saw lying dead upon them! "Dear friends," he said, weeping as he spoke, "may God have mercy on you and receive you into His Paradise! More loyal followers have I never seen. How is the fair land of France widowed of her bravest, and I can give you no help. Oliver, dear comrade, we must not part. If the enemy slay me not here, surely I shall be slain by sorrow. Come then, let us smite these heathen."

Thus did Roland again charge the enemy, his good sword Durendal in his hand; as the stag flies before the hounds, so did the heathen fly before Roland. "By my faith," cried the Archbishop when he saw him, "that is a right good knight! Such courage, and such a steed, and such arms I love well to see. If a man be not brave and a stout fighter, he had better by far be a monk in some cloister where he may pray all day long for our sins."

Now the heathen, when they saw how few the Frenchmen were, took fresh courage. And the Caliph, spurring his horse, rode against Oliver and smote him in the middle of his back, making his spear pass right through him. "That is a shrewd blow," he cried; "I have avenged my friends and countrymen upon you."

Then Oliver knew he was stricken to death, but he would not fall unavenged. With his great sword Hautclere he smote the Caliph on his head and cleft it to the teeth. "Curse on you, pagan. Neither your wife nor any woman in the land of your birth shall boast that you have taken a penny's worth from King Charles!" But to Roland he cried, "Come, comrade, help me; well I know that we two shall part in great sorrow this day."

Roland came with all speed, and saw his friend, how he lay all pale and fainting on the ground and how the blood gushed in great streams from his wound. "I know not what to do," he cried. "This is an ill chance that has befallen you. Truly France is bereaved of her bravest son." So saying he went near to swoon in the saddle as he sat. Then there befell a strange thing. Oliver had lost so much of his blood that he could not any more see clearly or know who it was that was near him. So he raised up his arm and smote with all his strength that yet remained to him on the helmet of Roland his friend. The helmet he cleft in twain to the visor; but by good fortune it wounded not the head. Roland looked at him and said in a gentle voice, "Did you this of set purpose? I am Roland your friend, and have not harmed you."

"Ah!" said Oliver, "I hear you speak, but I cannot see you. Pardon me that I struck you; it was not done of set purpose." "It harmed me not," answered Roland; "with all my heart and before God I forgive you." And this was the way these two friends parted at the last.

And now Oliver felt the pains of death come over him. He could no longer see nor hear. Therefore he turned his thoughts to making his peace with God, and clasping his hands lifted them to heaven and made his confession. "O Lord," he said, "take me into Paradise. And do Thou bless King Charles and the sweet land of France." And when he had said thus he died. And Roland looked at him as he lay. There was not upon earth a more sorrowful man than he. "Dear comrade," he said, "this is indeed an evil day. Many a year have we two been together. Never have I done wrong to you; never have you done wrong to me. How shall I bear to live without you?" And he swooned where he sat on his horse. But the stirrup held him up that he did not fall to the ground.

When Roland came to himself he looked about him and saw how great was the calamity that had befallen his army. For now there were left alive to him two only, Turpin the Archbishop and Walter of Hum. Walter had but that moment come down from the hills where he had been fighting so fiercely with the heathen that all his men were dead; now he cried to Roland for help. "Noble Count, where are you? I am Walter of Hum, and am not unworthy to be your friend. Help me therefore. For see how my spear is broken and my shield cleft in twain, my hauberk is in pieces, and my body sorely wounded. I am about to die; but I have sold my life at a great price." When Roland heard him cry he set spurs to his horse and galloped to him. "Walter," said he, "you are a brave warrior and a trustworthy. Tell me now where are the thousand valiant men whom you took from my army. They were right good soldiers, and I am in sore need of them."

"They are dead," answered Walter; "you will see them no more. A sore battle we had with the Saracens yonder on the hills; they had the men of Canaan there and the men of Armenia and the Giants; there were no better men in their army than these. We dealt with them so that they will not boast themselves of this day's work. But it cost us dear; all the men of France lie dead on the plain, and I am wounded to the death. And now, Roland, blame me not that I fled; for you are my lord, and all my trust is in you."

"I blame you not," said Roland, "only as long as you live help me against the heathen." And as he spake he took his cloak and rent it into strips and bound up Walter's wounds therewith. This done he and Walter and the Archbishop set fiercely on the enemy. Five-and-twenty did Roland slay, and Walter slew six, and the Archbishop five. Three valiant men of war they were; fast and firm they stood one by the other; hundreds there were of the heathen, but they dared not come near to these three valiant champions of France. They stood far off, and cast at the three spears and darts and javelins and weapons of every kind. Walter of Hum was slain forthwith; and the Archbishop's armour was broken, and he wounded, and his horse slain under him. Nevertheless he lifted himself from the ground, still keeping a good heart in his breast. "They have not overcome me yet"; said he, "as long as a good soldier lives, he does not yield."

Roland took his horn once more and sounded it, for he would know whether King Charles were coming. Ah me! it was a feeble blast that he blew. But the King heard it, and he halted and listened. "My lords!" said he, "things go ill for us, I doubt not. To-day we shall lose, I fear me much, my brave nephew Roland. I know by the sound of his horn that he has but a short time to live. Put your horses to their full speed, if you would come in time to help him, and let a blast be sounded by every trumpet that there is in the army." So all the trumpets in the host sounded a blast; all the valleys and hills re-echoed with the sound; sore discouraged were the heathen when they heard it. "King Charles has come again," they cried; "we are all as dead men. When he comes he shall not find Roland alive." Then four hundred of them, the strongest and most valiant knights that were in the army of the heathen, gathered themselves into one company, and made a yet fiercer assault on Roland.

Roland saw them coming, and waited for them without fear. So long as he lived he would not yield himself to the enemy or give place to them. "Better death than flight," said he, as he mounted his good steed Veillantif, and rode towards the enemy.

And by his side went Turpin the Archbishop on foot. Then said Roland to Turpin, "I am on horseback and you are on foot. But let us keep together; never will I leave you; we two will stand against these heathen dogs. They have not, I warrant, among them such a sword as Durendal." "Good," answered the Archbishop. "Shame to the man who does not smite his hardest. And though this be our last battle, I know well that King Charles will take ample vengeance for us."

When the heathen saw these two stand together they fell back in fear and hurled at them spears and darts and javelins without number. Roland's shield they broke and his hauberk; but him they hurt not; nevertheless they did him a grievous injury, for they killed his good steed Veillantif. Thirty wounds did Veillantif receive, and he fell dead under his master. At last the Archbishop was stricken and Roland stood alone, for the heathen had fled from his presence.

When Roland saw that the Archbishop was dead, his heart was sorely troubled in him. Never did he feel a greater sorrow for comrade slain, save Oliver only. "Charles of France," he said, "come as quickly as you may, many a gallant knight have you lost in Roncesvalles. But King Marsilas, on his part, has lost his army. For one that has fallen on this side there has fallen full forty on that." So saying he turned to the Archbishop; he crossed the dead man's hands upon his breast and said, "I commit thee to the Father's mercy. Never has man served his God with a better will, never since the beginning of the

140

world has there lived a sturdier champion of the faith. May God be good to you and give you all good things!"

Now Roland felt that his own death was near at hand. In one hand he took his horn, and in the other his good sword Durendal, and made his way the distance of a furlong or so till he came to a plain, and in the midst of the plain a little hill. On the top of the hill in the shade of two fair trees were four marble steps. There Roland fell in a swoon upon the grass. There a certain Saracen spied him. The fellow had feigned death, and had laid himself down among the slain, having covered his body and his face with blood. When he saw Roland, he raised himself from where he was lying among the slain and ran to the place, and, being full of pride and fury, seized the Count in his arms, crying aloud, "He is conquered, he is conquered, he is conquered, the famous nephew of King Charles! See, here is his sword; 'tis a noble spoil that I shall carry back with me to Arabia." Thereupon he took the sword in one hand, with the other he laid hold of Roland's beard. But as the man laid hold, Roland came to himself, and knew that some one was taking his sword from him. He opened his eyes but not a word did he speak save this only, "Fellow, you are none of ours," and he smote him a mighty blow upon his helmet. The steel he brake through and the head beneath, and laid the man dead at his feet. "Coward," he said, "what made you so bold that you dared lay hands on Roland? Whosoever knows him will think you a fool for your deed."

And now Roland knew that death was near at hand. He raised himself and gathered all his strength together—ah me! how pale his face was!—and took in his hand his good sword Durendal. Before him was a great rock and on this in his rage and pain he smote ten mighty blows. Loud rang the steel upon the stone; but it neither brake nor splintered. "Help me," he cried, "O Mary, our Lady. O my good sword, my Durendal, what an evil lot is mine! In the day when I must part with you, my power over you is lost. Many a battle I have won with your help; and many a kingdom have I conquered, that my Lord Charles possesses this day. Never has any one possessed you that would fly before another. So long as I live, you shall not be taken from me, so long have you been in the hands of a loyal knight."

Then he smote a second time with the sword, this time upon the marble steps. Loud rang the steel, but neither brake nor splintered. Then Roland began to bemoan himself, "O my good Durendal," he said, "how bright and clear thou art, shining as shines the sun! Well I mind me of the day when a voice that seemed to come from heaven bade King Charles give thee to a valiant captain; and forthwith the good King girded it on my side. Many a land have I conquered with thee for him, and now how great is my grief! Can I die and leave thee to be handled by some heathen?" And the third time he smote a rock with it. Loud rang the steel, but it brake not, bounding back as though it would rise to the sky. And when Count Roland saw that he could not break the sword, he spake again but with more content in his heart. "O Durendal," he said, "a fair sword art thou, and holy as fair. There are holy relics in thy hilt, relics of St. Peter and St. Denis and St. Basil. These heathen shall never possess thee; nor shalt thou be held but by a Christian hand."

And now Roland knew that death was very near to him. He laid himself down with his head upon the grass putting under him his horn and his sword, with his face turned towards the heathen foe. Ask you why he did so? To shew, forsooth, to Charlemagne and the men of France that he died in the midst of victory. This done he made a loud confession of his sins, stretching his hand to heaven. "Forgive me, Lord," he cried, "my sins, little and great, all that I have committed since the day of my birth to this hour in which I am stricken to death." So he prayed; and, as he lay, he thought of many things, of the countries which he had conquered, and of his dear Fatherland France, and of his kinsfolk, and of the good King Charles. Nor, as he thought, could he keep himself from sighs and tears; yet one thing he remembered beyond all others—to pray for forgiveness of his sins. "O Lord," he said, "Who art the God of truth, and didst save Daniel Thy prophet from the lions, do Thou save my soul and defend it against all perils!" So speaking he raised his right hand, with the gauntlet yet upon it, to the sky, and his head fell back upon his arm and the angels carried him to heaven. So died the great Count Roland.

# KING ALFRED

WE NOW come to the great King Alfred, the best and greatest of all English Kings. We know quite enough of his history to be able to say that he really deserves to be so called, though I must warn you that, just because he left so great a name behind him, people have been fond of attributing to him things which really belonged to others. Thus you may sometimes see nearly all English laws and customs attributed to Alfred, as if he had invented them all for himself. You will sometimes hear that Alfred founded Trial by Jury, divided England into Counties, and did all kinds of other things. Now the real truth is that the roots and beginnings of most of these things are very much older than the time of Alfred, while the particular forms in which we have them now are very much later. But people have a way of fancying that everything must have been invented by some particular man, and as Alfred was more famous than anybody else, they hit upon Alfred as the most likely person to have invented them.

But, putting aside fables, there is quite enough to show that there have been very few Kings, and very few men of any sort, so great and good as King

Alfred. Perhaps the only equally good King we read of is Saint Louis of France; and though he was quite as good, we cannot set him down as being so great and wise as Alfred. Certainly no King ever gave himself up more thoroughly than Alfred did fully to do the duties of his office. His whole life seems to have been spent in doing all that he could for the good of his people in every way. And it is wonderful in how many ways his powers showed themselves. That he was a brave warrior is in itself no particular praise in an age when almost every man was the same. But it is a great thing for a prince so large a part of whose time was spent in fighting to be able to say that all his wars were waged to set free his country from the most cruel enemies.

And we may admire too the wonderful way in which he kept his mind always straight and firm, never either giving way to bad luck or being puffed up by good luck. We read of nothing like pride or cruelty or injustice of any kind either towards his own people or towards his enemies. And if he was a brave warrior, he was many other things besides. He was a lawgiver; at least he collected and arranged the laws, and caused them to be most carefully administered. He was a scholar, and wrote and translated many books for the good of his people. He encouraged trade and enterprise of all kinds, and sent men to visit distant parts of the world, and bring home accounts of what they saw. And he was a thoroughly good man and a devout Christian in all relations of life. In short, one hardly knows any other character in all history so perfect; there is so much that is good in so many different ways; and though no doubt Alfred had his faults like other people, yet he clearly had none, at any rate in the greater part of his life, which took away at all seriously from his general goodness. One wonders that such a man was never canonized as a Saint; most certainly many people have received that name who did not deserve it nearly so well as he did.

Alfred, or, as his name should really be spelled, Ælfred,[1] was the youngest son of King Æthelwulf, and was born at Wantage in Berkshire in 849. His mother was Osburh daughter of Oslac the King's cup-bearer, who came of the royal house of the Jutes in Wight. Up to the age of twelve years Alfred was fond of hunting and other sports but he had not been taught any sort of learning, not so much as to read his own tongue. But he loved the old English songs; and one day his mother had a beautiful book of songs with rich pictures and fine painted initial letters, such as you may often see in ancient books. And she said to her children, "I will give this beautiful book to the one of you who shall first be able to read it." And Alfred said, "Mother, will you really give me the book when I have learned to read it?" And Osburh said, "Yes, my son." So Alfred went and found a master, and soon learned to read. Then he came to his mother, and read the songs in the beautiful book and took the book for his own.

---

[1] That is, the *rede* or counsel of the *elves*. A great many Old-English names are called after the elves or fairies.

In 868, when he was in his twentieth year, while his brother Æthelred was King, Alfred married. His wife's name was Ealhswyth; she was the daughter of Æthelred called the Mickle or Big, Alderman of the Gainas in Lincolnshire, and her mother Eadburh was of the royal house of the Mercians. It is said that on the very day of his marriage he was smitten with a strange disease, which for twenty years never quite left him, and fits of which might come on at any time. If this be true, it makes all the great things that he did even more wonderful.

Meanwhile the great Danish invasion had begun in the northern parts of England. There are many stories told in the old Northern Songs as to the cause of it. Some tell how Ragnar Lodbrog, a great hero of these Northern tales, was seized by Ælla, King of the Northumbrians, and was thrown into a dungeon full of serpents, and how, while he was dying of the bites of the serpents, he sang a wonderful death-song, telling of all his old fights, and calling on his sons to come and avenge him.

The year 871 the Danes for the first time entered Wessex. Nine great battles, besides smaller skirmishes, were fought this year, in some of which the English won and in others the Danes. One famous battle was at Ashdown, in Berkshire. We are told that the heathen men were in two divisions; one was commanded by their two Kings Bagsecg and Halfdene, and the other by five Earls, Sidroc the Old, Sidroc the Young, Osbeorn, Fræna, and Harold. And King Æthelred was set against the

Kings and Alfred the Ætheling against the Earls. And the heathen men came on against them. But King Æthelred heard mass in his tent. And men said, "Come forth, O King, to the fight, for the heathen men press hard upon us." And King Æthelred said, "I will serve God first and man after, so I will not come forth till all the words of the mass be ended." So King Æthelred abode praying, and the heathen men fought against Alfred the Ætheling. And Alfred said, "I cannot abide till the King my brother comes forth; I must either flee, or fight alone with the heathen men." So Alfred the Ætheling and his men fought against the five Earls. Now the heathen men stood on the higher ground and the Christians on the lower. Yet did Alfred go forth trusting in God, and he made his men hold close together with their shields, and they went forth like a wild boar against the hounds. And they fought against the heathen men and smote them, and slew the five Earls, Sidroc the Old, Sidroc the Young, Osbeorn, Fræna, and Harold. Then the mass was over, and King Æthelred came forth and fought against the two Kings, and slew Bagsecg the King with his own hand and smote the heathen men with a great slaughter and chased them even unto Reading.

In 871, on Æthelred's death, Alfred became King of the West-Saxons and Over-lord of all England, as his father had appointed so long before with the consent of his Wise Men.

The Danes did not come again into Wessex till 876. But though the West-Saxons had no fighting by land during these years, things were not quite quiet, for in 875 King Alfred had a fight at sea against some of the Danish pirates. This sea-fight is worth remembering as being, I suppose, the first victory won by the Englishmen at sea, where Englishmen have since won so many victories. King Alfred then fought against seven Danish ships, of which he took one and put the rest to flight. It is somewhat strange that we do not hear more than we do of warfare by sea in these times, especially when we remember how in earlier times the Angles and Saxons had roved about in their ships, very much as the Danes and other Northmen were doing now. It would seem that the English, after they settled in Britain, almost left off being a seafaring people. We find Alfred and other Kings doing what they could to keep up a fleet and to stir up a naval spirit among their people. And in some degree they did so; still we do not find the English, for a long while after this time, doing nearly so much by sea as they did by land. This was a pity; for ships might then, as in later times, have been wooden walls. It is much better to meet an enemy at sea, and to keep him from landing in your country, than to let him land, even if you can beat him when he has landed.

But in 876 the Danes came again into Wessex; and we thus come to the part of Alfred's life which is at once the saddest and the brightest. It is the time when his luck was lowest and when his spirit was highest. The army under Guthorm or Guthrum, the Danish King of East-Anglia, came suddenly to Wareham in Dorsetshire. The Chronicle says that they "bestole"—that is, came secretly or escaped—

from the West-Saxon army, which seems to have been waiting for them. This time Alfred made peace with the Danes, and they gave him some of their chief men for hostages, and they swore to go out of the land. They swore this on the holy bracelet, which was the most solemn oath in use among the heathen Northmen, and on which they had never before sworn at any of the times when they had made peace with the English. But they did not keep their oath any better for taking it in this more solemn way. The part of the host which had horses "bestole away." King Alfred rode after the Danish horse as far as Exeter, but he did not overtake them till they had got there, and were safe in the stronghold. Then they made peace, swearing oaths, and giving as many hostages as the King asked for.

And now we come to the terrible year 878, the greatest and saddest and most glorious in all Alfred's life. In the very beginning of the year, just after Twelfth-night, the Danish host again came suddenly—"bestole" as the Chronicle says—to Chippenham. Then "they rode through the West-Saxons' land, and there sat down, and mickle of the folk over the sea they drove, and of the others the most deal they rode over; all but the King Alfred; he with a little band hardly fared [went] after the woods and on the moor-fastnesses." This time of utter distress lasted only a very little while, for in a few months Alfred was again at the head of an army and able to fight against the Danes.

It was during this trouble that Alfred stayed in the hut of a neatherd or swineherd of his, who knew who he was, though his wife did not know him. One day the woman set some cakes to bake, and bade the King, who was sitting by the fire mending his bow and arrows, to tend them. Alfred thought more of his bow and arrows than he did of the cakes, and let them burn. Then the woman ran in and cried out, "There, don't you see the cakes on fire? Then wherefore turn them not? You are glad enough to eat them when they are piping hot."

We are told that this swineherd or neatherd afterwards became Bishop of Winchester. They say that his name was Denewulf, and that the King saw that, though he was in so lowly a rank, he was naturally a very wise man. So he had him taught, and at last gave him the Bishoprick.

I do not think that I can do better than tell you the next happening to Alfred, as it is in the Chronicle, only changing those words which you might not understand.

"And that ilk [same] winter was Iwer's and Healfdene's brother among the West-Saxons in Devonshire; and him there men slew and eight hundred men with him and forty men of his host. And there was the banner taken which they the Raven hight [call]. And after this Easter wrought King Alfred with his little band a work [fortress] at Athelney, and out of that work was he striving with the [Danish] host, and the army sold [gave] him hostages and mickle oaths, and eke they promised him that their King should receive baptism. And this they fulfilled. And three weeks after came King

Guthrum with thirty of the men that in the host were worthiest, at Aller, that is near Athelney. And him the King received at his baptism,[1] and his chrisom-loosing[2] was at Wedmore. And he was twelve nights with the King, and he honoured him and his feres [companions] with mickle fee [money]."

Thus you see how soon King Alfred's good luck came back to him again. The Raven was a famous banner of the Danes, said to have been worked by the daughters of Ragnar Lodbrog. It was thought to have wonderful powers, so that they could tell by the way in which the raven held his wings whether they would win or not in battle.

You see the time of utter distress lasted only from soon after Twelfth-night to Easter, and even during that time the taking of the Raven must have cheered the English a good deal. After Easter things began to mend, when Alfred built his fort at Athelney and began to skirmish with the Danes, and seven weeks later came the great victory at Ethandun, which set Wessex free. Some say that the white horse which is cut in the side of the chalk hills near Edington was cut then, that men might remember the great battle of Ethandun. But it has been altered in modern times to make it look more like a real horse.

---

[1] That is, was his godfather.
[2] That is, he laid aside the *chrisom* or white garment which a newly baptised person wore.

All this time Alfred seems to have kept his headquarters at Athelney. Thence they went to Wedmore. There the Wise Men came together, and Alfred and Guthorm (or, to give him the name by which he was baptised, Æthelstan) made a treaty. This treaty was very much better kept than any treaty with the Danes had ever been kept before. The Danes got much the larger part of England; still Alfred contrived to keep London. Some accounts say that only those of the Danes stayed in England who chose to become Christians, and that the rest went away into Gaul under a famous leader of theirs named Hasting. Anyhow, in 880 they went quite away into what was now their own land of East-Anglia, and divided it among themselves. Thus Alfred had quite freed his own Kingdom from the Danes, though he was obliged to leave so much of the island in their hands. And even through all these misfortunes, the Kingdom of Wessex did in some sort become greater. Remember that in 880, when Alfred had done so many great things, he was still only thirty-one years old.

We can see how much people always remembered and thought of Alfred, by there being many more stories told of him than of almost any other of the old Kings. One story is that Alfred, wishing to know what the Danes were about and how strong they were, set out one day from Athelney in the disguise of a minstrel or juggler, and went into the Danish camp, and stayed there several days, amusing the Danes with his playing, till he had seen all that he wanted, and then went back without any one finding him out. This is what you may call a soldier's story, while some of the others are rather what monks and clergymen would like to tell. Thus there is a tale which is told in a great many different ways, but of which the following is the oldest shape.

"Now King Alfred was driven from his Kingdom by the Danes, and he lay hid for three years in the isle of Glastonbury. And it came to pass on a day that all his folk were gone out to fish, save only Alfred himself and his wife and one servant whom he loved. And there came a pilgrim to the King, and begged for food. And the King said to his servant, 'What food have we in the house?' And his servant answered, 'My Lord, we have in the house but one loaf and a little wine.' Then the King gave thanks to God, and said, 'Give half of the loaf and half of the wine to this poor pilgrim.' So the servant did as his lord commanded him, and gave to the pilgrim half of the loaf and half of the wine, and the pilgrim gave great thanks to the King. And when the servant returned, he found the loaf whole, and the wine as much as there had been aforetime. And he greatly wondered, and he wondered also how the pilgrim had come into the isle, for that no man could come there save by water, and the pilgrim had no boat. And the King greatly wondered also. And at the ninth hour came back the folk who had gone to fish. And they had three boats full of fish, and they said, 'Lo, we have caught more fish this day than in all the three years that we have tarried in this island.' And the King was glad, and he and his folk were merry; yet he pondered much upon that which had come to pass. And when night came, the King went to his bed with Ealhswyth his wife. And the Lady slept, but the King lay awake and thought of all that had come to pass by day. And presently he saw a great light, like the brightness of the sun, and he saw an old man with black hair, clothed in priest's garments, and with a mitre on his head, and holding in his right hand a book of the Gospels adorned with gold and gems. And the old man blessed the King, and the King said unto him, 'Who art thou?' And he answered, 'Alfred, my son, rejoice; for I am he to whom thou didst this day give thine alms, and I am called Cuthberht the soldier of Christ. Now be strong and very courageous, and be of joyful heart, and hearken diligently to the things which I say unto thee; for henceforth I will be thy shield and thy friend, and I will watch over thee and over thy sons after thee. And now I will tell thee what thou must do. Rise up early in the morning, and blow thine horn thrice, that thy enemies may hear it and fear, and by the ninth hour thou shalt have around thee five hundred men harnassed for the battle. And this shall be a sign unto thee that thou mayest believe. And after seven days thou shalt have by God's gift and my help all the folk of this land gathered unto thee upon the mount that is called Assandun. And thus shalt thou fight against thine enemies, and doubt not that thou shalt overcome them. Be thou therefore glad of heart, and be strong and very courageous, and fear not, for God hath given thine enemies into thine hand. And He hath given thee also all this land and the Kingdom of thy fathers, to thee and to thy sons and to thy sons' sons after thee.

Be thou faithful to me and to my folk, because that unto thee is given all the land of Albion. Be thou righteous, because thou art chosen to be the King of all Britain. So may God be merciful unto thee, and I will be thy friend, and none of thine enemies shall ever be able to overcome thee.' Then was King Alfred glad at heart, and he was strong and very courageous, for that he knew that he would overcome his enemies by the help of God and Saint Cuthberht his patron. So in the morning he arose, and sailed to the land, and blew his horn three times, and when his friends heard it they were glad, and when his enemies heard it they feared. And by the ninth hour, according to the word of the Lord, there were gathered unto him five hundred men of the bravest and dearest of his friends. And he spake unto them and told them all that God had said unto him by the mouth of his servant Cuthberht, and he told them that, by the gift of God and by the help of Saint Cuthberht, they would overcome their enemies and win back their own land. And he bade them as Saint Cuthberht had taught him, to fear God alway and to be alway righteous toward all men. And he bade his son Edward who was by him to be faithful to God and Saint Cuthberht, and so he should alway have the victory over his enemies. So they went forth to battle and smote their enemies and overcame them, and King Alfred took the Kingdom of all Britain, and he ruled well and wisely over the just and the unjust for the rest of his days."

Now is there any truth in all this story? I think there is thus much, that Alfred, for some reason or other, thought he was under the special protection of Saint Cuthberht. For several years after 880 there was peace in the land, and for a good many more years still there was much less fighting than there had been before. It was no doubt at this time that Alfred was able to do all those things for the good of his people of which we hear so much. He had now more time than either before or after for making his laws, writing his books, founding his monasteries, and doing all that he did. You may wonder how he found time to do so much; but it was by the only way by which anybody can do anything, namely, by never wasting his time, and by having fixed times of the day for everything. Alfred did not, like most other writers of that time, write in Latin, so that hardly anybody but the clergy could read or understand what he wrote. He loved our own tongue, and was especially fond of the Old-English songs, and all that he wrote he wrote in English that all his people might understand. His works were chiefly translations from Latin books; what we should have valued most of all, his note-book or handbook, containing his remarks on various matters, is lost. He translated into English the History of Bæda, the History of Orosius, some of the works of Pope Gregory the Great, and the Consolation of Philosophy by Boethius. Perhaps you will ask why he did not rather translate some of the great and famous Greek and Latin writers of earlier times. Now we may be sure that King Alfred did not understand Greek at all; very few people in those days in the West of Europe knew any Greek, except those who needed to use the language for dealing with the men in the Eastern Empire who still spoke it. Indeed Alfred complains that, when he came to the Crown, very few people, even among the clergy, understood even Latin at all well. And as for Latin books, no doubt Alfred thought that the writings of Christians would be more edifying to his people than those of the old heathens. He chose the History of Orosius, as a general history of the world, and that of Bæda, as a particular history of England. Boethius was a Roman Consul in the beginning of the sixth century, who was put to death by the great Theodoric, King of the East-Goths, who then ruled over Italy. While he was in prison he wrote the book which King Alfred translated. He seems not to have been a Christian; at least there is not a single Christian expression in his book. But people fancied that he was not only a Christian, but a saint and a martyr, most likely because Theodoric, who put him to death, was not an orthodox Christian, but an Arian. Alfred, in translating his books, did not always care to translate them quite exactly, but he often altered and put in things of his own, if he thought he could thus make them more improving. So in translating Boethius, he altered a good deal, to make the wise heathen speak like a Christian. So in translating Orosius, where Orosius gives an account of the world, Alfred greatly enlarged the account of all the northern part of Europe, of which Alfred naturally knew much more than Orosius did.

Alfred was also very careful in the government of his Kingdom, especially in seeing that justice was properly administered. So men said of him in their songs, much as they had long before said of King Edwin in Northumberland, that he hung up golden bracelets by the roadside, and that no man dared to steal them. In his collection of laws, he chiefly put in order the laws of the older Kings, not adding many of his own, because he said that he did not know how those who came after him might like them.

King Alfred was very attentive to religious matters, and gave great alms to the poor and gifts to churches. He also founded two monasteries; one was for nuns, at Shaftesbury in Dorsetshire, of which he made his own daughter, Æthelgifu, abbess. The other was for monks at Athelney; you can easily see why he should build it there. He also sent several embassies to Rome, where he got Pope Marinus to grant certain privileges to the English School at Rome; the Pope also sent him what was thought to be a piece of the wood of the True Cross, that on which our Lord Jesus Christ died. He also sent an embassy to Jerusalem, and had letters from Abel the Patriarch there. And what seems stranger than all, he sent an embassy all the way to India, with alms for the Christians there, called the Christians of Saint Thomas and Saint Bartholomew.

Lastly, there seems some reason to think that the Chronicle began to be put together in its present shape in Alfred's time, and that it was regularly gone on with afterward, so that from the time of Alfred onward we have a history which was regularly written down as things happened.

All these things happened mainly in the middle years of the reign of Alfred, when there was so much less fighting than there was before and after, and when some years seem to have been quite peaceable. Guthorm-Æthelstan and his Danes in East-Anglia were for some years true to the treaty of Wedmore, and the other Danes seem just now to have been busy in invading Gaul and other parts of the continent rather than England. Also King Alfred had now got a fleet, so that he often met them at sea and kept them from landing. This he did in 882, and we do not find that any Danes landed again in England till 885. In that year part of the army which had been plundering along the coast of Flanders and Holland came over to England, landed in Kent, and besieged Rochester. But the citizens withstood them bravely, and Alfred gathered an army and drove the Danes to their ships. They seem then to have gone to Essex and to have plundered there with their ships, getting help from the Danes who were settled in East-Anglia, or at least from such of them as still were heathens. Alfred's fleet however quite overcame them and took away their treasure, but his fleet was again attacked and defeated by the East-Anglian Danes. It would seem that in some part of this war Guthorm-Æthelstan was helped by Hrolf, otherwise called Rollo, the great Northern chief.

The Danish wars began again in 893. For years now there was a great deal of fighting. Two large bodies of Danes, one of them under the famous chief Hasting, landed in Kent in 893 and fixed themselves in fortresses which they built. And the Danes who had settled in Northumberland and East-Anglia helped them, though they had all sworn oaths to King Alfred, and those in East-Anglia had also given hostages. There was fighting all over the south of England throughout 894, and the King had to go constantly backward and forward to keep up with the Danes. One time Alfred took a fort in Kent, in which were the wife and two sons of Hasting. Now Hasting had not long before given oaths and hostages to Alfred, and the two boys had been baptised, the King being godfather to one of them and Alderman Æthelred to the other. But Hasting did not at all keep to his oath, but went on plundering all the same. Still, when the boys and their mother were taken, Alfred would not do them any harm, but gave them up again to Hasting.

In 897 we read that Alfred made some improvements in his ships. "They were full-nigh twice as long as the others; some had sixty oars, some more; they were both swifter and steadier and eke higher than the others; they were neither on the Frisian shape nor on the Danish, but as himself thought that they useful might be." These new ships seem to have done good service, though one time they got aground, seemingly because they were so large, and the Danes were therefore able to sail out before them. These sea-fights along the south coast were nearly the last things that we hear of in Alfred's reign. The crews of two Danish ships were brought to Winchester to Alfred and there hanged. One cannot blame him for this, as these Danes were mere pirates, not engaged in any lawful war, and many of them had been spared, and had made oaths to Alfred, and had broken them, over and over again.

This was in 897; the rest of King Alfred's reign seems to have been spent in peace. In 901 the great King died himself. He was then only fifty-two years old. Alfred's wife, the Lady Ealhswyth, lived a little while after her husband, till 903 or 905. King Alfred was buried at Winchester in the New Minster which he himself began to found and which was finished by his son Edward. It then stood close to the Old Minster, that is, the cathedral church. Afterward it was moved out of the city and was called Hyde Abbey. But you cannot see King Alfred's grave there now, because everything has been destroyed, and the bones of the great King have been turned out, to make room for a prison.

# THE CID

AFTERWARDS the Castillians arrived, and they kissed his hands in homage, all, save only my Cid. And when King Don Alfonso saw that the Cid did not do homage and kiss his hand, as all the other chief persons had done, he said, "Since now ye have all received me for your Lord, and given me authority over ye, I would know of the Cid Ruydiez why he will not kiss my hand and acknowledge me; for I would do something for him, as I promised unto my father King Don Ferrando, when he commended him to me and to my brethren." And the Cid arose and said, "Sir, all whom you see here present, suspect that by your counsel the King Don Sancho your brother came to his death; and therefore I say unto you that, unless you clear yourself of this, as by right you should do, I will never kiss your hand, nor receive you for my lord." Then said the King, "Cid, what you say pleases me well; and here I swear to God and to St. Mary, that I never slew him, nor took counsel for his death. And I beseech ye therefore all, as friends and true vassals, that ye tell me how I may clear myself." And the chiefs who were present said, that he and twelve of the knights who came with him from Toledo, should make this oath in the church at St. Gadea at Burgos, and that so he should be cleared.

So the King and all his company took horse and went to Burgos. And when the day appointed for the oath was come, the King came forward upon a high stage that all the people might see him, and my Cid came to him to receive the oath; and my Cid took the book of the Gospels and opened it, and laid it upon the altar, and the King laid his hands upon it, and the Cid said unto him, "King Don Alfonso, you come here to swear concerning the death of King Don Sancho your brother, that you neither slew him nor took counsel for his death; say now you and these hidalgos, if ye swear this." And the King and the hidalgos answered and said, "Yea, we swear it." And the Cid said, "If ye knew of this thing, or gave command that it should be done, may you die even such a death as your brother the King Don Sancho, by the hand of a villain whom you trust; one who is not a hidalgo, from another land, not a Castillian"; and the King and the knights who were with him said "Amen." And the King's colour changed; and the Cid repeated the oath unto him a second time, and the King and the twelve knights said "Amen" to it in like manner, and in like manner the countenance of the King was changed again. And my Cid repeated the oath unto him a third time, and the King and the knights said "Amen." But the wrath of the King was exceedingly great, and he said to the Cid, "Ruydiez, why dost thou thus press me, man? To-day thou swearest me, and to-morrow thou wilt kiss my hand." And from that day forward there was no love toward my Cid in the heart of the King.

After this King Don Alfonso assembled together all his power and went against the Moors. And the Cid should have gone with him, but he fell sick and perforce therefore abode at home. And while the King was going through Andalusia, having the land at his mercy, a great power of the Moors assembled together on the other side, and entered the land, and did much evil. At this time the Cid was gathering strength; and when he heard that the Moors were in the country, laying waste before them, he gathered together what force he could, and went after them; and the Moors, when they heard this, began to fly. And the Cid followed them as far as Toledo, slaying and burning, and plundering and destroying, and laying hands on all whom he found, so that he brought back seven thousand prisoners, men and women; and he and all his people returned rich and with great honour. But when the King of Toledo heard of the hurt which he had received at the hands of the Cid, he sent to King Don Alfonso to complain thereof. And the King was greatly troubled. And he went with all speed to Burgos, and sent from thence to bid the Cid come unto him.

Now my Cid knew the evil disposition of the King toward him, and when he received his bidding he made answer that he would meet him between Burgos and Bivar. And the King went out from Burgos and came nigh unto Bivar; and the Cid came up to him and would have kissed his hand, but the King withheld it, and said angrily unto him,

"Ruydiez, quit my land." Then the Cid clapt spurs to the mule upon which he rode, and vaulted into a piece of ground which was his own inheritance, and answered, "Sir, I am not in your land, but in my own." And the King replied full wrathfully, "Go out of my kingdoms without any delay." And the Cid made answer, "Give me then thirty days' time, as is the right of the hidalgos"; and the King said he would not, but that if he were not gone in nine days' time he would come and look for him. The counts were well pleased at this; but all the people of the land were sorrowful. And then the King and the Cid parted. And the Cid sent for all his friends and his kinsmen and vassals, and told them how King Don Alfonso had banished him from the land, and asked of them who would follow him into banishment, and who would remain at home. Then Alvar Fañez, who was his cousin-german, came forward and said, "Cid, we will all go with you, through desert and through peopled country, and never fail you. In your service will we spend our mules and horses, our wealth and our garments, and ever while we live be unto you loyal friends and vassals." And they all confirmed what Alvar Fañez had said; and the Cid thanked them for their love, and said that there might come a time in which he should guerdon them.

And as he was about to depart he looked back upon his own home, and when he saw his hall deserted, the household chests unfastened, the doors open, no cloaks hanging up, no seats in the porch, no hawks upon the perches, the tears came into his eyes, and he said, "My enemies have done this. God be praised for all things." And he turned toward the East and knelt and said, "Holy Mary Mother, and all Saints, pray to God for me, that He may give me strength to destroy all the Pagans, and to win enough from them to requite my friends therewith, and all those who follow and help me." Then he called for Alvar Fañez and said unto him, "Cousin, the poor have no part in the wrong which the King hath done us; see now that no wrong be done unto them along our road," and he called for his horse.

My Cid Ruydiez entered Burgos, having sixty streamers in his company. And men and women went forth to see him, and the men of Burgos and the women of Burgos were at their windows, weeping, so great was their sorrow; and they said with one accord, "God, how good a vassal if he had but a good Lord!" and willingly would each have bade him come in, but no one dared so to do. For King Don Alfonso in his anger had sent letters to Burgos, saying that no man should give the Cid a lodging; and that whosoever disobeyed should lose all that he had, and moreover the eyes in his head. Great sorrow had these Christian folk at this, and they hid themselves when he came near them because they did not dare speak to him; and my Cid went to his Posada, and when he came to the door he found it fastened, for fear of the King. And his people called out with a loud voice, but they within made no answer. And the Cid rode up to the door, and took his foot out of the stirrup, and gave it a kick, but the door did not open with it, for it was well secured. A little girl of nine years old then came out of one of the houses and said unto him, "O Cid, the King hath forbidden us to receive you. We dare not open our doors to you, for we should lose our houses and all that we have, and the eyes in our head. Cid, our evil would not help you, but God and all His saints be with you." And when she had said this she returned into the house. And when the Cid knew what the King had done he turned away from the door and rode up to St. Mary's, and there he alighted and knelt down, and prayed with all his heart; and then he mounted again and rode out of the town and pitched his tent near Arlanzon, upon the sands. My Cid Ruydiez, he who in a happy hour first girt on his sword, took up his lodging upon the sands, because there was none who would receive him within their door. He had a good company round about him, and there he lodged.

Moreover the King had given orders that no food should be sold them in Burgos, so that they could not buy even a pennyworth. But Martin Antolinez, who was a good Burgalese, he supplied my Cid and all his company with bread and wine abundantly. "Campeador," said he to the Cid, "to-night we will rest here, and to-morrow we will be gone: I shall be accused for what I have done in serving you, and shall be in the King's displeasure; but following your fortunes, sooner or later, the King will have me for his friend, and if not, I do not care a fig for what I leave behind." Now this Martin Antolinez was nephew unto the Cid, being the son of his brother, Ferrando Diaz. And the Cid said unto him, "Martin Antolinez, you are a bold lancier; if I live I will double you your pay. You see I have nothing with me, and yet must provide for my companions. I will take two chests and fill them with sand, and do you go in secret to Rachel and Vidas, and tell them to come hither privately; for I cannot take my treasures with me because of their weight, and will pledge them in their hands. Let them come for the chests at night, that no man may see them. God knows that I do this thing more of necessity than of wilfulness; but by God's good help I shall redeem all." Now Rachel and Vidas were rich Jews, from whom the Cid used to receive money for his spoils. And Martin Antolinez went in quest of them, and he passed through Burgos and entered into the Castle; and when he saw them he said, "Ah Rachel and Vidas, my dear friends! now let me speak with ye in secret." And they three went apart. And he said to them, "Give me your hands that you will not discover me, neither to Moor nor Christian! I will make you rich men for ever. The Campeador went for the tribute and he took great wealth, and some of it he has kept for himself. He has two chests full of gold; ye know that the King is in anger against him, and he cannot carry these away with him without their being seen. He will leave them therefore in your hands, and you shall lend him money upon them, swearing with great oaths and upon your faith, that ye will not open them till a year be past." Rachel and Vidas took counsel together and answered, "We well knew he got something when he entered the land of the Moors; he who has treasures does not sleep without suspicion; we will take the chests, and place them where they shall not be seen. But tell us with what will the Cid be contented, and what gain will he give us for the year?" Martin Antolinez answered like a prudent man, "My Cid requires what is reasonable; he will ask but little to leave his treasures in safety. Men come to him from all parts. He must have six hundred marks." And the Jews said, "We will advance him so much." "Well then," said Martin Antolinez, "ye see that the night is advancing; the Cid is in haste, give us the marks." "This is not the way of business," said they; "we must take first, and then give." "Ye say well," replied the Burgalese: "come then to the Campeador, and we will help you to bring away the chests, so that neither Moors nor Christians may see us." So they went to horse and rode out together, and they did not cross the bridge, but rode through the water that no man might see them, and they came to the tent of the Cid.

Meantime the Cid had taken two chests, which were covered with leather of red and gold, and the nails which fastened down the leather were well gilt; they were ribbed with bands of iron, and each fastened with three locks; they were heavy, and he filled them with sand. And when Rachel and Vidas entered his tent with Martin Antolinez, they kissed his hand; and the Cid smiled and said to them, "Ye see that I am going out of the land, because of the King's displeasure; but I shall leave something with ye." And they made answer, "Martin Antolinez has covenanted with us, that we shall give you six hundred marks upon these chests, and keep them a full year, swearing not to open them till that time be expired, else shall we be perjured." "Take the chests," said Martin Antolinez; "I will go with you, and bring back the marks, for my Cid must move before cock-crow." So they took the chests, and though they were both strong men they could not raise them from the ground; and they were full glad of the bargain which they had made. And Rachel then went to the Cid and kissed his hand and said, "Now, Campeador, you are going from Castille among strange nations, and your gain will be great, even as your fortune is. I kiss your hand, Cid, and have a gift for you, a red skin; it is Moorish and honourable." And the Cid said, "It pleases me: give it me if ye have brought it; if not, reckon it upon the chests." And they departed with the chests, and Martin Antolinez and his people helped them, and went with them. And when they had placed the chests in safety, they spread a carpet in the middle of the hall, and laid a sheet upon it, and they threw down upon it three hundred marks of silver. Don Martin counted them, and took them without weighing. The other three hundred they paid in gold.

When Martin Antolinez came into the Cid's tent he said unto him, "I have sped well, Campeador! you have gained six hundred marks. Now then strike your tent and be gone. The time draws on, and you may be with your Lady Wife at St. Pedro de Cardeña, before the cock crows."

The cocks were crowing amain, and the day began to break, when the good Campeador reached St. Pedro's. The Abbot Don Sisebuto was saying matins, and Doña Ximena and five of her ladies of good lineage were with him, praying to God and St. Peter to help my Cid. And when he called at the gate and they knew his voice, God, what a joyful man was the Abbot Don Sisebuto! Out into the courtyard they went with torches and with tapers, and the Abbot gave thanks to God that he now beheld the face of my Cid. And the Cid told him all that had befallen him, and how he was a banished man; and he gave him fifty marks for himself, and a hundred for Doña Ximena and her children. "Abbot," said he, "I leave two little girls behind me, whom I commend to your care. Take you care of them and of my wife and of her ladies: when this money be gone, if it be not enough, supply them abundantly; for every mark which you spend upon them I will give the monastery four." And the Abbot promised to do this with a right good will. Then Doña Ximena came up weeping bitterly, and she said to her husband, "Lo now you are banished from the land by mischief-making men, and here am I with your daughters, who are little ones and of tender years, and we and you must be parted, even in your life-time. For the love of St. Mary tell me now what we shall do." And the Cid took the children in his arms, and held them to his heart and wept, for he dearly loved them. "Please God and St. Mary," said he, "I shall yet live to give these my daughters in marriage with my own hands, and to do you service yet, my honoured wife, whom I have ever loved, even as my own soul."

Now hath my Cid left the kingdom of King Don Alfonso, and entered the country of the Moors.

And at day-break they were near the brow of the Sierra, and they halted there upon the top of the mountains, and gave barley to their horses, and remained there until evening. And they set forward when the evening had closed, that none might see them, and continued their way all night, and before dawn they came near to Castrejon, which is upon the Henares. And Alvar Fañez said unto the Cid, that he would take with him two hundred horsemen, and scour the country and lay hands on whatever he could find, without fear either of King Alfonso or of the Moors. And he counselled him to remain in ambush where he was, and surprise the castle of Castrejon: and it seemed good unto my Cid. Away went Alvar Fañez, and the two hundred horsemen; and the Cid remained in ambush with the rest of his company. And as soon as it was morning, the Moors of Castrejon, knowing nothing of these who were so near them, opened the castle gates, and went out to their work as they were wont to do. And the Cid rose from ambush and fell upon them, and took all their flocks, and made straight for the gates, pursuing them. And there was a cry within the castle that the Christians were upon them, and they who were within ran to the gates to defend them, but my Cid came up sword in hand; eleven Moors did he slay with his own hand, and they forsook the gate and fled before him to hide themselves within, so that he won the castle presently, and took gold and silver, and whatever else he would.

Alvar Fañez meantime scoured the country along the Henares as far as Alcala, and he returned driving flocks and herds before him, with great stores of wearing apparel, and of other plunder. And when the Cid knew that he was nigh at hand he went out to meet him, and praised him greatly for what he had done, and gave thanks to God. And he gave order that all the spoils should be heaped together, both what Alvar Fañez had brought, and what had been taken in the castle; and he said to him, "Brother, of all this which God hath given us, take you the fifth, for you well deserve it"; but Minaya would not, saying, "You have need of it for our support." And the Cid divided the spoil among the knights and foot-soldiers, to each his due portion; to every horseman a hundred marks of silver, and half as much to the foot-soldiers: and because he could find none to whom to sell his fifth, he spake to the Moors telling them that they might come safely to purchase the spoil, and the prisoners also whom he had taken, both men prisoners and women. And they came, and valued the spoil and the prisoners, and gave for them three thousand marks of silver, which they paid within three days: they bought also much of the spoil which had been divided, making great gain, so that all who were in my Cid's company were full rich. And the heart of my Cid was joyous, and he sent to King Don Alfonso, telling him that he and his companions would yet do him service upon the Moors.

Then my Cid assembled together his good men and said unto them, "Friends, we cannot take up our abode in this castle, for there is no water in it, and moreover the King is at peace with these Moors, and I know that the treaty between them hath been written; so that if we should abide here he would come against us with all his power, and with all the power of the Moors, and we could not stand against him. If therefore it seem good unto you, let us leave the rest of our prisoners here, that we may be free from all encumbrance, like men who are to live by war." And it pleased them well that it should be so. And he said to them, "Ye have all had your shares, neither is there anything owing to any one among ye. Now then let us be ready to take horse betimes on the morrow, for I would not fight against my Lord the King." So on the morrow they went to horse and departed, being rich with the spoils which they had won: and they left the castle to the Moors, who remained blessing them for this bounty which they had received at their hands. Then my Cid and his company went up the Henares as fast as they could go; great were the spoils which they collected as they went along. And on the morrow they came against Alcocer. There my Cid pitched his tents upon a round hill, which was a great hill and a strong: and the river Salon ran near them, so that the water could not be cut off. My Cid thought to take Alcocer: so he pitched his tents securely, having the Sierra on one side, and the river on the other, and he made all his people dig a trench, that they might not be alarmed, neither by day nor by night.

When my Cid had thus encamped, he went to look at the Alcazar, and see if he could by any means enter it. And the Moors offered tribute to him, if he would leave them in peace; but this he would not do, and he lay before the town. And news went through all the land that the Cid was come among them. And my Cid lay before Alcocer fifteen weeks; and when he saw that the town did not surrender, he ordered his people to break up their camp, as if they were flying, and they took their way along the Salon, with their banners spread. And when the Moors saw this they rejoiced greatly, and they praised themselves for what they had done in withstanding him, and said that the Cid's bread and barley had failed him, and he had fled away, and left one of his tents behind him. And they said among themselves, "Let us pursue them and spoil them." And they went out after him, great and little, leaving the gates open and shouting as they went; and there was not left in the town a man who could bear arms. And when my Cid saw them coming he gave orders to quicken their speed, as if he was in fear, and would not let his people turn till the Moors were far from the town. But when he saw that there was a good distance between them and the gates, he bade his banner turn, and spurred toward them crying, "Lay on, knights, by God's mercy the spoil is our own." God! what a good joy was theirs that morning! My Cid's vassals laid on without mercy; in one hour, and in a little space, three hundred Moors were slain, and my Cid won the place, and planted his banner upon the highest point of the castle. And the Cid said, "Blessed be God and all His saints, we have bettered our quarters both for horses and men." And he said to Alvar Fañez and all his knights, "Hear me, we shall get nothing by killing these Moors—let us take them and they shall show us their treasures which they have hidden in their houses, and we will dwell here and they shall serve us." In this manner did my Cid win Alcocer, and take up his abode therein.

In three weeks time after this returned Alvar Fañez from Castille. And my Cid rode up to him, and embraced him without speaking, and kissed his mouth and the eyes in his head. God, how joyful was that whole host because Alvar Fañez was returned! for he brought them greetings from their kinswomen and their brethren and the fair comrades whom they had left behind. God, how joyful was my Cid with the fleecy beard, that Minaya had purchased the thousand masses, and had brought him the biddings of his wife and daughters! God, what a joyful man was he!

Now it came to pass that the days of King Almudafar were fulfilled: and he left his two sons Zulema and Abenalfange, and Zulema had the kingdom of Zaragoza, and Abenalfange the kingdom of Denia. And Zulema put his kingdom under my Cid's protection, and bade all his people obey him even as they would himself. Now there began to be great enmity between the two brethren, and they made war upon each other. And the Count Don Ramon Berenguer of Barcelona helped Abenalfange, and was enemy to the Cid because he defended Zulema. And my Cid chose out two hundred horsemen and went out by night, and fell upon the lands of Alcañiz and brought away great booty. Great was the talk among the Moors; how my Cid was over-running the country.

177

When Don Ramon Berenguer the Count of Barcelona heard this, it troubled him to the heart, and he held it for a great dishonour, because that part of the land of the Moors was in his keeping. And he spake boastfully saying, "Great wrong doth that Cid of Bivar offer unto me; he ravages the lands which are in my keeping, and I have never renounced his friendship; but since he goes on in this way I must take vengeance." So he and King Abenalfange gathered together a great power both of Moors and Christians, and went in pursuit of the Cid, and after three days and two nights they came up with him in the pine-forest of Tebar. And when the Cid heard this he sent to Don Ramon saying, that the booty which he had won was none of his, and bidding him let him go on his way in peace: but the Count made answer, that my Cid should now learn whom he had dishonoured. Then my Cid sent the booty forward, and bade his knights make ready. "They are coming upon us," said he, "with a great power both of Moors and Christians, to take from us the spoils which we have so hardly won, and without doing battle we cannot be quit of them; for if we should proceed they would follow till they overtook us: therefore let the battle be here, and I trust in God that we shall win more honour, and something to boot. They come down the hill, drest in their hose, with their gay saddles, and their girths wet. Before they get upon the plain ground let us give them the points of our lances; and Ramon Berenguer will then see whom he has overtaken to-day in the pine-forest of Tebar, thinking to despoil

178

him of booty won from the enemies of God and of the faith."

While my Cid was speaking, his knights had taken their arms, and were ready on horseback for the charge. Presently they saw the Frenchmen coming down the hill, and when they had not yet set foot upon the plain ground, my Cid bade his people charge, which they did with a right good will, thrusting their spears so stiffly, that by God's good pleasure not a man whom they encountered but lost his seat. The Count's people stood firm round their Lord; but my Cid was in search of him, and when he saw where he was, he made up to him, clearing the way as he went, and gave him such a stroke with his lance that he felled him. When the Frenchmen saw their Lord in this plight they fled away and left him; and the pursuit lasted three leagues, and would have been continued farther if the conquerors had not had tired horses. Thus was Count Ramon Berenguer made prisoner, and my Cid won from him that day the good sword Colada, which was worth more than a thousand marks of silver. That night did my Cid and his men make merry, rejoicing over their gains. And the Count was taken to my Cid's tent, and a good supper was set before him; nevertheless he would not eat, though my Cid besought him so to do. And on the morrow my Cid ordered a feast to be made, that he might do pleasure to the Count, but the Count said that for all Spain he would not eat one mouthful, but would rather die, since he had been beaten in battle by such a set of ragged fellows. And Ruydiez said to him, "Eat and drink, Count, for this is the chance of war; if you do as I say you shall be free; and if not you will never return again into your own lands." And Don Ramond answered, "Eat you, Don Rodrigo, for your fortune is fair and you deserve it; take you your pleasure, but leave me to die." And in this mood he continued for three days, refusing all food. But then my Cid said to him, "Take food, Count, and be sure that I will set you free, you and any two of your knights, and give you wherewith to return into your own country." And when Don Ramond heard this, he took comfort and said, "If you will indeed do this thing I shall marvel at you as long as I live." "Eat then," said Ruydiez, "and I will do it: but mark you, of the spoil which we have taken from you I will give you nothing; for to that you have no claim neither by right nor custom, and besides we want it for ourselves, being banished men, who must live by taking from you and from others as long as it shall please God." Then was the Count full joyful, being well pleased that what should be given him was not of the spoils which he had lost; and he called for water and washed his hands, and chose two of his kinsmen to be set free with him. And my Cid sate at the table with them, and said, "If you do not eat well, Count, you and I shall not part yet." Never since he was Count did he eat with better will than that day! And when they had done he said, "Now, Cid, if it be your pleasure let us depart." And my Cid clothed him and his kinsmen well with goodly skins and mantles, and gave them each a goodly palfrey, with rich caparisons, and he rode out with them on their way. And when he took leave of the Count he said to him, "Now go freely, and I thank you for what you have left behind; if you wish to play for it again let me know, and you shall either have something back in its stead, or leave what you bring to be added to it." The Count answered, "Cid, you jest safely now, for I have paid you and all your company for this twelve-months, and shall not be coming to see you again so soon."

Then Count Ramond pricked on more than apace, and many times looked behind him, fearing that my Cid would repent what he had done, and send to take him back to prison, which the perfect one would not have done for the whole world, for never did he do disloyal thing.

At last after long and pitiful fighting it was bruited abroad throughout all lands, how the Cid Ruydiez had won the noble city of Valencia.

And now the Cid bethought him of Doña Ximena his wife, and of his daughters Doña Elvira and Doña Sol, whom he had left in the monastery of St. Pedro de Cardeña and he called for Alvar Fañez and Martin Antolinez of Burgos, and spake with them, and besought them that they would go to Castille, to King Don Alfonso and take him a present from the riches which God had given them; and the present should be a hundred horses, saddled and bridled; and that they would kiss the King's hand for him, and beseech him to send to him his wife Doña Ximena, and his daughters; and that they would tell the King all the mercy which God had shown him, and how he was at his service with Valencia and with all that he had. Moreover he bade them take a thousand marks of silver to the monastery of St. Pedro de Cardeña, and give them to the Abbot, and thirty marks of gold for his wife and daughters, that they might prepare themselves and come in honourable guise. And he ordered three hundred marks of gold to be given them, and three hundred marks of silver, to redeem the chests full of sand which he had pledged in Burgos to the Jews; and he bade them ask Rachel and Vidas to forgive him the deceit of the sand, for he had done it because of his great need.

Then Alvar Fañez and Martin Antolinez dispeeded themselves of the King, and took their way toward Burgos. When they reached Burgos they sent for Rachel and for Vidas, and demanded from them the chests, and paid unto them the three hundred marks of gold and the three hundred of silver as the Cid had commanded, and they besought them to forgive the Cid the deceit of the chests, for it was done because of his great necessity. And they said they heartily forgave him, and held themselves well paid; and they prayed God to grant him long life and good health, and to give him power to advance Christendom, and put down Pagandom. And when it was known through the city of Burgos the goodness and the gentleness which the Cid had shown to these merchants in redeeming from them the chests full of sand and earth and stones, the people held it for a great wonder, and there was not a place in all Burgos where they did not talk of the gentleness and loyalty of the Cid; and they besought blessings upon him, and prayed that he and his people might be advanced in honour. When they had done this, they went to the monastery of St. Pedro de Cardeña, and the porter of the King went with them, and gave order everywhere that everything which they wanted should be given them. If they were well received, and if there was great joy in St. Pedro de Cardeña over them, it is not a thing to ask, for Doña Ximena and her daughters were like people beside themselves with the great joy which they had, and they came running out on foot to meet them, weeping plenteously.

After a long life-time of adventure the Cid sickened of a malady. And the day before his weakness waxed great, he ordered the gates of Valencia to be shut, and went to the Church of St. Peter; and there the Bishop Don Hieronymo being present, and all the clergy who were in Valencia, and the knights and honourable men and honourable dames, as many as the church could hold, the Cid Ruydiez stood up, and made a full noble preaching, showing that no man, however honourable or fortunate he may be in this world, can escape death, to which, said he, "I am now full near; and since ye know that this body of mine hath never yet been conquered, nor put to shame, I beseech ye let not this befall it at the end, for the good fortune of man is only accomplished at his end." Then he took leave of the people, weeping plenteously, and returned to the Alcazar, and betook himself to his bed, and never rose from it again; and every day he waxed weaker and weaker. He called for the caskets of gold in which was the balsam and the myrrh which the

Soldan of Persia had sent him; and when these were put before him he bade them bring him the golden cup, of which he was wont to drink; and he took of that balsam and of that myrrh as much as a little spoonful, and mingled it in the cup with rose-water, and drank of it; and for the seven days which he lived he neither ate nor drank aught else than a little of that myrrh and balsam mingled with water. And every day after he did this, his body and his countenance appeared fairer and fresher than before, and his voice clearer, though he waxed weaker and weaker daily, so that he could not move in his bed.

On the twenty-ninth day, being the day before he departed, he called for Doña Ximena, and for the Bishop Don Hieronymo, and Don Alvar Fañez Minaya, and Pero Bermudez, and his trusty Gil Diaz; and when they were all five before him, he began to direct them what they should do after his death; and he said to them, "Ye know that King Bucar will presently be here to besiege this city, with seven and thirty Kings whom he bringeth with him, and with a mighty power of Moors. Now therefore the first thing which ye do after I have departed, wash my body with rose-water many times and well, and when it has been well washed and made clean, ye shall dry it well, and anoint it with this myrrh and balsam, from these golden caskets, from head to foot, so that every part shall be anointed. And you, my Doña Ximena, and your women, see that ye utter no cries, neither make any lamentation for me, that the Moors may not know of my death. And when the day shall come in which King Bucar arrives, order all the people of Valencia to go upon the walls, and sound your trumpets and tambours and make the greatest rejoicings that ye can. For certes ye cannot keep the city, neither abide therein after they know of my death. And see that sumpter beasts be laden with all that there is in Valencia, so that nothing which can profit may be left. And this I leave especially to your charge, Gil Diaz. Then saddle ye my horse Bavieca, and arm him well; and apparel my body full seemlily, and place me upon the horse, and fasten and tie me thereon so that it cannot fall: and fasten my sword Tizona in my hand. And let the Bishop Don Hieronymo go on one side of me, and my trusty Gil Diaz on the other, and he shall lead my horse. You, Pero Bermudez, shall bear my banner, as you were wont to bear it; and you, Alvar Fañez, my cousin, gather your company together, and put the host in order as you are wont to do. And go ye forth and fight with King Bucar: for be ye certain and doubt not that ye shall win this battle; God hath granted me this. And when ye have won the fight, and the Moors are discomfited, ye may spoil the field at pleasure. Ye will find great riches."

And this noble Baron yielded up his soul, which was pure and without spot, to God, on that Sunday which is called Quinquagesima, being the twenty and ninth of May, in the year of our Lord one thousand and ninety and nine, and in the seventy and third year of his life. After he had thus made his end they washed his body and embalmed it as he had commanded. And then all the honourable men, and all the clergy who were in Valencia, assembled and carried it to the Church of St. Mary of the Virtues, which is near the Alcazar, and there kept their vigil, and said prayer and performed masses, as was meet for so honourable a man.

Three days after the Cid had departed King Bucar came into the port of Valencia, and landed with all his power. And there came with him thirty and six Kings, and one Moorish Queen, and she brought with her two hundred horsewomen, all negresses like herself, all having their hair shorn save a tuft on the top, and they were all armed in coats of mail and with Turkish bows. King Bucar ordered his tents to be pitched round about Valencia. And his people thought that the Cid dared not come out against them, and they were the more encouraged, and began to think of making engines wherewith to combat the city.

All this while the company of the Cid were preparing all things to go into Castille, as he had commanded before his death; and his trusty Gil Diaz did nothing else but labour at this. And the body of the Cid was prepared and the virtue of the balsam and myrrh was such that the flesh remained firm and fair, having its natural colour and his countenance as it was wont to be, and the eyes open, and his long beard in order, so that there was not a man who would have thought him dead if he had seen him. And on the second day after he had departed, Gil Diaz placed the body upon a right noble saddle. And he took two boards and fitted them to the body, one to the breast and the other to the shoulders; these were so hollowed out and fitted that they met at the sides and under the arms, and these boards were fastened into the saddle, so that the body could not move. All this was done by the morning of the twelfth day; and all that day the people of the Cid were busied in making ready their arms, and in loading beasts with all that they had. When it was midnight they took the body of the Cid fastened to the saddle as it was, and placed it upon his horse Bavieca, and fastened the saddle well: and the body sate so upright and well that it seemed as if he was alive. And it had on painted hose of black and white, so cunningly painted that no man who saw them would have thought but that they were grieves, unless he had laid his hand upon them; and they put on it a surcoat of green sendal, having his arms blazoned thereon, and a helmet of parchment, which was cunningly painted that every one might have believed it to be iron; and his shield was hung around his neck, and they placed the sword Tizona in his hand, and they raised his arm, and fastened it up so subtly that it was a marvel to see how upright he held the sword. And the Bishop Don Hieronymo went on one side of him, and the trusty Gil Diaz on the other, and he led the horse Bavieca, as the Cid had commanded him. And when all this had been made ready, they went out from Valencia at midnight, through the gate of Roseros, which is towards Castille. Pero Bermudez went first with the banner of the Cid, and with him five hundred knights who guarded it, all well appointed. Then came the body of the Cid with an hundred knights, all chosen men, and behind them Doña Ximena with all her company, and six hundred knights in the rear.

All these went out so silently, and with such a measured pace, that it seemed as if there were only a score. And by the time that they had all gone out it was broad day.

Now, while the Bishop Don Hieronymo and Gil Diaz led away the body of the Cid, and Doña Ximena, and the baggage, Alvar Fañez Minaya fell upon the Moors. First he attacked the tents of that Moorish Queen, the Negress, who lay nearest to the city; and this onset was so sudden, that they killed full a hundred and fifty Moors before they had time to take arms or go to horse. But that Moorish Negress, so skilful in drawing the Turkish bow, that they called her the Star of the Archers, was the first that got on horseback, and with some fifty that were with her, did some hurt to the company of the Cid; but in fine they slew her, and her people fled to the camp. And so great was the uproar and confusion, that few there were who took arms, but instead thereof they turned their backs and fled toward the sea. And when King Bucar and his Kings saw this they were astonished. And it seemed to them that there came against them on the part of the Christians full seventy thousand knights, all as white as snow: and before them a knight of great stature upon a white horse. And King Bucar and the other Kings were so greatly dismayed that they never checked the reins till they had ridden into the sea; and the company of the Cid rode after them, smiting and slaying and giving them no respite. And when the Moors came to the sea, so great was the press among them to get to the ships, that more than ten thousand died in the water. And King Bucar and they who escaped with him hoisted sails and went their way, and never more turned their heads.

Then Alvar Fañez and his people went after the Bishop Don Hieronymo and Gil Diaz, who, with the body of the Cid, and Doña Ximena, and the baggage, had gone on till they were clear of the host, and then waited for those who were gone against the Moors. And so great was the spoil, gold, and silver, and other precious things that the poorest man among the Christians, horseman or on foot, became rich with what he won that day. And when they were all met together, they took the road toward Castille; and they halted that night in a village which is called Siete Aguas, that is to say, the Seven Waters, which is nine leagues from Valencia.

When the company of the Cid departed from the Siete Aguas, they held their way by short journeys. And the Cid went alway upon his horse Bavieca, as they had brought him out from Valencia, save only that he wore no arms, but was clad in right noble garments. Great was the concourse of people to see the Cid Ruydiez coming in that guise. They came from all the country round about, and when they saw him their wonder was the greater, and hardly could they be persuaded that he was dead.

At this time King Don Alfonso abode in Toledo, and when the letters came unto him saying how the Cid Campeador was departed, and after what manner he had discomfited King Bucar, and how they brought him in this goodly manner upon his horse Bavieca, he set out from Toledo, taking long journeys till he came to San Pedro de Cardeña to do honour to the Cid at his funeral. And when the King Don Alfonso saw so great a company and in such goodly array, and the Cid Ruydiez so nobly clad and upon his horse Bavieca, he was greatly astonished. And the King beheld his countenance, and seeing it so fresh and comely, and his eyes so bright and fair, and so even and open that he seemed alive, he marvelled greatly.

On the third day after the coming of King Don Alfonso, they would have interred the body of the Cid, but when the King heard what Doña Ximena had said, that while it was so fair and comely it should not be laid in a coffin, he held that what she said was good. And he sent for the ivory chair which had been carried to the Cortes of Toledo, and gave order that it should be placed on the right of the altar of St. Peter; and he laid a cloth of gold upon it, and he ordered a graven tabernacle to be made over the chair, richly wrought with azure and gold. And he himself, and the King of Navarre and the Infante of Aragon, and the Bishop Don Hieronymo, to do honour to the Cid, helped to take his body from between the two boards, in which it had been fastened at Valencia. And when they had taken it out, the body was so firm that it bent not on either side, and the flesh so firm and comely, that it seemed as if he were yet alive. And the King thought that what they purported to do and had thus begun, might full well be effected. And they clad the body in cloth of purple, which the Soldan of Persia had sent him, and put him on hose of the same, and set him in his ivory chair; and in his left hand they placed his sword Tizona in its scabbard, and the strings of his mantle in his right. And in this fashion the body of the Cid remained there ten years and more, till it was taken thence and buried.

Gil Diaz took great delight in tending the horse Bavieca, so that there were few days in which he did not lead him to water, and bring him back with his own hand. And from the day in which the dead body of the Cid was taken off his back, never man was suffered to bestride that horse, but he was alway led when they took him to water, and when they brought him back. And this good horse lived two years and a half after the death of his master the Cid, and then he died also, having lived full forty years. And Gil Diaz buried him before the gate of the monastery, in the public place, on the right hand; and he planted two elms upon the grave, the one at his head and the other at his feet, and these elms grew and became great trees, and are yet to be seen before the gate of the monastery.

# ROBIN HOOD

BECAUSE of the hardness towards the English people of William the Conqueror, and of William's successors to several generations, many an Englishman exiled himself from town and passed his life in the greenwood. These men were called "outlaws." First they went forth out of love for the ancient liberties of England. Then in their living in the forest, they put themselves without the law by their ways of gaining their livelihood. Of such men none were more renowned than Robin Hood and his company.

We do not know anything about Robin Hood, who he was, or where he lived, or what evil deed he had done. Any man might kill him and never pay penalty for it. But, outlaw or not, the poor people loved him and looked on him as their friend, and many a stout fellow came to join him, and led a merry life in the greenwood, with moss and fern for bed, and for meat the King's deer, which it was death to slay. Tillers of the land, yeomen, and some say knights, went on their ways freely, for of them Robin took no toll; but lordly churchmen with money-bags well filled, or proud bishops with their richly dressed followers, trembled as they drew near to Sherwood Forest—who was to know whether behind every tree there did not lurk Robin Hood or one of his men?

One day Robin was walking alone in the wood, and reached a river spanned by a very narrow bridge, over which one man only could pass. In the midst stood a stranger, and Robin bade him go back and let him go over. "I am no man of yours," was all the answer Robin got, and in anger he drew his bow and fitted an arrow to it, "Would you shoot a man who has no arms but a staff?" asked the stranger in scorn; and with shame Robin laid down his bow, and unbuckled an oaken stick at his side. "We will fight till one of us falls into the water," he said; and fight they did, till the stranger planted a blow so well that Robin rolled over into the river. "You are a brave soul," said he, when he had waded to land, and he blew a blast with his horn which brought fifty good fellows, clad in green, to the little bridge. "Have you fallen into the river that your clothes are wet?" asked one; and Robin made answer, "No, but this stranger, fighting on the bridge, got the better of me, and tumbled me into the stream."

At this the foresters seized the stranger, and would have ducked him had not their leader bade them stop, and begged the stranger to stay with them and make one of themselves. "Here is my hand," replied the stranger, "and my heart with it. My name, if you would know it, is John Little."

"That must be altered," cried Will Scarlett; "we will call a feast, and henceforth, because he is full seven feet tall and round the waist at least an ell, he shall be called Little John."

And thus it was done; but at the feast Little John, who always liked to know exactly what work he had to do, put some questions to Robin Hood. "Before I join hands with you, tell me first what sort of life is this you lead? How am I to know whose goods I shall take, and whose I shall leave? Whom I shall beat, and whom I shall refrain from beating?"

And Robin answered: "Look that you harm not any tiller of the ground, nor any yeoman of the greenwood—no knight, no squire, unless you have heard him ill spoken of. But if bishops or archbishops come your way, see that you spoil them, and mark that you always hold in your mind the High Sheriff of Nottingham."

This being settled, Robin Hood declared Little John to be second in command to himself among the brotherhood of the forest, and the new outlaw never forgot to "hold in his mind" the High Sheriff of Nottingham, who was the bitterest enemy the foresters had.

## THE BALLAD OF ROBIN HOOD, THE BUTCHER AND THE SHERIFF

Upon a time it chanced so,
  Bold Robin in forest did spy
A jolly butcher, with a bonny fine mare,
  With his flesh to the market did hie.

"Good morrow, good fellow," said jolly Robin,
    "What food hast thou? tell unto me;
  Thy trade to me tell, and where thou dost dwell,
    For I like well thy company."

  The butcher he answer'd jolly Robin,
    "No matter where I dwell;
  For a butcher I am, and to Nottingham
    I am going, my flesh to sell."

"What's the price of thy flesh?" said jolly Robin,
    "Come, tell it soon unto me;
  And the price of thy mare, be she never so dear,
    For a butcher fain would I be."

"The price of my flesh," the butcher replied,
    "I soon will tell unto thee;
  With my bonny mare, and they are not dear,
    Four marks thou must give unto me."

"Four marks I will give thee," said jolly Robin,
    "Four marks shall be thy fee;
  The money come count, and let me mount,
    For a butcher I fain would be."

  Now Robin he is to Nottingham gone,
    His butcher's trade to begin;
  With good intent to the Sheriff he went,
    And there he took up his inn.

  When other butchers did open their meat,
    Bold Robin got gold and fee,
  For he sold more meat for one penny
    Than others did sell for three.

  Which made the butchers of Nottingham
    To study as they did stand,

Saying, "Surely he is some prodigal
    That has sold his father's land."

"This is a mad blade," the butchers still said;
    Said the Sheriff, "He is some prodigal,
That some land has sold for silver and gold,
    And now he doth mean to spend all.

"Hast thou any horn-beasts," the Sheriff asked,
    "Good fellow, to sell to me?"
"Yes, that I have, good Master Sheriff,
    I have hundreds, two or three.

"And a hundred acres of good free land,
    If you please it to see:
And I'll make you as good assurance of it,
    As ever my father made me."

The Sheriff he saddled his good palfrey,
    And with three hundred pounds of gold,
Away he went with bold Robin Hood,
    His horned beasts to behold.

Away then the Sheriff and Robin did ride,
    To the forest of merry Sherwood;
Then the Sheriff did say, "God keep us this day
    From a man they call Robin Hood."
But when a little farther they came,
    Bold Robin he chanced to spy
A hundred head of good red deer,
    Come tripping the Sheriff full nigh.

"How like you my horn-beasts, good Master Sheriff?
    They be fat and fair to see";
"I tell thee, good fellow, I would I were gone,
    For I like not thy company."

196

Then Robin set his horn to his mouth,
    And blew but blasts three;
Then quickly anon there came Little John,
    And all his company.

"What is your will?" then said Little John,
    "Good master, come tell unto me";
"I have brought hither the Sheriff of Nottingham
    This day to dine with thee."

Then Robin took his cloak from his back
    And laid it upon the ground;
And out of the Sheriff's portmanteau
    He took three hundred pound.

He then led the Sheriff through the wood,
    And set him on his dapple grey;
"Commend Robin Hood to your wife at home,"
    He said, and went laughing away.

Now Robin Hood had no liking for a company of idle men about him, and sent off Little John and Will Scarlett to the great road known as Watling Street, with orders to hide among the trees and wait till some adventure might come to them; and if they took captive earl or baron, abbot or knight, he was to be brought unharmed back to Robin Hood.

But all along Watling Street the road was bare; white and hard it lay in the sun, without the tiniest cloud of dust to show that a rich company might be coming: east and west the land lay still.

At length, just where a side path turned into the broad highway, there rode a knight, and a sorrier man than he never sat a horse on summer day. One foot only was in the stirrup, the other hung carelessly by his side; his head was bowed, the reins dropped loose, and his horse went on as he would. At so sad a sight the hearts of the outlaws were filled with pity, and Little John fell on his knees and bade the knight welcome in the name of his master.

"Who is your master?" asked the knight.

"Robin Hood," answered Little John.

"I have heard much good of him," replied the knight, "and will go with you gladly."

Then they all set off together, tears running down the knight's cheeks as he rode, but he said nothing, neither was anything said to him. And in this wise they came to Robin Hood.

"Welcome, Sir Knight," cried he, "and thrice welcome, for I waited to break my fast till you or some other had come to me."

"God save you, good Robin," answered the knight, and after they had washed themselves in the stream they sat down to dine off bread, with flesh of the King's deer, and swans and pheasants. "Such a dinner have I not had for three weeks and more," said the knight. "And if I ever come again this way, good Robin, I will give you as fine a dinner as you have given me."

"I thank you," replied Robin, "my dinner is always welcome; still, I am none so greedy but I can wait for it. But before you go, pay me, I pray you, for the food which you have had. It was never the custom for a yeoman to pay for a knight."

"My bag is empty," said the knight, "save for ten shillings only."

"Go, Little John, and look in his wallet," said Robin, "and, Sir Knight, if in truth you have no more, not one penny will I take; nay, I will give you all that you shall need."

So Little John spread out the knight's mantle, and opened the bag, and therein lay ten shillings and naught besides.

"What tidings, Little John?" cried his master.

"Sir, the knight speaks truly," said Little John.

"Then tell me, Sir Knight, whether it is your own ill doings which have brought you to this sorry pass."

"For an hundred years my fathers have dwelt in the forest," answered the knight, "and four hundred pounds might they spend yearly. But within two years misfortune has befallen me, and my wife and children also."

"How did this evil come to pass?" asked Robin.

"Through my own folly," answered the knight, "and because of my great love I bore my son, who would never be guided of my counsel, and slew, ere he was twenty years old, a knight of Lancaster and his squire. For their deaths I had to pay a large sum, which I could not raise without giving my lands in pledge to the rich Abbot of St. Mary's. If I cannot bring him the money by a certain day they will be lost to me for ever."

"What is the sum?" asked Robin. "Tell me truly."

"It is four hundred pounds," said the knight.

"And what will you do if you lose your lands?" asked Robin again.

"Hide myself over the sea," said the knight, "and bid farewell to my friends and country. There is no better way open to me."

At this tears fell from his eyes, and he turned him to depart. "Good day, my friend," he said to Robin, "I cannot pay you what I should—" But Robin held him fast. "Where are your friends?" asked he.

"Sir, they have all forsaken me since I became poor, and they turn away their heads if we meet upon the road, though when I was rich they were ever in my castle."

When Little John and Will Scarlett and the rest heard this they wept for very shame and fury.

"Little John," said Robin, "go to my treasure chest, and bring me thence four hundred pounds. And be sure you count it truly."

So Little John went, and Will Scarlett, and they brought back the money.

"Sir," said Little John, when Robin had counted it and found it no more and no less, "look at his clothes, how thin they are! You have stores of garments, green and scarlet, in your coffers—no merchant in England can boast the like. I will measure some out with my bow." And thus he did.

"Master," spoke Little John again, "there is still something else. You must give him a horse, that he may go as beseems his quality to the Abbey."

"Take the grey horse," said Robin, "and put a new saddle on it, and take likewise a good palfrey and a pair of boots, with gilt spurs on them. And as it were a shame for a knight to ride by himself on this errand, I will lend you Little John as squire—perchance he may stand you in yeoman's stead."

"When shall we meet again?" asked the knight.

"This day twelve months," said Robin, "under the greenwood tree."

Then the knight rode on his way, with Little John behind him, and as he went he thought of Robin Hood and his men, and blessed them for the goodness they had shown towards him.

"To-morrow," he said to Little John, "I must be at the Abbey of St. Mary, which is in the city of York, for if I am but so much as a day late my lands are lost for ever, and though I were to bring the money I should not be suffered to redeem them."

Now the Abbot had been counting the days as well as the knight, and the next morning he said to his monks: "This day year there came a knight and borrowed of me four hundred pounds, giving his lands in surety. And if he come not to pay his debt ere midnight tolls they will be ours forever."

"It is full early yet," answered the Prior, "he may still be coming."

"He is far beyond the sea," said the Abbot, "and suffers from hunger and cold. How is he to get here?"

"It were a shame," said the Prior, "for you to take his lands. And you do him much wrong if you drive such a hard bargain."

"He is dead or hanged," spake a fat-headed monk who was the cellarer, "and we shall have his four hundred pounds to spend on our gardens and our wines," and he went with the Abbot to attend the court of justice wherein the knight's lands would be declared forfeited by the High Justiciar.

"If he come not this day," cried the Abbot, rubbing his hands, "if he come not this day, they will be ours."

"He will not come yet," said the Justiciar, but he knew not that the knight was already at the outer gate, and Little John with him.

"Welcome, Sir Knight," said the porter. "The horse that you ride is the noblest that ever I saw. Let me lead them both to the stable, that they may have food and rest."

"They shall not pass these gates," answered the knight, sternly, and he entered the hall alone, where the monks were sitting at meat, and knelt down and bowed to them.

"I have come back, my lord," he said to the Abbot, who had just returned from the court. "I have come back this day as I promised."

"Have you brought my money? What do you here without it?" cried the Abbot in angry tones.

"I have come to pray you for a longer day," answered the knight, meekly.

"The day was fixed and cannot be gainsaid," replied the Justiciar; "I am with the Abbot."

"Good Sir Abbot, be my friend," prayed the knight again, "and give me one chance more to get the money and free my lands. I will serve you day and night till I have four hundred pounds to redeem them."

But the Abbot only swore a great oath, and vowed that the money must be paid that day or the lands be forfeited.

The knight stood up straight and tall: "It is well," said he, "to prove one's friends against the hour of need," and he looked the Abbot full in the face, and the Abbot felt uneasy, he did not know why, and hated the knight more than ever. "Out of my hall, false knight!" cried he, pretending to a courage which he did not feel. But the knight stayed where he was, and answered him, "You lie, Abbot. Never was I false, and that I have shown in jousts and in tourneys."

"Give him two hundred pounds more," said the Justiciar to the Abbot, "and keep the lands yourself."

"No, by Heaven!" answered the knight, "not if you offered me a thousand pounds would I do it! Neither Justiciar, abbot, nor monk shall be heir of mine." Then he strode up to a table and emptied out four hundred pounds. "Take your gold, Sir Abbot, which you lent to me a year agone. Had you but received me civilly, I would have paid you something more.

> Now have I kept my day!
> Now shall I have my land again,
> For aught that you may say."

So he passed out of the hall singing merrily, leaving the Abbot staring silently after him, and rode back to his house in Verisdale, where his wife met him at the gate.

> "Welcome, my lord," said his lady,
> "Sir, lost is all your good."
> "Be merry, dame," said the knight,
> "And pray for Robin Hood.

But for his kindness, we would have been beggars."

After this the knight dwelt at home, looking after his lands and saving his money carefully till the four hundred pounds lay ready for Robin Hood. Then he bought a hundred bows and a hundred arrows, and every arrow was an ell long, and had a head of silver and peacock's feathers. And clothing himself in white and red, and with a hundred men in his train, he set off to Sherwood Forest.

On the way he passed an open space near a bridge where there was a wrestling, and the knight stopped and looked, for he himself had taken many a prize in that sport. Here the prizes were such as to fill any man with envy; a fine horse, saddled and bridled, a great white bull, a pair of gloves, and a ring of bright red gold. There was not a yeoman present who did not hope to win one of them. But when the wrestling was over, the yeoman who had beaten them all was a man who kept apart from his fellows, and was said to think much of himself. Therefore the men grudged him his skill, and set upon him with blows, and would have killed him, had not the knight, for love of Robin Hood, taken pity on him, while his followers fought with the crowd, and would not suffer them to touch the prizes a better man had won.

When the wrestling was finished the knight rode on, and there under the greenwood tree, in the place appointed, he found Robin Hood and his merry men waiting for him, according to the tryst that they had fixed last year:

"God save thee, Robin Hood,
   And all this company."
"Welcome be thou, gentle knight,
   And right welcome to me."

"Hast thou thy land again?" said Robin,

"Truth then thou tell me."
"Yea, for God," said the knight,
"And that thank I God and thee."

"Have here four hundred pounds," said the knight,
"The which you lent to me;
And here are also twenty marks
For your courtesie."

But Robin would not take the money. Then he noticed the bows and arrows which the knight had brought, and asked what they were. "A poor present to you," answered the knight, and Robin, who would not be outdone, sent Little John once more to his treasury, and bade him bring forth four hundred pounds, which was given to the knight. After that they parted, in much love, and Robin prayed the knight if he were in any strait "to let him know at the greenwood tree, and while there was any gold there he should have it."

Now the King had no mind that Robin Hood should do as he willed, and called his knights to follow him to Nottingham, where they would lay plans how best to take captive the felon. Here they heard sad tales of Robin's misdoings, and how of the many herds of wild deer that had been wont to roam the forest in some places scarce one remained. This was the work of Robin Hood and his merry men, on whom the king swore vengeance with a great oath.

"I would I had this Robin Hood in my hands," cried he, "and an end should soon be put to his doings." So spake the King; but an old knight, full of days and wisdom, answered him and warned him that the task of taking Robin Hood would be a sore one, and best let alone. The King, who had seen the vanity of his hot words the moment that he had uttered them, listened to the old man, and resolved to bide his time, if perchance some day Robin should fall into his power.

All this time and for six weeks later that he dwelt in Nottingham the King could hear nothing of Robin, who seemed to have vanished into the earth with his merry men, though one by one the deer were vanishing too!

At last one day a forester came to the King, and told him that if he would see Robin he must come with him and take five of his best knights. The King eagerly sprang up to do his bidding, and the six men clad in monk's clothes mounted their palfreys and rode down to the Abbey, the King wearing an Abbot's broad hat over his crown and singing as he passed through the greenwood.

Suddenly at the turn of the path Robin and his archers appeared before them.

"By your leave, Sir Abbot," said Robin, seizing the King's bridle, "you will stay a while with us. Know that we are yeomen, who live upon the King's deer, and other food have we none. Now you have abbeys and churches, and gold in plenty; therefore give us some of it, in the name of holy charity."

"I have no more than forty pounds with me," answered the King, "but sorry I am it is not a hundred, for you should have had it all."

So Robin took the forty pounds, and gave half to his men, and then told the King he might go on his way. "I thank you," said the King, "but I would have you know that our liege lord has bid me bear you his seal, and pray you to come to Nottingham."

At this message Robin bent his knee.

> "I love no man in all the world
> So well as I do my King,"

he cried, "and, Sir Abbot, for thy tidings, which fill my heart with joy, to-day thou shalt dine with me, for love of my King." Then he led the King into an open place, and Robin took a horn and blew it loud, and at its blast seven-score of young men came speedily to do his will.

"They are quicker to do his bidding than my men are to do mine," said the King to himself.

Speedily the foresters set out the dinner, venison and white bread, and Robin and Little John served the King. "Make good cheer, Abbot, for charity," said Robin, "and then you shall see what sort of life we lead, that so you may tell our King."

When he had finished eating the archers took their bows, and hung rose-garlands up with a string, and every man was to shoot through the garland. If he failed, he should have a buffet on the head from Robin.

Good bowmen as they were, few managed to stand the test. Little John and Will Scarlett, and

Much, all shot wide of the mark, and at length no one was left in but Robin himself and Gilbert of the White Hand. Then Robin fired his last bolt, and it fell three fingers from the garland. "Master," said Gilbert, "you have lost, stand forth and take your punishment."

"I will take it," answered Robin, "but, Sir Abbot, I pray you that I may suffer it at your hands."

The King hesitated. "It did not become him," he said, "to smite such a stout yeoman," but Robin bade him smite on; so he turned up his sleeve, and gave Robin such a buffet on the head that he rolled upon the ground.

"There is pith in your arm," said Robin. "Come, shoot a-main with me." And the King took up a bow, and in so doing his hat fell back and Robin saw his face.

"My lord the King of England, now I know you well," cried he, and he fell on his knees and all the outlaws with him. "Mercy I ask, my lord the King, for my men and me."

"Mercy I grant," then said the King, "and therefore I came hither, to bid you and your men leave the greenwood and dwell in my court with me."

"So it shall be," answered Robin, "I and my men will come to your court, and see how your service liketh us."

"Have you any green cloth," asked the King, "that you could sell to me?" and Robin brought out thirty yards and more, and clad the King and his men in coats of Lincoln green. "Now we will all ride to Nottingham," said he, and they went merrily, shooting by the way.

The people of Nottingham saw them coming, and trembled as they watched the dark mass of Lincoln green drawing near over the fields. "I fear lest our King be slain," whispered one to another, "and if Robin Hood gets into the town there is not one of us whose life is safe"; and every man, woman, and child made ready to fly.

The King laughed out when he saw their fright, and called them back. Right glad were they to hear his voice, and they feasted and made merry. A few days later the King returned to London, and Robin dwelt in his court for twelve months. By that time he had spent a hundred pounds, for he gave largely to the knights and squires he met, and great renown he had for his openhandedness.

But his men who had been born under the shadow of the forest, could not live amid streets and houses. One by one they slipped away, till only Little John and Will Scarlett were left. Then Robin himself grew home-sick, and at the sight of some young men shooting thought upon the time when he was accounted the best archer in all England, and went straightway to the King and begged for leave to go on a pilgrimage to Bernisdale.

"I may not say you nay," answered the King; "seven nights you may be gone and no more." And

Robin thanked him, and that evening set out for the greenwood.

It was early morning when he reached it at last, and listened thirstily to the notes of singing birds, great and small.

"It seems long since I was here," he said to himself; "It would give me great joy if I could bring down a deer once more," and he shot a great hart, and blew his horn, and all the outlaws of the forest came flocking round him. "Welcome," they said, "our dear master, back to the greenwood tree," and they threw off their caps and fell on their knees before him in delight at his return.

For two and twenty years Robin Hood dwelt in Sherwood forest after he had run away from court, and naught that the King could say would tempt him back again. At the end of that time he fell ill; he neither ate nor drank, and had no care for the things he loved. "I must go to merry Kirkley," said he, "and have my blood let."

But Will Scarlett, who heard his words, spoke roundly to him. "Not by *my* leave, nor without a hundred bowmen at your back. For there abides an evil man, who is sure to quarrel with you, and you will need us badly."

"If you are afraid, Will Scarlett, you may stay at home, for me," said Robin, "and in truth no man will I take with me, save Little John only, to carry my bow."

"Bear your bow yourself, master, and I will bear mine."

"Very well, let it be so," said Robin, and they went on merrily enough till they came to some women weeping sorely near a stream.

"What is the matter, good wives?" said Robin Hood.

"We weep for Robin Hood and his dear body, which to-day must let blood," was the answer.

"Pray why do you weep for me?" asked Robin; "the Prioress is the daughter of my aunt, and well I know she would not do me harm for all the world." And he passed on, with Little John at his side.

Soon they reached the Priory, where they were let in by the Prioress herself, who bade them welcome heartily, and not the less because Robin handed her twenty pounds in gold as payment for his stay, and told her if he cost her more, she was to let him know of it. Then she began to bleed him, and for long Robin said nothing, giving her credit for kindness and for knowing her art, but at length so much blood came from him that he suspected treason. He tried to open the door, for she had left him alone in the room, but it was locked fast, and while the blood was still flowing he could not escape from the casement. So he lay down for many hours, and none came near him, and at length the blood stopped. Slowly Robin uprose and staggered to the lattice-window, and blew thrice on his horn; but the blast was so low, and so little like what Robin was wont to give, that Little John, who was watching for some sound, felt that his master must be nigh to death.

At this thought he started to his feet, and ran swiftly to the Priory. He broke the locks of all the doors that stood between him and Robin Hood, and soon entered the chamber where his master lay, white, with nigh all his blood gone from him.

"I crave a boon of you, dear master," cried Little John.

"And what is that boon," said Robin Hood, "which Little John begs of me?" And Little John answered, "It is to burn Kirkley Hall, and all the nunnery."

But Robin Hood, in spite of the wrong that had been done him, would not listen to Little John's cry for revenge. "I never hurt a woman in all my life," he said, "nor a man that was in her company. But now my time is done. That know I well. So give me my bow and a broad arrow, and wheresoever it falls there shall my grave be digged. Lay a green sod under my head and another at my feet, and put beside me my bow, which ever made sweetest music to my ears, and see that green and gravel make my grave. And, Little John, take care that I have length enough and breadth enough to lie in." So Robin he loosened his last arrow from the string. He then died. And where the arrow fell Robin was buried.

# RICHARD THE LION-HEARTED

KING RICHARD, with his chief nobles, disembarked at Acre an hour before noon on the 8th day of June, 1191. I had the good fortune to see him without difficulty, by the favour of one who has a charge in the ordering of the harbour. Nor was this a small thing, for there was such a press and crowding of men.

The King was as noble a warrior as ever I have seen. Some that I have known were taller of stature, but never one that bore himself more bravely and showed more likelihood of strength and courage. They that are learned in such things said that his arms were over-long for the height of his body; but this is scarce a fault in a swordsman, another inch of length adding I know not how much of strength to a blow. He was of a ruddy complexion, his eyes blue, with a most uncommon fire in them, such as few could dare to look into if his wrath was kindled, his countenance, such as befitted a ruler of men, being of an aspect both generous and commanding.

Some ten days after his coming to the camp King Richard was taken with sickness. This was never altogether absent, but it grew worse, as might indeed be looked for, in the heats of summer. The King sickened on the day which the Christians celebrate as the Feast of St. Barnabas.[1] I was called to see him, having, as I have said, no small fame as a healer. Never have I seen a sick man more intractable. My medicine he swallowed readily, I may say, even greedily. Had I suffered it, he would have taken it at intervals shorter by far than I ordered. Doubtless he thought that the more a man has of a good thing, the better it is for him. (So indeed many believe, and of other things besides medicine, but wholly without reason). But in this I hindered him, leaving with those who ministered to him sufficient for one dose only.

He was troubled about many things, about the siege, which, as he justly thought, had already been too much drawn out, about King Philip of France, whom he loved not nor trusted, about his engines of war, of which the greater part had not yet reached the camp; the ships that bore them having been outsailed by the rest of the fleet. His fever was of the intermittent sort, coming upon him on alternate days. On the days when he was whole, or as nearly whole as a man sick of this ague may ever be, he was busy in the field, causing such engines as he had to be set in convenient places for the assault of the town, and in other cares such as fall to a general.

[1] The longest day according to the old calendar. So the old adage has it: "Barnaby bright, Barnaby bright; Longest day and shortest night."

When he was perforce shut in his pavilion by access of the fever, he suffered himself to take no rest. Messengers were coming and going from morning to night with news of the siege—he could never hear enough of the doings of the French King—and there were always near him men skilful in the working and making of engines. One would show him some new thing pictured upon paper; another would bring a little image, so to speak, of an engine, made in wood or iron. Never was a child more occupied with a toy than was King Richard with these things. I am myself no judge of such matters, but I have heard it said by men well acquainted with them, that the King had a marvellous understanding of such contrivances. But these cares were a great hindrance to recovery. So at least I judged, and doubtless it had been thus in the case of most men. But the King was not as others, and, as it seemed to me, he drove away his disease by sheer force of will.

On a certain evening when King Richard was mending apace of his fever one came to his tent—an English knight, Hugh Brown by name—who brought the news that the King of the French had commanded that a general assault should be made on the town the very next day. The King would fain know the cause of this sudden resolve. "Well," said the English knight, "it came about, as I understand, in this fashion. The Turks have this day destroyed two engines of King Philip on which he had spent much time and gold." "Aye!" said King Richard, "I know the two; the cat and the mantlet. They are pretty contrivings the both of them, but I set not such store on them as does my brother of France." And here I should say that the cat was like to a tent made of hides long and narrow and low upon the ground, with a pointed end as it might be a ploughshare, which could be brought up to the walls by men moving it from within, and so sheltered from the stones and darts of the enemy. As for the mantlet, it was made in somewhat the same fashion, only it was less in size, nor was it to be brought near to the wall. King Philip loved dearly to sit in it, cross-bow in hand—the French, I noted, like rather the cross-bow, the English the long-bow—and would shoot his bolts at any Turk that might show himself upon the walls.

But to come back to the knight's story. "An hour or so after noon, when the cat had been brought close to the wall, and the mantlet was in its accustomed place, some fifty yards distant, the Turks made an attack on both at the same moment of time. On to the cat they dropped a heavy beam; and when this with its weight had broken in the roof, or I should rather say the back of the cat, a great quantity of brushwood, and after the brushwood a whole pailful of Greek fire—the machine was over near to the wall, so that these things could be dropped on it from above.[1] At the mantlet they aimed bolts from a strong engine which they had newly put in place, and by ill luck broke it through. And verily before the nimblest-tongued priest in the whole realm of

---

[1] A composition, supposedly of asphalt, nitre and sulphur. It burnt under water.

England could say a hunting-mass, both were in a blaze."

What the man might mean by the priest and the hunting-mass I knew not then, but heard after, that when a noble will go forth hunting, the service which they call the mass is shortened to the utmost, and the priest that can say it more speedily than his brethren is best esteemed.

"And my brother of France," cried the King, "how fared he?" "He had as narrow an escape with his life," answered the knight, "as ever had Christian king. His mantle, nay his very hair was singed, and as for his cross-bow, he was constrained to leave it behind." "And he gave commands for the assault in his anger?" said the King. " 'Tis even so," answered Sir Hugh.

"My brother of France is, methinks, too greedy of gain and glory; if he had been willing to ask our help, he had done better." But King Richard sorrowed for the brave men, fellow-soldiers of the Cross with him, who had fallen to no purpose. Nevertheless, in his secret heart, he was not ill-pleased that the French King had not taken the town of Acre.

On the second day after the failure of the French assault upon the town, King Richard would make his own essay. He was not yet wholly recovered of his sickness; but it would have passed the wit of man to devise means by which he could be kept within his pavilion; nor must it be forgotten that such restraint might have done him more of harm than of good. So his physicians, for he had those who regularly waited on him (though I make bold to say that he trusted in me rather than in them), gave him the permission which he had taken. He had caused a mantlet to be built for him which was brought up to the edge of the ditch with which the town was surrounded. In this he sat, with a cross-bow in hand, and shot not a few of the enemy, being skilful beyond the common in the use of this weapon. But towns are not taken by the shooting of bolts, howsoever well aimed they may be. This may not be done save by coming to close quarters.

It was on the thirty-fourth day after the coming of King Richard that the town was given up. Proclamation was made throughout the camp that no one should trespass by deed or word against the departing Turks. And, indeed, he who would insult men so brave would be of a poor and churlish spirit. To the last they bore themselves with great courage and dignity. On the morning of the day of their departure they dressed themselves in their richest apparel, and being so drest showed themselves on the walls. This done, they laid aside their garments, piling them in a great heap in the market-place, and so marched forth from the town, each clad in his shirt only, but with a most cheerful contenance.

When the last of the Turks had left the town the Christian army entered. Half of it was given to the French king, who had for his own abode the House of the Templars, and half to King Richard, to whom was assigned the palace of the Caliph. In like manner the prisoners and all the treasure were equally divided.

For one shameful deed the English King must answer. Of this deed I will now tell the story. When the army had had sufficient rest—and the King knew well that no army must have more than is sufficient, suffering more from excess than from defect in this matter—and it was now time to advance, there arose a great question touching the agreement made when the town was given up. There was much going to and fro of messengers and embassies between the English King and the Caliph Saladin, much debating, and many accusations bandied to and fro. Even to this day no man can speak certainly of what was done or not done in this matter. What I write, I write according to the best of my knowledge. First, then, it is beyond all doubt that the Caliph did not send either the Holy Cross or the money which had been covenanted, or the prisoners whom he had promised to deliver up; but as to the cause wherefore he did not send them there is no agreement, the Christians affirming one thing, the followers of Mahomet another. As to the Holy Cross, let that be put out of the account. No man that I ever talked with—and I have talked with many—ever saw it. 'Tis much to be doubted whether it was in being. As to the money, that the Caliph had it, or a great portion of it, at hand, is certainly true. It was seen and counted by King Richard's own envoys. As to the prisoners, it is hard to discover the truth. For my part, I believe that the Caliph was ready to deliver up all that he had in his own hands or could find elsewhere, but that he had promised more in respect of this than he was able to perform. Many of those whom he had covenanted to restore were dead, either of disease or by violence. As for disease, it must be noted that a sick man was likely to fare worse in the hands of Turks; as for violence, there was not much diversity between the Christians and the followers of Mahomet. But this may be said, that one who invades the land of others is like to suffer worse injury should he come into their power than he would have the disposition to inflict upon them. Whatever, then, the cause, the Caliph had engaged in this matter far more than he was able to perform. But he did not fail from want of good faith. I take it that it was from the matter of the money that there came the breaking of the agreement. To put it very shortly, the Caliph said, "Restore to me the hostages and you shall receive the gold"; King Richard said, "Send on the gold and you shall receive the hostages." And neither was the Caliph willing to trust the good faith of the King, nor the King the good faith of the Caliph.

So there was delay after delay, much talk to no purpose, and the hearts of men, both on one side and on the other, growing more hot with anger from day to day. And there was also the need which increased from day to day, as, indeed, it needs must, for the Christians to be about the business on which they came. They had taken the town of Acre, but that was but the beginning of their enterprise, for they had to conquer the whole land. And how could the army march with a whole multitude of prisoners in their hands? It would need no small number of men to keep watch over them, lest they should escape, or, what was more to be feared, do an injury to the army. What could be worse in a doubtful battle than that there should be these enemies in its very midst? I set these things down because I would not do an injustice to the English King, whom I have always held as one to be greatly admired. Nevertheless I say again, that in the matter of the prisoners he did a shameful deed. For on the 20th day of August he commanded that all the prisoners that were in his hands, whether they had been taken in battle, or delivered up as hostages for the fulfilment of the covenant, should be led out of the city and slain. These were in number between two and three thousand. Some the King kept alive, for whom, as being of high nobility and great wealth, he hoped to receive a ransom; others were saved by private persons, a few for compassion's sake; and others in the hope of gain. But the greater part were slain without mercy, the soldiers falling upon them, without arms and helpless as they were.

It was soon made plain to all that the spirit of the Caliph and his Turks was not broken by the losing of Acre. Rather were they stirred up by it to more earnestness and courage; nor did they forget how their countrymen had been cruelly slaughtered. For a time they were content to watch the King's army as it went on its way, taking such occasion as offered itself of plundering or slaying. If any lagged behind, falling out of the line of march by reason of weariness, or seeking refreshment on the way, as when there was a spring of water near to the road, or a vineyard with grapes—'twas just the time of the ripening of grapes—then the Turkish horsemen would be upon him. Such loiterers escaped but seldom. And for this business the Turks had a particular fitness, so quickly did they come and depart. The Christian knights were clad in armour, a great defense, indeed, against arrows and stones, but a great hindrance if a man would move quickly; the horses also had armour on them. Why do they set men on horses but that they may go speedily to and fro as occasion may call? but these knights are like to fortresses rather than to riders. A man on foot can easily outrun them; as for the Turks who rode on horses from the desert—than which there is no creature on earth lighter and speedier—they flew from the Christian who would pursue them, as a bird flies from a child who would catch it.

All this while the Turks were close at hand, and ready to assault the King's army so soon as a convenient occasion would arise. But they did not take King Richard unaware, for indeed he was as watchful as he was brave.

I will now set forth as briefly as may be the order of the army as it was set out for battle at Arsuf. On the right hand of the army was the sea, its front being set towards the south. In the van were the Templars, and next to these the Frenchmen in two divisions, the second being led by that Guy who called himself King of Jerusalem, and after the Frenchmen King Richard with his Englishmen; last of all, holding the rear-guard, were the Hospitallers.

These are ever rivals of the Templars, and it was the King's custom so to order his disposition that this rivalry should work for the common good. On one day the Templars would lead, and the Hospitallers bring up the rear; on another each would take the other's place; and there was ever a mighty contention between the two companies which would bear itself the better. These two posts, it should be said, were the most full of peril; nor was any part of the army save only these two companies suffered to hold either the one or the other. Between the divisions there was a small space, not more than sufficient to mark one from the other: otherwise the soldiers stood and marched in as close array as might be. Also they moved very slowly, travelling less than a league in the space of two hours. And even the King with some chosen knights rode up and down the lines, watching at the same time the Turks, so that whenever they might make assault the army might be ready to meet them.

Now King Richard's commandment had been that the Christians should on no account break their lines to attack the enemy, but should only defend themselves as best they could. There is nothing harder in the whole duty of a soldier than so to stand; even they who have been men of war from their youth grow greatly impatient; as for the younger sort they often fail to endure altogether. Many a man will sooner throw himself upon almost sure death than abide danger less by far standing still. And so it could be seen that day in the Christian army. The first to fail were the men that carried the cross-bows; nor, indeed, is it to be wondered at that when they had spent their store of bolts, they, having but short swords wherewith to defend themselves, should be ill content to hold their place. Many I did see throw away their bows and fly, thrusting themselves by main force into the ranks of the men-at-arms, who liked not to beat them back, nor yet to suffer them to pass. And they themselves had much ado to hold their ground, for it was a very fierce assault that they had to endure. In the first place there was such a shower of darts and stones and arrows that the very light of the sun itself was darkened, a thing which I had always before judged to be a fable, but saw that day to be possible. The greater part of them, it is true, fell without effect to the ground, for of twenty missiles scarce one served its purpose, but some were not cast in vain. As for the number, they lay so thick upon the ground that a man might gather twenty into his hand without moving from his place.

About noon the Knights Hospitallers themselves, than whom, as I have said, there were no braver men in the whole army, sent word to the King that they could bear up no longer, unless they should be suffered to charge the enemy. But they got small comfort from the King. "Close up your lines," he said to the messenger, "and be patient. Be sure that you shall not miss your reward." A second time did they send to him, the Master of the Company himself going on the errand, but he also came back with nothing done. Now the King's plan was this, that when the Turks should have spent their strength, and should also, through over-confidence and contempt of their adversaries, have fallen into disorder, then the trumpets should sound, and the whole army with one consent and moving all together, so that the whole of its strength should be put, as it were, into one blow, should fall upon the enemy. 'Twas a wisely conceived plan, save in this that there was needed for the full carrying out more than the King was like to find. He laid upon his soldiers a greater burden of patience than they could bear.

As for the King, he was, I can scarce doubt, glad at heart that the season of waiting was over. Certain it is that not only did he not seek to call back his men from the charge—doubtless he knew full well that to do this was beyond the power of mortal—but he himself joined in it with the greatest vehemence; none that saw him but must have believed that the affair was altogether to his liking. If others were before him at the first, but a short time had passed when he was to be seen in the front rank, aye, and before it. Where he rode, it was as if Azrael had passed, for the dead lay upon the ground on either side.

Never had the Caliph Saladin suffered so great a defeat as that which fell upon him in the battle of Arsuf; never, indeed, after that day did he dare to meet King Richard in the open field. Nevertheless, from that very day did the hope of the Christians that they should accomplish the end of their warfare grow less and less. But, if any one ask what was the cause of this falling, and who should bear the blame, I, for one, know not what answer should be made to him. There was not one in the whole army more brave and more generous in this matter than King Richard; yet even he, I hold, had not a wholly single heart. He was ever thinking of worldly things; he desired greatly to win the city of Jerusalem, yet he desired it as much for his own sake, for his own glory and renown, and the increase of his royal power, as for any other cause.

There is no need to tell of all the combats, skirmishes, and the like that took place, how on one day a company of the Templars fell into an ambush, how on another the Hospitallers suffered some damage. For the most part the Christians had the better in these things, and this not a little because of the great skill and valour of the English King. Nevertheless, the fortunes of the army seemed to go backwards rather than forwards.

About this time the King began to have dealings for peace with the Caliph Saladin, sending an embassage to him, and receiving the like from him. But it was ever thus that the King asked more than he looked for the Caliph to give; and the Caliph promised more than he had the purpose to fulfil. There were many courtesies passed between them, and gifts also. King Richard would send a set of hawks, and, indeed, he had not much that he could give; but the presents that came from the Caliph were of exceeding richness and splendour; there was a tent made of cloth of gold, and horses such as Kings only have in their stalls, and rare beasts and birds, and snow from Lebanon, for the cooling of wines, and many other things, both for show and for use, of which it were long to tell. And these things, for all that they were costly, served the Caliph's purpose well, and for this reason, they seemed to show his good will, and all the while he was busy destroying the towns and laying waste the country. Of these things the King heard something, but not all, for in the matter of news he was ill served. And all the while the Turks ceased not to do all the mischief that they could, slaying such as strayed from the camp, yea, and coming into the camp itself, and doing men to death in their very tents, and Saladin, or rather Saphadin, his brother, for he it was who held converse with King Richard, when complaints were made of their deeds, affirmed that they were done by robbers and others who were not subject to him, and paid no reverence to his commands; of which pretence there need be said this only, that these robbers or murderers, whether they were the Caliph's men or no, never harmed any but such as were his enemies.

For all this King Richard still strove by all means that he could devise to come to a peaceful agreement with his adversaries. Nor did he refuse any instrument by which he might hope to compass this end.

When a whole moon had been wasted in parleying and the sending of messengers to and fro, the King, seeing that he must accomplish his purpose by force of arms or not at all, led his army towards the Holy City. It would serve no profitable end to tell of the other places where he pitched his camp, or of the days which he tarried in this or that. Let it suffice to say that in a month's time he traversed so much space only as an army well equipped might pass over in a single day's march; and that about twenty-one days after the winter solstice the army of the Christians came to a certain place which is named the Casal of Beitenoble, and which in ancient times was, if I err not, a city of the priests. There it tarried some twelve days, being much troubled by storms and rains, for the winds blew and the rains fell during the whole of this time, in such a fashion as I have never seen. As for the tents, only such as were appointed with ropes and so forth could be kept in their place, so violent were the blasts, so that the greater part of the army lay under the open sky, not a little to the damage of their health. The horses also were in evil case. These creatures, all men know, suffer from much sickness, and multitudes of them perished. Also there was a great scarcity of victuals; for the corn and even the biscuit were spoilt by the rain, and the hogs' flesh grew corrupt.

Though not a few died of sickness, yet did the host daily grow greater. Many who had stayed behind in various cities, their zeal having grown stale, now came back to the camp, judging that they would do well to take part in an enterprise that was now near to success. Also many that had tarried on the march for the cause of sickness now made shift to come to the camp. Some I saw carried in litters, and others that could scarce set one foot before the other crawled painfully along the road. Many of these were slain by the Turks, but not the less did the rest brave the dangers of the journey. And in the camp there was a great furbishing of arms and armour, and trimming of the plumes of helmets, for it was counted an unseemly thing that any man should enter such a place as the Holy City save in his best array.

On a certain evening, some eleven days after the coming of the army to Beitenoble, there was a council held in the tent of King Richard, at which were present the Master of the Templars and the Master of the Hospitallers, and other chief men in the army. About an hour after sunset the council came to an end; darkness had long since fallen, but it chanced to be full moon, and the faces of them that had been present at the council were plain to be seen. Before ever a word was said, it was manifest to all that a great misfortune had befallen them. For the faces of these men were clouded with discouragement. And straightway all the multitude that had been gathered together departed every man to his own place. There needed no proclaiming that neither on the morrow nor on any other day would there be a marching to the Holy City.

On the 8th day of January the army departed from Beitenoble, and on the 20th it came, after much toil and suffering, for the rain and tempest scarcely abated for a single hour through the twelve days, to the city of Ascalon.

For some little time, King Richard and his army dwelt in peace in the city of Ascalon. Nor can it be denied that they gathered strength; the sick, being duly handled by their physicians, were restored to a sound body, and they that were wearied with the labours of long-continued warfare had rest and refreshment. Nevertheless it may be doubted whether the King was able to advance the cause at all which he had in hand, namely, the taking of the Holy City. And the chief cause was this, that the Christians, not having for the present a common foe with whom to contend, began to quarrel among themselves more grievously than ever. So the King and the French, among whom, now that the French King had departed to his own land, a certain Duke of Burgundy was chief, fell out, and this with such heat, that the duke departed from Ascalon to Acre in great haste, and all the Frenchmen followed him.

Now about this same time there came a messenger to King Richard bearing a letter from one that he had set to rule in England in his stead while he should be absent from his kingdom. In this letter there were written many things about the doings of Prince John the King's brother: how he had commerce with the French to the King's damage, and was troubling all loyal men, and had taken all the money that was in the treasury. When the King heard these things he was sore distraught. And indeed he was in a great strait. On the one hand there was the purpose for which he had come on his present journey, the taking again of the Holy City; and, on the other, there was the loss of his own kingdom at home. For in the letter it was plainly written that if he was not speedy in returning, all the realm of England would be lost to him.

At the first he made no doubt of departing with but as little delay as might be. "I must be gone," he said, "or my kingdom will not be worth a silver penny." But before many days his purpose was changed. 'Twas said that a holy man, a priest of the land of France, took courage to speak to him and set before him his duty in this matter. He said that the hearts of all were sorely troubled by the King's purpose to depart—and this was most certainly true, seeing that they who were most jealous of the King and chafed most at his command were not less dismayed by the news of his departure than were his best friends. "Think too," he is reported to have spoken, "how that you will greatly dim your kingly renown. You have done well, O King, and God has manifestly bestowed His blessings on you. Will you then be ungrateful, and, if your royal grace will suffer me to say so much, unfaithful to Him? Verily there is a great reward laid up for him that recovers the Holy City out of the hands of the heathen, and will you give this up on the bare rumour of mischief that may befall your estate in this world?" So the holy man is reported to have spoken. Such words may have had weight with the King, who was ever greatly moved by eloquent words. But I also believe that when he came to himself he judged that there was no great need of haste in the matter; that the Prince John his brother was not greatly loved, nor was ever like to be; that when the people of England had had a year's trial of his rule, if such should come to pass, they would be the less likely to stand by him; and, moreover, that if Richard should go back to his country in high esteem among all men, as having set up yet again a Christian Kingdom in the Holy City, his enemies would be brought nought by the mere rumour of his coming. Certain it is that, let the cause be what it might, he caused it to be made known throughout the army that they would set out for the Holy City in three days' time.

Again there was great joy in the army; again the sick rose from their beds, and the lame threw away their crutches, that they might go without hindrance on this great journey. Again did the army come almost in sight of the Holy City; again were all things ready for the assault. And then once more the more skilful and prudent of the leaders hindered the matter. It was not well, they said to run into such danger. It might well be that if they should assail the city they would not take it; it was well-nigh certain that even if they should take it, they could not hold it to any good purpose. And so it came to pass that King Richard and the army having once more come to Beitenoble, once more departed, leaving their task unaccomplished.

When the leaders had taken this resolve that they would turn back and the army was now about to depart, there came to King Richard a certain man-at-arms, who was well acquainted with the country, for indeed, he had travelled on foot as a pilgrim from the coast to Jerusalem, and this not once only but twice or thrice. This man said, "My lord King, if you are minded to see the Holy City, you can do so at little pains. If you will ride a mile or so you will come to a hill from whence you can see the walls, and the hill on which the temple was built and other of the Holy places." But the King answered, "I thank you much, nor, indeed, is there any sight in the whole world on which I would more gladly look with my eyes, but I am not worthy of so great a favour. If it had been the will of God that I should see His city, I do not doubt that I had done so, not as one who looks upon some spectacle from far, but as the conqueror in some great battle looks upon the thing that he has won. But of this grace I, by reason I doubt not of my sins, have been judged unworthy." And when he had so spoken he turned his horse's head to the west, as being minded to return yet again to the sea-coast. And this he did.

I have spoken of the King's courage and skill in arms and wisdom in leadership, nor need I say these things again. But one thing I will add, namely, that of all the men that came to this land from the West none left behind him so great a fame as did King Richard. So if a mother was minded to make a crying child hold his peace, she would say, "Hush, child, or King Richard shall have thee"; or if a horse started unaware, his rider would say, "Dost see King Richard in the bush?"

On the 9th day of October, 1192, did King Richard set sail to return to his own country. But it fared ill with him on his journey. For it fell out that he was separated from all his friends, and that when he was in this case a certain duke, with whom he had had a strife, laid hands upon him, and laid him in prison. There he remained for the space of a year and more, fretting much, I doubt not, against his condition, for never surely was a man more impatient of bonds. But he could not escape, nor did his friends so much as know where he was. And when this was discovered by some strange chance, there was yet much delay, nor indeed was he set free till there had been paid for him a ransom of many thousands of gold pieces. Not many years after he was slain by a chance arrow shot from the walls of a certain castle which he was besieging, being then in the forty-second year of his age.

# SAINT LOUIS

KING LOUIS sailing from Cyprus about the 24th day of May, 1249, came with a fair wind to Egypt in some four days, having a great fleet of ships, numbering in all, it was said, some eighteen hundred, great and small. And now there fell upon him the first stroke of misfortune. There arose a strong wind from the south which scattered the fleet, so that not more than a third part remained with the King. As for the others, they were blown far to the north, even to the town of Acre, and, though none were cast away, it was many days before they could return. Now the King's purpose was to lay siege to the town of Damietta, a town which is built on the midmost of the seven mouths of the Nile. It was commonly agreed that whoever should hold possession of this said town of Damietta might go whithersoever he would in the whole land of Egypt, and further, that whosoever should be master of Egypt could do what he would in the land of Palestine.

When the King came with what was left to him over against the city of Damietta there was much debate between him and his counsellors as to what might best be done. "I have no mind," said he, "to turn back, having, by the grace of God, come so

236

far. Say you that I should do well to wait for those who have been separated from us? That I would gladly do, for it grieves me much that they lose, so far, their share in this great enterprise. But two reasons constrain me to do otherwise. First, it would put the infidel in great heart if they should see me so delay to make trial of them; and, second, there is here no harbour or safe anchorage where I might wait. Nay, my lords, it is my purpose to attack the enemy without delay, for the Lord our God can save by few or by many."

The King being thus steadfastly resolved to have no more delay, his nobles and knights could not choose but obey him. This being so, they strove among themselves who should be the first to come to blows with the enemy. There were small boats with the larger of the ships, and these were filled with men and rowed to the shore. This was not done wholly without loss, for some slipped as they descended from the ships, or missed their feet, the boat moving from under them with the motion of the waves, so that some were drowned and others hardly saved.

Meanwhile they took the great flag of Saint Denys, from the ship in which it was, and carried it to the shore. But when the King saw the flag on the shore he would tarry no longer, but leapt into the sea, accoutred as he was, and the water came up to his armpits. When he saw the Saracens, he said to the knight that followed him, "Who are these?" And the knight answered, "These, sir, are the Saracens." When he heard this he put his lance in rest, and held his shield before him, and would have charged them, but his counsellors would not suffer it.

When the enemy saw that the King and his men had landed, they sent a message to the Sultan by carrier-pigeons; this they did three times. But it so chanced that the Sultan was in a fit of the fever which troubled him in the summer time, and he sent no answer. Then his men, thinking that he was dead, for they knew already that he was sick, fled straightway from the town of Damietta. When the King knew this for certain, the bishops that were in the army sang the *Te Deum* with great joy. The army which King Louis brought with him numbered thirty thousand men.

The army being thus established in the town of Damietta, there was much debate as to what should be done. The King was set upon assailing the enemy without delay. "It is by delay," he said, and said truly, "that these enterprises have been ruined heretofore, for not only does an army grow less and less with every day by sickness—keep it as carefully as you will, such loss must needs happen—but the first fire of zeal begins to burn low." To such purpose the King spoke to his counsellors, nor could they gainsay his words. Yet they had to urge on the other part reasons so weighty that they could not be resisted.

The truth is that there could not have been chosen a worse time for the waging of war in Egypt than that at which the King arrived. Whereas other rivers overflow their banks in the winter season, the

Nile overflows his in summer, and this he does because his stream is swollen, not by rains that fall in the land of Egypt, for such rains are more scanty than in any other country of the world, but by those that fall in countries far inland and, haply, by the melting of snows. So it is that in that part of Egypt which is nearest to the sea the river begins to rise in the month of June, and for a quarter of a year or so thereafter an army must rest perforce. The King was very ill served in his ministers when he was suffered to remain in ignorance of these things. Nevertheless, the case being so, he had no choice but to accept the counsel of delay. It was agreed, therefore, that the army should tarry in Damietta till the floods of the river should have ceased.

In the beginning of the month of December the King set out for Cairo with his army. Now the Sultan had sent five hundred of his knights, the bravest warriors and the best mounted that he could find in his whole army, to the end that they should harass the King's army as much as might be. Now the King being very careful of the lives of his men, as knowing that a soldier lost could not be replaced, had given a strict commandment that no one should presume to leave the line of march and charge the enemy. When the Turks saw this, or, haply, had learnt from their spies that the King had given this commandment, they grew bolder and bolder, till one of them, riding up to the line, overthrew one of the Knights Templar. This was done under the very eyes of the Master of the Temple, who, when he saw it, could no longer endure to be quiet. So he cried to his brethren, "At them, good sirs, for this is more than can be borne." So he spurred his horse, and the other Templars with him, and charged the Turks. And because their horses were fresh and the horses of the Turks weary, they bore them down. It was said that not one of the five hundred escaped, many being ridden down, and the rest being drowned in the river.

After this the King encamped between the two branches of the Nile, that which flows by Damietta and that which is the next to it toward the sunsetting. On the other side of this branch was ranged the army of the Sultan, to hinder the Christians from passing, an easy thing seeing that there was no ford, nor any place where a man might cross save by swimming.

While they were in this strait there came a Bedouin to the camp, who said that for five hundred pieces of gold he would show them a good ford. When the Constable Imbert, to whom the Bedouin had spoken of this ford, told the matter to the King, the King said, "I will give the gold right willingly; only be sure that the man perform his part of the bargain." So the constable parleyed with the man; but the Bedouin would not depart from his purpose. "Give me the gold," said he, "and I will show you the ford." And because the King was in a strait, he consented; so the man received the five hundred pieces, and he showed the ford to certain that were sent with him.

It was agreed that the Duke of Burgundy and other nobles who were not of France should keep guard in the camp, and that the King with his brothers should ford the river at the place which the Arab should show. So, all being ready, at daybreak they came down to the water. A ford there was, but not such as a man would choose save in the greatest need.

The King, having with him the main body of the army, crossed amidst a great sounding of horns and trumpets. It was a noble sight to see, and nothing in it nobler and more admirable than the King himself. A fairer knight there never was, and he stood with a gilded helmet on his head, and a long German sword in his hand, being by his head and shoulders taller than the crowd. Then he and his knights charged the Saracens, who by this time had taken a stand again on the river bank. It was a great feat of arms. No man drew long-bow that day or plied cross-bow. The Crusaders and the Saracens fought with mace and sword, neither keeping their ranks, but all being confused together.

But the Crusaders, for all their valour, could scarce hold their own, because the enemy outnumbered them by much. Also there was a division of counsel among them. Also there came a messenger from them that were shut up in Mansoura, telling the King how hard pressed they were, and in what instant need of succour.

And now the Saracens grew more and more confident, for they were greatly the better in numbers; and if, man for man and in the matter of arms and armour, they were scarce equal to the Crusaders, yet the difference was not so great. They pushed on, therefore, and drove the Christians back to the river. These were very hard pressed, and some were for swimming across the river to the camp, but by this time their horses were weary, and not a few perished by drowning.

Nevertheless as time passed the Crusaders fared somewhat better, for they drew more together, and the enemy, seeing that they still held their ground, and being themselves not a little weary, drew back. In the end the King and such of the chiefs as were left got back into the camp. Right glad they were to rest, for the battle had been long and fierce.

But they had but little peace, for that very night the Saracens made an attack upon the camp. A great disturbance they made, and most unwelcome to men who had been fighting all the day. But they did not work much harm. Many valiant deeds were done by the Christians.

But the Saracens were making ready for attacking the camp with more force than before. And their leader could be seen from the camp, taking account of the Crusaders, and strengthening his battalions where he thought that the King's camp might be most conveniently assailed.

The first attack was made on the Count of Anjou. He held that part of the camp that was nearest to the city of Cairo. Some of the enemy were on horseback and some on foot; there were some also that threw Greek fire among the count's men. Between them they pressed the count so sorely that he was fain to send to the King for help. This the King gave without loss of time; he led the men himself, and it was not long before they chased the Saracens from this part of the field.

When the battle was over the King called the barons to his tent, and thanked them for all that they had done, and gave them great encouragement, saying that as they had driven back the Saracens over and again, it would, beyond doubt, go well with them in the end.

And now the army was sore distressed for want both of food and of water. In Damietta, indeed, there were yet stores of barley, rice, and other grains; but in the camp scarce anything that could be eaten. Some small fishes were caught in the river; but these were very ill savoured, and all the more so—so, at least, it seemed to such as eat them under constraint of hunger—because they fed on dead bodies, of which many were thrown into the river. For a while some portion of the stores that were in the city were carried across the river to the camp. But this the Saracens hindered, for by this time their ships had the mastery over the ships of the Christians. They kept, therefore, the river, suffering nothing to pass. If anything was carried across, it was but a trifle. Some things the country people brought into the camp, but these were not to be purchased save for large sums of money, and money was by this time scarce even among the richer sort. And when it was judged expedient that the King's army should cross the river again and return to the camp, things were worse rather than better, so far as victuals were concerned. It was well that the army should be brought together, both for attack and for defence, but with the greater multitude the famine grew worse and worse.

After a while there was a treating for peace between the King and the Saracens; and for a while it seemed as if they might come to an agreement, and this not without advantage to the King. But the matter came to naught, because the Saracens would have the King himself as a hostage for the due performance of the treaty. The Christians would have given the King's brothers, and these were willing to go; but the King they could not give. "It would be better," said one of the bravest knights in the army, and in this matter he spake the mind of all, "that we should all be taken captive or slain, than that we should leave the King in pledge."

The King, seeing that the condition of the army still grew from bad to worse, and that if they tarried they would all be dead men, commanded that they should make their way into the town of Damietta. And this the army began to do the very next night. Now the first thing to be cared for was the taking of the sick, of whom there was a great multitude, on board the ships. But while this was being done, the Saracens entered the camp on the other side. When the sailors who were busy in embarking the sick saw this, they loosed the cables by which they were moored to the shore, and made as if they would fly. Now the King was on the bank of the river, and there was a galley in waiting for him, whereon, if he had been so minded, he might easily have escaped. Nor could he have been blamed therefor, because he was afflicted with the dysentery that prevailed in the camp. But this he would not do; "Nay," he said, "I will stay with my people." But when there was now no hope of safety, one of his officers took him, mounted as he was on a pony, to a village hard by, defending him all the way from such as chanced to fall in with him—but none knew that he was the King. When he was come to the village they took him into a house that there was, and laid him down almost dead. A good woman of Paris that was there took his head upon her lap, and there was no one but thought that he would die before nightfall. Then one of the nobles coming in asked the King whether he should not go to the chief of the Saracens, and see whether a treaty might not yet be made on such terms as they would. The King said yes; so he went. Now there was a company of the Saracens round the house, whither by this time not a few of the Christians had assembled. And one of the King's officers cried—whether from fear or with traitorous intent cannot be said—"Sir knights, surrender yourselves! The King will have it so; if you do not, the King will perish." So the knights gave up their swords, and the Saracens took them as prisoners. When the chief of the Saracens, with whom the noble aforesaid was talking, saw them, he said, "There can be no talk of truce and agreement with these men; they are prisoners."

And now the question was not of a treaty but a ransom. About this there was no little debate between the Sultan and the King. First the Sultan required that the King should surrender to him the castles of the Knights Templars and of the Hospitallers of St. John. "Nay," said the King, "that I cannot do, for they are not mine to give." This answer greatly provoked the Sultan, and he threatened to put the King to the torture, to which the King answered this only, that he was a prisoner in their hands, and that they could do with him as they would.

When they saw that they could not turn him from his purpose by threats or by fear, they asked him how much money he was willing to pay to the Sultan for his ransom, such money being over and above the rendering up of the town of Damietta. Then the King made answer: "If the Sultan will take a reasonable sum in money for ransom, I will recommend it to the Queen that she should pay the same." "Nay," said the envoy of the Sultan, "why do you not say outright that you will have it so?" "Because," answered the King, "in this matter it is for the Queen to say yea or nay. I am a prisoner, and my royal power is gone from me." So it was agreed that if the Queen would pay a thousand thousand gold pieces by way of ransom, the King should go free. Said the King, "Will the Sultan swear to this bargain?" They said that he would. So it was agreed that the King should pay for the ransom of his army a thousand thousand gold pieces, and for his own ransom the town of Damietta, "for," said he, "a

246

King cannot be bought and sold for money." When the Sultan heard this, he said, "On my word, this is a noble thing of the Frenchman that he makes no bargaining concerning so great a thing. Tell him that I give him as a free gift the fifth part of the sum which he has covenanted to pay."

All things were now settled, and there were but four days before the fulfilling of the treaty, when the King should give up Damietta to the Sultan, and the Sultan, on his part, should suffer the King and his people to go free. But lo! there came to pass that which was like to bring the whole matter to nothing. The emirs of the Sultan made a conspiracy against him. "Know this," they said one to another, "that so soon as he shall find himself master of Damietta, he will slay us. Let us therefore be beforehand with him." And it was agreed that this should be done. First, when the Sultan was going to his chamber after a banquet which he had given to the emirs, one, who was, indeed, his sword-bearer, dealt him a blow and struck off his hand. But the Sultan, being young and nimble, escaped into a strong tower that was hard by his chamber, and three of his priests were with him. The emirs called upon him to give himself up. "That," said he, "I will do, if you will give me a promise of my life." "Nay," they answered, "we will give you no promises. If you surrender not of your own free will, then will we compel you." Then they threw Greek fire at the tower, and the tower, which was built of pine-wood, caught fire on the instant. When the Sultan saw this he ran down with all the speed that he could, seeking to reach the river, if so be he could find a ship. But the emirs and their men were ranged along the way, nor was it long before they slew him. And he that dealt him the last blow came to the King, his hand yet dripping with blood, and said, "What will you give me? I have slain your enemy, who would assuredly have done you to death had he lived." But the King answered him not a word.

Now the covenant between the King and the Saracen chiefs was renewed, nor was any change made in the conditions; only the payment was differently ordered; that is to say, one-half of the ransom was to be paid before the King left the place where he was, and the other half in the town of Acre.

Then the emirs on the one part and the King on the other took the oaths that were held to be the most binding on them. The King indeed held staunchly by his faith, and when the emirs would have had him swear in a way that he thought to be unseemly to him as a Christian man he would not. And the emirs paid him the more honour and reverence for this very cause. It was said, indeed, that they would have made him Sultan of Cairo, if he had been minded to receive that dignity at their hands; furthermore, some that knew the King affirmed that he was not altogether set against it. But none knew for certain the truth in the matter. Yet it was well said by one of the emirs, "There surely never was better or more steadfast Christian than this King Louis. Verily if he had been made our sultan he would never have been content till he had either made us all Christians, or, failing this, had put us all to the sword."

And now there came a time of great peril to the prisoners. First the town of Damietta was given up to the Saracens, the gates being opened and their flag hoisted on the towers.

On the next day the paying of the ransom was begun. When the money was counted it was found to be short by some thirty thousand pieces. These were taken from the treasury of the Templars much against their will, but the necessities of the prisoners prevailed.

As for the King, there could not have been a man more loyal in the fulfilling of his promise. When one of those that counted the money said that the Saracens had received less than their due by some ten thousand pieces, the King would not suffer but that the whole matter should be looked into, lest the Saracens should have wrong. The counter, indeed, averred that this thing was said in jest; but the King answered that such a jest was out of season, and that above all things it was necessary that a Christian should show good faith.

Not many days after the paying of the ransom the King sent for his chief counsellors and opened his mind to them in the matter of his return to France. He said, "The Queen, my mother, begs me to come back to France, saying that my kingdom is in great peril seeing, that I have no peace, nor even a truce, with England. Tell me, then, what you think.

And because it is a great matter, I give you eight days to consider it."

After this the King went to Acre, where he tarried till what was left over of the ransom was paid.

On the day appointed the counsellors came before the King, who said to them, "What do you advise? Shall I go, or shall I stay?" They said that they had chosen one from among them, a certain Guy Malvoisin, to speak for them. Thereupon this Guy said, "These lords have taken counsel together, and are agreed that you cannot tarry in this country without damage to yourself and your kingdom. For think how that of all the knights whom you had in Cyprus, two thousand eight hundred in number, there remain with you here in Acre scarce one hundred. Our counsel, therefore, is that you return to France, and there gather another army, with which you may come hither again and take vengeance on your enemies for their trespasses against God and against you."

Then the King turned to a certain John, who was Count of Jaffa, and asked him for his judgment. Count John answered: "Ask me not, sire; my domain is here, and if I bid you stay, then it will be said that I did this for my own profit." But when the King was urgent for his advice he said, "If you stay for a year it will be for your honour." And one other of the counsellors gave the same judgment; but all the rest were urgent for the King's return. Then the King said, "I will tell you eight days hence what it is my pleasure to do."

On the day appointed they all came together again, and the King said, "I thank you, my lords, for your counsel—both those who have advised my going back and those who have advised my staying. Now I hold that if I stay, my kingdom of France will be in no peril, seeing that the Queen, my mother, is well able to keep it in charge; but that if I depart, then the kingdom of Jerusalem will most certainly be lost, because no man will be bold enough to stay after I am gone. Now, it was for the sake of this same kingdom of Jerusalem that I have come hither. My purpose, therefore, is to stay." There was no little trouble among the barons when they heard these words. There were some among them who could not hold back their tears. But though the King resolved himself to stay, yet he commanded his brothers to depart. And this they did before many days.

While the King tarried at Acre there came to him messengers from the Old Man of the Mountain. One of the messengers was the spokesman, and had his place in front; the second had in his hand three daggers, to signify what danger threatened him who should not listen to the message; the third carried a shroud of buckram for him who should be smitten with the daggers. The King said to the first envoy, "Speak on." Then the envoy said, "My master says, 'Know you me?'" The King answered, "I know him not, for I have never seen him; yet I have often heard others talk of him." "Why, then," went on the envoy, "have you not sent him such gifts as would have gained his friendship, even as the Emperor of

Germany and the King of Hungary and other princes have done, yea, and do now year after year, knowing well that they cannot live save by my lord's pleasure?" The King made no answer, but bade the envoys come again in the afternoon. When they came they found the King sitting with the Master of the Templars on one side and the Master of the Hospitallers on the other. Now the Old Man is in great awe of these two, for he knows that if he slay them there will be put in their place other two as good or better. The envoys were not a little disturbed when they saw the two. And the Master of the Templars said, "Your lord is over bold to send you with such a message for the King. Now be sure that we would have drowned you in the sea, but that so doing might be a wrong to him. Go now to your lord, and come again in fourteen days with such a token and such gifts as may suffice for the making of peace."

So the envoys departed, and came again in the time appointed, and they brought with them the shirt of the Old Man and his ring, which was of the finest gold, and with these things this message: "As man wears no garment that is nearer to him than his shirt, so the Old Man would have the King nearer to him than any other King upon earth; and as a ring is the sign of marriage by which two are made one, so the Old Man would have himself and the King to be one." Other gifts there were, an elephant of crystal, very cunningly wrought, and a monster which they call a giraffe, also of crystal, and draughts and chessmen, all finely made. The King, on his part, sent to the Old Man a great store of jewels, and scarlet cloth, and dishes of gold and bridles of silver.

While the King was at Jaffa it was told him that if he desired to make a pilgrimage to Jerusalem the Sultan of Damascus would give him a safe-conduct. The King consulted his nobles on the matter, and both he and they were of one mind in the matter, to wit, that he should not go. "For," said they, "if the King should go as a pilgrim, when he has not been able to take the Holy City itself out of the hands of the infidel, then will other Kings in time to come do the same. They will be content to go as pilgrims, but will take no thought as to the city, whether it be held by Christian or infidel."

After these things the King went to the city of Sidon and fortified it with strong walls, for he was greatly unwilling to give up his hope of winning the whole land out of the hands of the infidel. But when he had brought this work to an end, there came news to him from his own country that the Queen his mother, who was charged with the government thereof, was dead. Then he took counsel with his nobles what he should do, and it seemed to them that he must of necessity return to France. One among them put the case before the King as follows:

"Sire, we see that it will not profit the kingdom of Jerusalem that you tarry longer here. You have done what was in your power. You have fortified the city of Sidon, and Cæsarea, and Jaffa, and you have made the city of Acre much stronger than it was. And now for your own kingdom's sake, you must needs depart." And to this the King gave his consent, though with an unwilling heart. So he departed, and this, as it chanced, on his birthday. As the ship went forth from the harbour he said to the Lord of Joinville, who stood by him, "On this day I was born." And the Lord of Joinville said to him, "Truly, sire, I should say that you are beginning another life, now that you are safely quit of this land of death."

Some seventeen years after the things last recorded, I took a journey to the Island of Sardinia, and made my abode at a town on the west coast, called Neapolis. When I had sojourned there two months there came in sight on a certain day a great fleet of ships, which those who were acquainted with such things declared to be from the land of France. As for the crowd that came ashore that day, it were best to say little. It is more to the purpose to say that I met with one whom I knew, having consorted with him in time past, and this the more constantly because he followed the same occupation as I. I asked him, "How came you hither? If you are bound for Palestine, this is but a short stage in your journey." He answered me with something of a smile in his eye, though his mouth was set, "Where could we more conveniently halt than here, for we are bound for Tunis?" "For Tunis?" said I; "but how shall this help you for the taking of Jerusalem?" "That," said he, "you must ask of some one that has more wisdom than I. But this I know that the King was told, by whom I know not, that the Bey of Tunis desired to be baptised. This, then, is cause sufficient for him. Are you minded to come with me? If so, I can find you a place in the King's ship, for it is in it that I sail."

When I heard that, I consented without delay. So that night I gave my friend the shelter of my lodging; and the next day he took me with him, and commended me to one of the chief officers of the ship, bearing witness to my skill as a physician. On the fourth day we sailed, and came in two days, the wind blowing from the north, to the harbour of Tunis. As for the King, I saw him but once. His valets carried him up on the deck; and, to tell the truth, he looked as little fit for doing feats of arms as man could look. But I thought that the sickness which takes many men upon the sea might be the cause.

Scarce had the army landed than there began a most grievous sickness. In truth the place for the camp had been ill chosen, for there was a little stream into which much of the filth of the city was wont to run. From this there came a most evil smell. Many also, for want of good water, would drink of the stream, than which there could be no more deadly thing.

On the very day after he landed from his ship the King fell sick. His physician being disabled by the same malady, I was called in to the King's help; and from the first I saw that, save by a miracle, he could not live. On the fourth day he died, making as good and devout an end as any that I have ever seen. He would know the truth, for he was not one of those who buoy themselves up with false hopes. And when he knew it, then first with the help of the priests that attended him he prepared his soul, and afterward he gave what time remained to teaching the son who should be King after him how he should best do his duty to God and man.

I heard much from him who had put it in my mind to come from the island of Sardinia concerning King Louis. Never, he told me, was a King more bent on doing justice and judgment. These he maintained with his whole heart and strength, not having any respect of persons, or having regard to his own profit. Though he held bishops and priests in great reverence, being most careful of all the offices of religion, yet he would withstand even these when they seemed to seek that which was not fair and just. He was a lover of peace far beyond the wont of Kings, who indeed, for the most part, care but little for it, so that men say in a proverb, "War is the game of Kings." Of the poor he was a great and constant favourer. Every day he had a multitude of them fed at his cost in his palace, and sometimes he would serve himself, and it was his custom on a certain day to wash the feet of poor men. In his eating and drinking he was as temperate as man could be, drinking, for example, but one cup of wine, and that largely mingled with water. In all things wherein great men ofttimes offend he was wholly blameless and beyond reproach. Of all men that I had any knowledge of, whether by sight or by hearing, in this business of the Crusades there was not one who could be so much as named in comparison with King Louis. To King Louis religion was as life itself. It filled, as it were, his whole soul; he judged of all things by it; he hungered and thirsted after it. And yet of all who bore the cross this man, being, as he was, so much the most faithful to his vow, by far the truest cross-bearer of all, yet failed the most utterly. Of such things I have not the wit to judge; yet this, methinks, is manifest, that the Kingdom of God is not set forward by the power of armies. I do believe that if King Louis, being what he was, a man after God's own heart, had come, not with the sword, but preaching the truth by his life, he had done more for the cause that he had at heart. As it was, he furthered it not at all, so far as I can discern, but rather set it back. That he did not gain for Christendom so much as a single foot of earth is not so much to be lamented, as that he made wider the breach between Christian men and the followers of Mahomet. And this he did, though he was in very truth the most Christlike of all the men that I have ever seen.

# WILLIAM TELL

WILLIAM TELL was born toward the close of the thirteenth century. I cannot tell you the precise year of his birth; but in the year 1307 he was a married man, and lived with his wife and children, in the village of Bürglen, near the great town of Altdorf, in the canton of Uri.

Tell maintained his family chiefly by hunting the chamois, and shooting other wild game. So skilful was he in the use of the bow, that the fame of his exploits in that way had obtained for him the name of "The Crossbowman of Bürglen." He was also very skilful in the management of boats upon the lakes. His father had followed the profession of a pilot, and William Tell, though he preferred the life of a hunter, understood the navigation of the lakes better than almost any boatman in the canton of Uri. It was a saying, "That William Tell knew how to handle the rudder as expertly as the bow." In short, he was a person of strong natural talents, who observed on everything he saw, and acquired all the knowledge he could.

Switzerland was at that time in a state of slavery to Albert, Duke of Austria, who had recently been selected Emperor of Germany. He had taken great offence with the Swiss, because they wished Count Adolph of Nassau to be elected Emperor of Germany instead of him. The first use he made of his power was to punish the Swiss for having favoured the cause of his rival; and he was so unwise as to declare publicly, "that he would no longer treat them as subjects, but as slaves." In pursuance of this wicked resolution he deprived them of many of their rights and privileges, and altered their ancient laws and customs.

By these proceedings the Emperor rendered his government very unpopular, and when he found that the people expressed dissatisfaction, he built castles and fortresses all over the country, and filled them with soldiers to awe the people into submission. In each of these fortresses he placed a governor, who exercised despotic power in the district over which his sway extended. The inhabitants of the canton Uri, in particular, had to complain of the oppression of their German governor, Gessler, who had committed several murders, and acted in such a manner as to excite general indignation, by his pride, cruelty, and injustice. The whole country was indeed ripe for a revolt, in case an opportunity should occur of throwing off the German yoke.

One cold autumnal evening, the blaze of the cheerful fire which the wife of William Tell had kindled on the hearth, against her husband's return, gleamed through the rude latticed casements of their cottage window. The earthern floor of the humble dwelling had been freshly swept; a clean cloth of the matron's own spinning, was spread on the homely board, which was garnished with wooden bowls and spoons of the most snowy whiteness; and a kettle of fish-soup, with herbs, was stewing over the fire. Some flat oaten cakes, designed to be eaten hot with butter, were baking on the hearth.

The babe was sleeping peacefully in the cradle; two or three of the other little ones, weary with their sportive play, had been laid in their cribs. Henric and Lewis, two lovely boys of five and six years old, having promised to be very good, if allowed to sit up till their father's return, were watching their mother, who was employed in roasting a fine fat quail which their cousin, Lalotte, who had arrived at the discreet age of fourteen, was basting, and spinning the string by which it was suspended before the fire.

"Mother," said Henric, "if my father does not come home very soon, that quail will be done too much."

"What then?" asked Lalotte.

"I was thinking, cousin Lalotte, that it would be a pity for it to be spoiled, after you and mother have taken so much pains in cooking it; and it smells so very good."

"Oh, fie! you greedy child; you want to eat the bird that is cooking for your father's supper," said Lalotte. "If I were my aunt, I would send you to bed only for thinking of such a thing."

"You are not the mistress—you are not the mistress!" cried the sturdy rebel Henric; "and I shall not go to bed at your desire."

"But you shall go to bed, young sir, if your cousin Lalotte tells you so to do," said his father, who had entered during the dispute.

"Alack!" cried Henric turning to his little brother, "if we had only been patient, Lewis, we should have tasted the nice quail, and heard all our father's news into the bargain."

"There now, see what you have lost by being naughty children," cried Lalotte, as she led the offenders into their little bedroom.

"Thy father's news is not for thy young ears, my boys," murmured William Tell, as the door closed after the unconscious children.

"There is a sadness in thy voice and trouble on thy brow," said the anxious wife of Tell, looking earnestly in his face. "Wilt thou not trust me with the cause of thy care?"

"Annette," replied Tell, "thou hast been a good and faithful wife to me—yea, and a prudent counsellor and friend in the time of need. Why, then, should I do a thing and conceal it from thee, my well-beloved?"

"What is it thou hast done, my husband?"

"That for which thou wilt blame me, perchance."

"Nay, say not so; thou art a good man."

"Thou knowest, my loving wife, the sad state of slavery to which this unhappy country of Switzerland is reduced by the unlawful oppression of our foreign rulers," said Tell.

"I do," she replied; "but what have peasants to do with matters so much above them?"

"Much!" returned Tell. "If the good laws made by the worthies of the olden time, for the comfort and protection of all ranks of people, be set at naught by strangers, and all the ancient institutions, which were the pride and the glory of our land, be overthrown, by those to whom we owe neither the love of children, nor the allegiance of subjects, then, methinks, good wife, it becomes the duty of peasants to stand forth in defence of their rights. I have engaged myself, with three-and-thirty of my valiant countrymen, who met this night on the little promontory of land that juts into a lonely angle of the Lake, to concert with them means for the deliverance of my country."

"But how can three-and-thirty men hope to oppose the power of those who enthral Switzerland?" asked the wife of Tell.

"Great objects are often effected by small instruments," replied he. "The whole population of Switzerland is exasperated against the German tyrants, who have of late abused their power so far as to rouse the indignation even of women and of children against them. The father of Arnold Melchthal, one of the 'Brothers of Rütli,' as our band is called, was recently put to a cruel death by the unjust sentence of Gessler, the governor of our own canton of Uri; and who knoweth, gentle wife, whether his jealous caprice may not induce him to single me out for his next victim?"

"Single thee out, my husband!" exclaimed Annette turning pale. "Nay, what accusation could he bring against thee?"

"That of being the friend of my country, which is, of course, a crime not to be forgiven by a person of Gessler's disposition."

"But Gessler is too much exalted above our humble sphere of life, to be aware of a peasant's sentiments on such matters," said Annette.

"Gessler will not permit us to indulge the thoughts of our hearts in secret," said Tell; "for he hath recently devised a shrewd test, whereby he is enabled to discern the freeman from the slave throughout this province."

"And what is the test which the governor of Uri employeth for that purpose?"

"Thou hast heard our good pastor read in the Scripture of the prophet Daniel, of the golden image, which the tyrant Nebuchadnezzar caused to be erected. He made a decree that all nations and people of the world should bow down and worship it, and that those who refused to do so should be cast into a burning fiery furnace. Rememberest thou this, my beloved?"

"Certainly," Annette replied. "But what hath Gessler to do with that presumptuous folly of the King of Babylon?"

"Gessler," replied Tell, "imitates the presumption, albeit it is not in his power to rival the grandeur, of Nebuchadnezzar; for he hath set up an idol in the market-place of Altdorf, to which he requireth blind homage to be paid by fools and cowards. Now, the King of Babylon's idol, the prophet tells us, was of solid gold, a metal which the world is, I grieve to say, too prone to worship; but Gessler's paltry Baal is but the empty ducal bonnet of Austria, which he hath exalted on a pole; and he commands the men of Uri to bow down before it, under penalty of death. Wouldst thou wish thy husband to degrade the name of a Swiss, by stooping to such an action?"

"No," she replied, "I should blush for thee, if thou wert capable of such baseness."

"Thou hast spoken like a free woman," he exclaimed. "Yea, and thou shalt be the mother of free children: for the first time I go to Altdorf I will resist the edict, which enjoins me and my countrymen to pay homage to the senseless bauble which the German governor hath exalted in the market-place."

"But why go to Altdorf at all, my husband?" said the wife to Tell.

"My business calls me to Altdorf, and I shall go thither like an honest man, in the performance of my duty," replied Tell. "Thinkest thou that I am either to confess myself a slave, by bending my body to an empty cap, or to permit it to be a scarecrow, that shall fright me from entering the capital city of my native province, lest I should draw upon myself the penalty of refusing to perform a contemptible action, enjoined by a wicked man? No, no, my sweet wife; I shall go to Altdorf, when occasion may require, without considering myself bound to observe Gessler's foolish edict."

The return of Lalotte put an end to this discourse; and Annette began to assist her in taking up the supper.

Lalotte was the orphan of Tell's brother. Her parents had both died when she and her brother Philip were very young, and they had been adopted into the family of her kind uncle soon after his marriage with Annette. Lalotte was affectionate, sprightly, and industrious. She assisted her aunt in the household work and the dairy; and it was her business to take charge of the children, whom she carefully instructed in such things as she knew, and laboured to render them virtuous and obedient.

Philip, her brother, who was about a year older than herself, had been unfortunately a spoiled child. He was self-willed and intractable, and, though far from a bad disposition, was always getting himself and others into scrapes and difficulties.

That night his place at the board was vacant, which his uncle observing, said,

"Lalotte, where is your brother Philip?"

265

"Absent, uncle, I am sorry to say," replied Lalotte.

"It is not usual for Philip to desert the supper meal," observed Tell, "even if he be absent the rest of the day. I am afraid he is after no good."

A hasty step was heard; and Lalotte exclaimed, "I should not wonder if that were my scrapegrace brother!"

"It does not sound well of you to call him so, Lalotte, though he is a sad plague to us all," said Tell.

The door was hastily opened, and Philip bounced in out of breath, and covered with mud. He flung himself on a wooden settle beside the fire, and gave way to fits of laughter.

"How now, Philip! what is the cause of all this?" asked Tell gravely.

"Hurrah!" shouted he, springing from his seat, and capering about, "I have done such a deed!"

"Some notable piece of folly, no doubt," observed his uncle; "what is it, boy?"

"A deed that will render my name famous throughout the whole province of Uri, my good uncle. Everybody is talking about it in Altdorf at this very moment," exclaimed Philip, rubbing his hands.

"You have long been celebrated there as the ringleader of mischief," observed Tell; "but I doubt whether you will have much reason to exult in the evil reputation you have acquired, Philip. Therefore go to bed, and when you say your prayers, ask for grace to reform your evil habits."

"My good uncle," replied Philip, "be content. This night I have turned patriot, raised a rabble of boys, and pelted down the fool's cap which old Gessler had stuck up in the market-place of Altdorf, for Switzers to pay homage to. Is not that a glorious deed!"

"It is of a piece with the rest of your folly. Were you called upon to pay homage to the cap?"

"By no means, uncle, else must I perforce have made my obeisance to the empty bonnet of the Emperor-Duke of Austria. But this exploit of mine was after dark, when one boy could not be distinguished from another; and there were fully fifty of us engaged in pelting at the mock majesty till down it came, feathers and all, souse into the mud. Then, oh stars! how we all ran! But it was my stone that hit it, take notice: ha! ha! ha!"

"Your head must be as devoid of brains as the empty cap you pelted, Philip, or you never would have engaged in any such adventure."

"How, uncle!" cried Philip in amaze; "would you have me pay homage to the ducal bonnet without a head in it?"

"It seems you were not required to do so, Philip; therefore you had no pretext for raising a riot to break the peace."

"But, uncle, do you intend to yield obedience to the governor's tyrannous edict?"

"Philip," replied Tell, "I am a man, and of age to form a correct judgment of the things which it may be expedient to do or proper to refuse. But it is not meet for idle boys to breed riots and commit acts of open violence, calculated to plunge a whole country into confusion."

Philip withdrew with an air of great mortification and the family soon after retired to rest.

The next day William Tell took his thoughtless nephew with him, on a hunting excursion, since it was necessary he should find some better occupation than throwing stones. After several days they returned, loaded with the skins of the chamois that had been slain by the unerring arrow of Tell.

His wife and children hastened to the cottage door to welcome him, when they beheld him coming. "Behold, my beloved," said Tell, "how well I have sped in the chase! These skins will bring in a mine of wealth against the winter season. To-morrow is Altdorf fair and I shall go thither to sell them."

"Hurrah!" shouted Philip. "Is Altdorf fair to-morrow? Oh, my faith, I had forgotten it. Well, I shall go thither, and have some fun."

"And I mean to go too, cousin Philip," said Henric.

"Not so fast, young men," cried Tell. "Altdorf fair will be full of soldiers and turbulent people, and is not a proper place for rash boys and children."

"But you will take care of us, father, dear father," said Henric, stroking his father's arm caressingly.

"I shall have enough to do to take care of myself, Henric," replied Tell. "So you must be a good boy, and stay with your mother."

"But I won't be a good boy, if you leave me at home," muttered the little rebel.

"Then you must be whipped, sir," said his father; "for we love you too well to permit you to be naughty without punishing you."

On hearing this, Henric began to weep with anger. So his father told Lalotte to put him to bed without his supper.

Now Philip was a silly, good-natured fellow, and fancied that his little cousin, Henric, of whom he was very fond, was ill-treated by his father. So he took an opportunity of slipping a sweet-cake into his pouch, from the supper-board, with which he slily stole to Henric's crib.

"Never mind my cross uncle, sweet cousin," said he: "see, I have brought you a nice cake."

"Oh! I don't care about cakes," cried Henric. "I want to go to Altdorf fair to-morrow."

"And you shall go to Altdorf fair," said Philip.

"But how can I go, when father says he won't take me?" sobbed Henric.

"There, dry your eyes, and go to sleep," whispered Philip; "as soon as my uncle is gone I will take you to the fair with me; for I mean to go, in spite of all he has said to the contrary."

"But what will mother say?" asked Henric.

"We won't let her know anything about it," said Philip.

"But Lalotte won't let us go; for Lalotte is very cross, and wants to master me."

"A fig for Lalotte!" cried the rude Philip; "do you think I care for her?"

"I won't care for Lalotte when I grow a great big boy like you, cousin Philip; but she makes me mind her now," said Henric.

"Never fear; we will find some way of outwitting Mademoiselle Lalotte to-morrow," said Philip.

The next morning William Tell rose at an early hour, and proceeded to the fair at Altdorf, to sell his chamois skins.

Philip instead of getting up, and offering to carry them for his uncle, lay in bed till after he was gone. He was pondering on his undutiful scheme of taking little Henric to the fair, in defiance of Tell's express commands that both should stay at home that day.

Henric could eat no breakfast that morning for thinking of the project in which Philip had tempted him to engage. His kind mother patted his curly head, and gave him a piece of honeycomb for not crying to go to the fair. He blushed crimson-red at this commendation, and was just going to tell his mother all about it, when Philip, guessing his thoughts, held up his finger, and shook his head at him.

When his mother and Lalotte went into the dairy to churn the butter they begged Henric and Philip to take care of Lewis and the other little ones, so that they should not get into any mischief. No sooner, however, were they gone, than Philip said,

"Now, Henric, is our time to make our escape, and go to the fair."

"But," said Henric, "my mother gave me some sweet and honeycomb just now, for being a good boy; and it will be very naughty of me to disobey my father's commands after that. So, dear Philip, I was thinking that I would stay at home to-day, if you would stay too, and make little boats for me to float on the lake."

"I shall do no such thing, I promise you," replied Philip; "for I mean to go to the fair, and see the fun. You may stay at home, if you like—for I don't want to be plagued with your company."

"Oh, dear!" cried Henric, "but I want very much to go to the fair, and see the fun too."

"Come along then," said Philip; "or we shall not get there in time to see the tumblers, or the apes and dancing bears, or the fire-eaters, or any other of the shows."

It was nearly two hours before the truants were missed by Henric's mother and Lalotte; for they were all that time busy in the dairy. At length they heard the children cry; on which, Lalotte ran into the room, and found no one with them but Lewis.

"What a shame," cried Lalotte, "for that lazy boy Philip, to leave all these little ones, with only you, Lewis. Where is Henric, pray?"

"Oh! Henric is gone to the fair with cousin Philip," lisped little Lewis.

"Oh that wicked Philip!" cried Lalotte. "Aunt! aunt! Philip has run off to Altdorf fair, and taken Henric with him!"

"My dear Lalotte," said her aunt, "you must put on your hood and sabots, and run after them. Perhaps, as you are light-footed, you can overtake them, and bring Henric back. I am sure, some mischief will befall him."

Lalotte hastily threw her gray serge cloak about her, and drew the hood over her head. She slipped her little feet into her sabots, or wooden shoes, and took the road to Altdorf, hurrying along as fast as she could, in hope of overtaking the truants before they reached the town.

More than once the little maiden thought of turning back, but the remembrance of Philip's rash and inconsiderate temper filled her with alarm for the safety of the child whom he had tempted away from home. She reflected that, as her uncle was at Altdorf, it would be her wisest course to proceed thither to seek him out, and to inform him of his little boy being then in the fair.

Lalotte entered the market-place of Altdorf, at the moment when her uncle, having disposed of his chamois-skins to advantage, was crossing from the carriers' stalls to a clothier's booth to purchase woollen cloths for winter garments. Fairs were formerly marts, where merchants and artisans brought their goods for sale; and persons resorted thither, not for the purpose of riot and revelling, but to purchase useful commodities, clothing, and household goods at the best advantage.

William Tell had been requested by his careful wife to purchase a variety of articles for the use of the family. He was so intent in performing all her biddings, to the best of his ability, that he never once thought of the cap which the insolent governor, Gessler, had erected in the market-place, till he found himself opposite to the lofty pole on which it was exalted. He would have passed it unconsciously had he not been stopped by the German soldiers, who were under arms on either side the pole, to enforce obedience to the insulting edict of the governor of Uri. Tell then paused, and, raising his eyes to the object to which the captain of the guard, with an authoritative gesture, directed his attention, beheld the ducal cap of Austria just above him.

The colour mounted to the cheek of the free-born hunter of the Alps, at the sight of this badge of slavery of his fallen country. Casting an indignant glance upon the foreign soldiers who had impeded his progress, he moved sternly forward, without offering the prescribed act of homage to the cap.

"Stop!" cried the captain of the guard; "you are incurring the penalty of death, rash man, by your disobedience to the edict of his excellency the Governor of Uri."

"Indeed!" replied Tell. "I was not aware that I was doing anything unlawful."

"You have insulted the majesty of our lord the Emperor by passing that cap without bowing to it," said the officer.

"I wist not that more respect were due to an empty cap, than to a cloak and doublet, or a pair of hose," replied Tell.

"Insolent traitor! dost thou presume to level thy rude gibes at the badge of royalty?" cried the governor, stepping forward from behind the soldiers, where he had been listening to the dispute between Tell and the officer.

Poor Lalotte, meantime, having caught a glimpse of her uncle's tall, manly figure through the crowd, had pressed near enough to hear the alarming dialogue in which he had been engaged with the German soldiers. While, pale with terror, she stood listening with breathless attention, she recognised Philip at no great distance, with little Henric in his arms, among the spectators.

The thoughtless Philip was evidently neither aware how near he was to his uncle, nor of the peril in which he stood. With foolish glee, he was pointing out the cap to little Henric; and though Lalotte could not hear what he was saying, she fancied he was rashly boasting to the child of the share in the exploit of pelting it down a few nights previous.

While her attention was thus painfully excited she heard some of the people round her saying,

"Who is it that has ventured to resist the governor's decree?"

"It is William Tell, the crossbow-man of Bürglen," replied many voices.

"William Tell!" said one of the soldiers; "why it was his kinsman who raised a rabble to insult the ducal bonnet the other night."

"Ay, it was the scapegrace, Philip Tell, who assailed the cap of our sovereign with stones, till he struck it down," cried another.

"Behold where the young villain stands," exclaimed a third, pointing to Philip.

"Hallo, hallo! seize the young traitor, in the name of the Emperor and the governor!" shouted the Germans.

"Run, Philip, run—run for your life!" cried a party of his youthful associates.

Philip hastily set his little cousin on his feet, and started off with the speed of the wild chamois of the Alpine mountains; leaving little Henric to shift for himself.

"The child, the child! the precious boy! he will be trampled to death!" shrieked Lalotte.

Henric had caught sight of his father among the crowd while Philip was holding him up to look at the ducal cap, and he had been much alarmed lest his father should see him. But the moment he found himself abandoned by Philip, he lifted up his voice, and screamed with all his might, "Father, father!"

The helplessness, the distress, together with the uncommon beauty of the child, moved the heart of a peasant near him, to compassion. "Who is your father, my fair boy?" said he. "Point him out, and I will lead you to him."

"My father is William Tell, the crossbow-man of Bürglen," said the child. "There he is, close to the cap on the pole yonder."

"Is *he* your father, poor babe?" said the peasant. "Well, you will find him in rare trouble, and I hope you may not be the means of adding to it, my little man."

No sooner had the kind man cleared the way through the crowd for his young companion, and conducted him within a few yards of the spot where William Tell stood, than the urchin drew his hand away from his new friend, and running to his father, flung his little arms about his knees, sobbing,

"Father, dear father, pray forgive me this once, and I will never disobey you again."

Henric made his appearance at an unlucky moment both for his father and himself; for the cruel governor of Uri, exasperated at the manly courage of Tell, seized the boy by the arm and sternly demanded if he were his son.

"Harm not the child, I pray thee," cried Tell: "he is my first born."

"It is not my intention to do him harm," replied the governor. "If any mischief befall the child, it will be by thy own hand, traitor. Here," cried he to one of his soldiers, "take this boy, tie him beneath yon linden-tree, in the centre of the market-place, and place an apple on his head——"

"What means this?" cried Tell.

"I am minded to see a specimen of your skill as an archer," replied Gessler. "I am told that you are the best marksman in all Uri; and, therefore, your life being forfeited by your presumptuous act of disobedience, I am inclined, out of the clemency of my nature, to allow you a chance of saving it. This you may do, if you can shoot an arrow so truly aimed as to cleave the apple upon thy boy's head. But if thou either miss the apple, or slay the child, then shall the sentence of death be instantly executed."

"Unfeeling tyrant!" exclaimed Tell; "dost thou think that I could endeavour to preserve my own life by risking that of my precious child?"

"Nay," replied Gessler, "I thought I was doing thee a great favour by offering thee an alternative, whereby thou mightest preserve thy forfeited life by a lucky chance."

"A lucky chance!" exclaimed Tell: "and dost thou believe that I would stake my child's life on such a desperate chance as the cast of an arrow launched by the agitated hand of an anxious father, at such a mark as that? Nay, look at the child thyself, my lord. Though he be no kin to thee, and thou knowest none of his pretty ways and winning wiles, whereby he endeareth himself to a parent's heart— yet consider his innocent countenance, the artless beauty of his features, and the rosy freshness of his rounded cheeks, which are dimpling with joy at the sight of me, though the tears yet hang upon them— and then say, whether thou couldst find in thine heart to aim an arrow that perchance might harm him?"

"I swear," replied Gessler, "that thou shalt either shoot the arrow, or die!"

"My choice is soon made," said Tell, dropping the bow from his hand. "Let me die!"

"Ay, but the child shall be slain before thy face ere thine own sentence be executed, traitor!" cried the governor, "if thou shoot not at him."

"Give me the bow once more!" exclaimed Tell, in a hoarse, deep voice; "but in mercy let some one turn the child's face away from me. If I meet the glance of those sweet eyes of his, it will unnerve my

278

hand; and then, perchance, the shaft, on whose true aim his life and mine depend, may err."

Lalotte, knowing that all depended on his remaining quiet, as soon as the soldiers had placed him with his face averted from his father, sprang forward, and whispered in Henric's ear, "Stand firm, dear boy, without moving, for five minutes, and you will be forgiven for your fault of this morning."

There was a sudden pause of awe and expectation among the dense crowd that had gathered round the group planted within a bow-shot of the linden-tree beneath which the child was bound. Tell, whose arms were now released, unbuckled the quiver that was slung across his shoulder, and carefully examined his arrows, one by one. He selected two: one of them he placed in his girdle, the other he fitted to his bow-string; and then he raised his eyes to Heaven, and his lips moved in prayer. He relied not upon his own skill but he asked the assistance of One in whose hands are the issues of life and death; and he did not ask in vain. The trembling, agitated hand that a moment before shook with the strong emotion of a parent's anxious fears, became suddenly firm and steady; his swimming eyes resumed their keen, clear sight, and his mind recovered its wonted energy of purpose at the proper moment.

Lalotte's young voice was the first to proclaim, aloud, "The arrow hath cleft the apple in twain! and the child is safe."

"God hath sped my shaft, and blessed be His name!" exclaimed the pious archer, on whose ear the thunders of applause, with which the assembled multitude hailed his successful shot, had fallen unheeded.

The soldiers now unbound the child; and Lalotte fearlessly advanced, and led him to his father. But before the fond parent could fold his darling to his bosom, the tyrant Gessler sternly demanded for what purpose he had reserved the second arrow, which he had seen him select and place in his belt.

"That arrow," replied Tell, giving way to a sudden burst of passion, "that arrow was designed to avenge the death of my child, if I had slain him with the other."

"How to avenge?" exclaimed the governor, furiously. "To avenge, saidst thou? and on whom didst thou intend thy vengeance would fall?"

"On thee, tyrant!" replied Tell, fixing his eyes sternly on the governor. "My next mark would have been thy bosom, had I failed in my first. Thou perceivest that mine is not a shaft to miscarry."

"Well, thou hast spoken frankly," said Gessler; "and since I have promised thee thy life I will not swerve from my word. But as I have now reason for personal apprehensions from thy malice, I shall closet thee henceforth so safely in the dungeons of Küssnacht, that the light of sun or moon shall never more visit thine eyes; and thy fatal bow shall hereafter be harmless."

On this the guard once more laid hands on the intrepid archer, whom they seized and bound, in spite of the entreaties of Lalotte, and the cries and tears of little Henric, who hung weeping about his father.

"Take him home to his mother, Lalotte; and bear my last fond greetings to her and the little ones, whom I, peradventure, shall see no more," said Tell, bursting into tears. The mighty heart which had remained firm and unshaken in the midst of all his perils and trials, now melted within him at the sight of his child's tears, the remembrance of his home, and anticipations of the sufferings of his tender wife.

The inhuman Gessler scarcely permitted his prisoner the satisfaction of a parting embrace with Henric and Lalotte, ere he ordered him to be hurried on board a small vessel in which he embarked also with his armed followers. He commanded the crew to row to Brunnen, where it was his intention to land, and, passing through the territory of Schwyz, to lodge the captive Tell in the dungeon of Küssnacht, and there to immure him for life.

The sails were hoisted and the vessel under weigh, when suddenly one of those storms common on the lake of Uri overtook them, accompanied with such violent gusts of wind, that the terrified pilot forsook the helm; and the bark, with the governor and his crew, was in danger of being ingulfed in the raging waters. Gessler, like most wicked people, was in great terror at the prospect of death, when one of his attendants reminded him that the prisoner,

William Tell, was no less skilful in the management of a boat than in the exercise of the bow. So he ordered that Tell should be unbound, and placed at the helm.

The boat, steered by the master-hand of the intrepid Tell, now kept its course steadily through the mountain surge; and Tell observed, "that by the grace of God, he trusted a deliverance was at hand."

As the prow of the vessel was driven inland, Tell perceived a solitary table rock and called aloud the rowers to redouble their efforts, till they should have passed the precipice ahead. At the instant they came abreast this point he snatched his bow from the plank, where it was lying forgotten during the storm, and, turning the helm suddenly toward the rock, he sprang lightly on shore, scaled the mountain, and was out of sight and beyond reach of pursuit, before any on board had recovered from consternation.

Tell, meantime, entered Schwyz, and having reached the heights which border the main road to Küssnacht, concealed himself among the brushwood in a small hollow of the road, where he knew Gessler would pass on his way to his own castle, in case he and his followers escaped and came safely to shore. This, it appeared they did, and having effected a landing at Brunnen, they took horse, and proceeded towards Küssnacht, in the direction of the only road to the castle.

While they were passing the spot where Tell lay concealed, he heard the cruel tyrant denouncing the most deadly vengeance, not only on himself, but his helpless family: "If I live to return to Altdorf," he exclaimed, "I will destroy the whole brood of the traitor Tell, mother and children, in the same hour."

"Monster, thou shalt return to Altdorf no more!" murmured Tell. So, raising himself up in his lair, and fitting an arrow to his bow, he took deadly aim at the relentless bosom that was planning the destruction of all his family.

The arrow flew as truly to the mark as that which he had shot in the market-place of Altdorf, and the tyrant Gessler fell from his horse, pierced with a mortal wound.

The daring archer thought that he had taken his aim unseen by human eye; but, to his surprise, a familiar voice whispered in his ear, "Bravo, uncle! that was the best-aimed shaft you ever shot. Gessler is down, and we are a free people now."

"Thou incorrigible varlet, what brings thee here?" replied Tell, in an undervoice, giving Philip a rough grip of the arm.

"It is no time to answer questions," returned Philip. "The Rütli band are waiting for thee, if so be thou canst escape from this dangerous place; and my business here was to give thee notice of the same."

On this, Tell softly crept from the thicket, and, followed by his nephew, took the road to Stienen, which under cover of darkness, they reached that night.

Philip, by the way, after expressing much contrition for having seduced little Henric to go to the fair with him, informed his uncle that Henric and Lalotte had been safely conducted home by one of the band of the Rütli who chanced to be at Altdorf fair.

When they reached Stienen Tell was received with open arms by Stauffacher, the leader of the Rütli band; and with him and the other confederates, he so well concerted measures for the deliverance of Switzerland from the German yoke, that, in the course of a few days, the whole country was in arms. The Emperor of Germany's forces were everywhere defeated; and on the first day of the year, 1308, the independence of Switzerland was declared.

His grateful countrymen would have chosen William Tell for their sovereign, but he nobly rejected the offer, declaring that he was perfectly contented with the station of life in which he was born, and wished to be remembered in history by no other title than that of the Deliverer of Switzerland.

This true patriot lived happily in the bosom of his family for many years, and had the satisfaction of seeing his children grow up in the fear of God and the practice of virtue.

# ROBERT BRUCE

I HOPE you have not forgotten, my dear child, that all the cruel wars of Scotland arose out of the debate between the great lords who claimed the throne after King Alexander the Third's death. The Scottish nobility rashly submitted the decision of that matter to King Edward I of England, and thus opened the way to his endeavouring to seize the kingdom of Scotland to himself. It was natural that such of the people as were still determined to fight for the deliverance of their country from the English, should look round for some other King, under whom they might unite themselves, to combat the power of England.

Amongst these, the principal candidates, were two powerful noblemen. The first was Robert Bruce, Earl of Carrick; the other was John Comyn, or Cuming, of Badenoch, usually called the Red Comyn, to distinguish him from his kinsman, the Black Comyn, so named from his swarthy complexion. These two great and powerful barons had taken part with Sir William Wallace in the wars against England; but, after his defeat, being careful of losing their great estates, and considering the freedom of Scotland as beyond the possibility of being recovered, both Bruce and Comyn had not only submitted themselves to Edward, and acknowledged his title as King of Scotland, but even borne arms, along with the English, against such of their countrymen as still continued to resist the usurper. But the feelings of Bruce concerning the baseness of this conduct, are said, by the old tradition of Scotland, to have been awakened by the following incident. In one of the numerous battles, or skirmishes, which took place at the time between the English and their adherents on the one side, and the insurgent or patriotic Scots upon the other, Robert the Bruce was present, and assisted the English to gain the victory. After the battle was over, he sat down to dinner among his southern friends and allies, without washing his hands, on which there still remained spots of the blood which he had shed during the action. The English lords, observing this whispered to each other in mockery, "Look at that Scotsman, who is eating his own blood!" Bruce heard what they said, and began to reflect that the blood upon his hands might be indeed called his own, since it was that of his brave countrymen who were fighting for the independence of Scotland, whilst he was assisting its oppressors, who only laughed at and mocked him for his unnatural conduct. He was so much shocked and disgusted that he arose from table, and, going into a neighbouring chapel, shed many tears, and, asking pardon of God for the great crime he had been guilty of, made a solemn vow that he would atone for it by doing all in his power to deliver Scotland from the foreign yoke. Accordingly, he left, it is said, the English army, and never joined it again, but remained watching an opportunity for restoring the freedom of his country.

Now, this Robert the Bruce was held the best warrior in Scotland. He was very wise and prudent, and an excellent general; that is, he knew how to conduct an army, and place them in order for battle, as well or better than any great man of his time. He was generous, too, and courteous by nature; but he had some faults, which perhaps belonged as much to the fierce period in which he lived as to his own character. He was rash and passionate, and in his passion he was sometimes relentless and cruel.

Robert the Bruce had fixed his purpose, as I told you, to attempt once again to drive the English out of Scotland, and he desired to prevail upon Sir John, the Red Comyn, who was his rival in his pretensions to the throne, to join with him in expelling the foreign enemy by their common efforts. With this purpose, Bruce requested an interview with John Comyn. They met in the Church of the Minorites in Dunfries, before the high altar. What passed betwixt them is not known with certainty; but they quarrelled, either concerning their mutual pretensions to the Crown, or because Comyn refused to join Bruce in the proposed insurrection against the English; or, as many writers say, because Bruce charged Comyn with having betrayed to the English his purpose of rising up against King Edward. It is, however, certain, that these two haughty barons came to high and abusive words, until at length Bruce forgot the sacred character of the place in which they stood, and struck Comyn a blow with his dagger. Having done this rash deed, he instantly ran out of the church and called for his horse. Two friends of Bruce were in attendance on him. Seeing him pale, bloody, and in much agitation they eagerly inquired what was the matter.

"I doubt," said Bruce, "that I have slain the Red Comyn."

"Do you leave such a matter in doubt?" said one, "I will make sicker!"—that is, I will make certain. Accordingly, he and his companion rushed into the church and made the matter certain with a vengeance, by dispatching the wounded Comyn with their daggers. His uncle, Sir Robert Comyn, was slain at the same time.

This slaughter of Comyn was a rash and cruel action. It was followed by the displeasure of Heaven; for no man ever went through more misfortunes than Robert Bruce, although he at length rose to great honour. After the deed was done, Bruce might be called desperate. He had committed an action which was sure to bring down upon him the vengeance of all Comyn's relations, the resentment of the King of England, and the displeasure of the Church, on account of having slain his enemy within consecrated ground. He determined, therefore, to bid them all defiance at once, and to assert his pretensions to the throne of Scotland. He drew his own followers together, summoned to meet him such barons as still entertained hopes of the freedom of the country, and was crowned King at the Abbey of Scone, the usual place where the Kings of Scotland assumed their authority.

Everything relating to the ceremony was hastily performed. A small circlet of gold was hurriedly made, to represent the ancient crown of Scotland, which Edward had carried off to England. The Earl of Fife, descendant of the brave Macduff, whose duty it was to have placed the crown on the King's head, would not give his attendance, but the ceremonial was performed by his sister, Isabella, Countess of Buchan.

Edward was dreadfully incensed when he heard that, after all the pains which he had taken, and all the blood which had been spilled, the Scots were making this new attempt to shake off his authority. Though now old, feeble, and sickly, he made a solemn vow, in presence of all his court, that he would take the most ample vengeance upon Robert the Bruce and his adherents; after which he would never again draw his sword upon a Christian, but would only fight against the unbelieving Saracens for the recovery of the Holy Land. He marched against Bruce accordingly, at the head of a powerful army.

The commencement of Bruce's undertaking was most disastrous. He was crowned on the twenty-ninth of March, 1306. On the eighteenth of May he was excommunicated by the Pope, on account of the murder of Comyn within consecrated ground, a sentence which excluded him from all benefits of religion, and authorized any one to kill him. Finally, on the nineteenth of June, the new King was completely defeated near Methven by the English Earl of Pembroke. Robert's horse was killed under him in the action, and he was for a moment a prisoner. But he had fallen into the power of a Scottish knight, who, though he served in the English army, did not choose to be the instrument of putting Bruce into their hands, and allowed him to escape.

Bruce, with a few brave adherents, among whom was the young lord of Douglas, who was afterward called the Good Lord James, retired into the Highland mountains. The Bruce's wife, now Queen of Scotland, with several other ladies, accompanied her husband and his few followers during their wanderings. There was no way of providing for them save by hunting and fishing. Driven from one place in the Highlands to another, starved out of some districts, and forced from others by the opposition of the inhabitants, Bruce attempted to force his way into Lorn; but he found enemies everywhere. The MacDougals, a powerful family, then called Lords of Lorn, were friendly to the English, and attacked Bruce and his wandering companions as soon as they attempted to enter their territory. The chief, called John of Lorn, hated Bruce on account of his having slain the Red Comyn, to whom this MacDougal was nearly related. Bruce was again defeated by this chief. He directed his men to retreat through a narrow pass, and, placing himself last of the party, he fought with and slew such of the enemy as attempted to press hard on them. Three followers of MacDougal, a father and two sons, called MacAndrosser, all very strong men, when they saw Bruce thus protecting the retreat of his followers, rushed on the King at once. Bruce was on horseback, in the strait pass betwixt a precipitous rock and a deep lake. He struck the first man a blow with his sword, as cut off his hand and freed the bridle. The man bled to death. The other brother had meantime grasped Bruce by the leg, and was attempting to throw him from horseback. The King, setting spurs to his horse, made the animal suddenly spring forward, so that the Highlander fell under the horse's feet, and, as he was endeavouring to rise again, Bruce cleft his head in two with his sword. The father, seeing his two sons thus slain, flew desperately at the King, and grasped him by the mantle so close to his body, that he could not have room to wield his long sword. But with the heavy pummel of that weapon the King struck this third assailant so dreadful a blow, that he dashed out his brains. Still, however, the Highlander kept his dying grasp on the King's mantle; so that, to be free of the dead body, Bruce was obliged to undo the brooch, or clasp, by which it was fastened, and leave that, and the mantle itself, behind him. The brooch, which fell thus into the possession of MacDougal of Lorn, is still preserved in that ancient family as a memorial.

The King met with many such encounters amidst his dangerous and dismal wanderings; yet, though almost always defeated by the superior numbers of the English, and of such Scots as sided with them, he still kept up his own spirits and those of his followers. He was a better scholar than was usual in those days, when, except clergymen, few people learned to read and write. But King Robert could do both very well; and we are told that he sometimes read aloud to his companions, to amuse them, when they were crossing the great Highland lakes, in such wretched leaky boats as they could find for that purpose. Loch Lomond, in particular, is said to have been the scene of such a lecture. You may see by this, how useful it is to possess knowledge.

At last dangers increased so much around the brave King Robert, that he was obliged to separate himself from his Queen and her ladies. So Bruce left his Queen, with the Countess of Buchan and others, in the only castle which remained to him, which was called Kildrummie, and is situated near the head of the river Don in Aberdeenshire. The King also left his brother, Nigel Bruce, to defend the castle against the English; and he himself, with his second brother Edward, who was a very brave man, went over to an island called Rachrin, on the coast of Ireland, where Bruce and the few men who followed his fortunes passed the winter of 1306. In the meantime the castle of Kildrummie was taken by the English, and Nigel Bruce, a beautiful and brave youth, was cruelly put to death by the victors. The ladies who had attended on Robert's Queen, as well as the Queen herself, and the Countess of Buchan, were thrown into strict confinement.

The Countess of Buchan had given Edward great offence by being the person who placed the crown on the head of Robert Bruce. She was imprisoned within the Castle of Berwick, in a cage. The cage was a strong wooden and iron piece of frame-work, placed within an apartment, and resembling one of those places in which wild-beasts are confined. There were such cages in most old prisons to which captives were consigned, who were to be confined with peculiar rigour.

The news of the taking of Kildrummie, the captivity of his wife, and the execution of his brother, reached Bruce while he was residing in a miserable dwelling at Rachrin, and reduced him to the point of despair. After receiving the intelligence from Scotland, Bruce was lying one morning on his wretched bed, and deliberating with himself whether he had not better resign all thoughts of again attempting to make good his right to the Scottish crown, and, dismissing his followers, transport himself and his brothers to the Holy Land, and spend the rest of his life in fighting against the Saracens. But then, on the other hand, he thought it would be both criminal and cowardly to give up his attempts to restore freedom to Scotland while there yet remained the least chance of his being successful in an undertaking, which, rightly considered, was much more his duty than to drive the infidels out of Palestine.

While he was divided betwixt these reflections, and doubtful of what he should do, Bruce was looking upward to the roof of the cabin in which he lay; and his eye was attracted by a spider, which, hanging at the end of a long thread of its own spinning, was endeavouring to swing itself from one beam in the roof to another, for the purpose of fixing the line on which it meant to stretch its web. The insect made the attempt again and again without success; at length Bruce counted that it had tried to carry its point six times, and been as often unable to do so. It came into his head that he had himself fought just six battles against the English and their allies, and that the poor persevering spider was exactly in the same situation with himself, having made as many trials and been as often disappointed in what it aimed at. "Now," thought Bruce, "as I have no means of knowing what is best to be done, I will be guided by the luck which shall attend this spider. If the insect shall make another effort to fix its thread, and shall be successful, I will venture a seventh time to try my fortune in Scotland; but if the spider shall fail, I will go to the wars in Palestine, and never return to my native country more."

While Bruce was forming this resolution the spider made another exertion with all the force it could muster, and fairly succeeded in fastening its thread to the beam which it had so often in vain attempted to reach. Bruce seeing the success of the spider, resolved to try his own fortune; and as he had never before gained a victory, so he never afterward sustained any considerable or decisive check or defeat. I have often met with people of the name of Bruce, so completely persuaded of the truth of this story, that they would not on any account kill a spider, because it was that insect which had shown the example of perseverance, and given a signal of good luck to their great namesake.

Having determined to renew his efforts to obtain possession of Scotland, the Bruce removed himself and his followers from Rachrin to the island of Arran, which lies in the mouth of the Clyde. The King landed, and inquired of the first woman he met what armed men were in the island. She returned for answer that there had arrived there very lately a body of armed strangers, who had defeated an English governor of the castle, and were now amusing themselves with hunting about the island. The King, having caused himself to be guided to the woods which these strangers most frequented, there blew his horn repeatedly. Now, the chief of the strangers who had taken the castle was James Douglas, one of the best of Bruce's friends, and he was accompanied by some of the bravest of that patriotic band. When he heard Robert Bruce's horn, he knew the sound well, and cried out, that yonder was the King, he knew by his manner of blowing. So he and his companions hastened to meet King Robert. They could not help weeping when they considered their own forlorn condition, but they were stout-hearted men, and yet looked forward to freeing their country.

The Bruce was now where the people were most likely to be attached to him. He continued to keep himself concealed in his own earldom of Carrick, and in the neighboring country of Galloway, until he should have matters ready for a general attack upon the English. He was obliged, in the meantime, to keep very few men with him, both for the sake of secrecy, and from the difficulty of finding provisions.

Now, many of the people of Galloway were unfriendly to Bruce. They lived under the government of one MacDougal, related to the Lord of Lorn, who had defeated Bruce. These Galloway men had heard that Bruce was in their country, having no more than sixty men with him; so they resolved to attack him by surprise, and for this purpose they got together and brought with them two or three bloodhounds. At that time bloodhounds, or sleuthhounds, were used for the purpose of pursuing great criminals. The men of Galloway thought that if they missed taking Bruce, or killing him at the first onset, and if he should escape into the woods, they would find him out by means of these bloodhounds.

The good King Robert Bruce, who was always watchful and vigilant, received some information of the intention of the party to come upon him suddenly and by night. Accordingly, he quartered his little troop of sixty men on the side of a deep and swift-running river, that had very steep and rocky banks. There was but one ford by which this river could be crossed in that neighbourhood, and that ford was deep and narrow, so that two men could scarcely get through abreast; the ground on which they were to land, on the side where the King was, was steep, and the path which led upward from the water's edge to the top of the bank, extremely narrow and difficult.

Bruce caused his men to lie down to take some sleep, at a place about half a mile distant from the river, while he himself, with two attendants, went down to watch the ford. He stood looking at the ford, and thinking how easily the enemy might be kept from passing there, provided it was bravely defended, when he heard, always coming nearer and nearer, the baying of a hound. This was the bloodhound which was tracing the King's steps to the ford where he had crossed, and two hundred Galloway men were along with the animal, and guided by it. Bruce at first thought of going back to awaken his men; but then he reflected that it might be only some shepherd's dog. "My men," said he, "are sorely tired; I will not disturb their sleep for the yelping of a cur, till I know something more of the matter." So he stood and listened; and by and by, as the cry of the hound came nearer, he began to hear a trampling of horses, and the voices of men, and the ringing and clattering of armour, and then he was sure the enemy were coming to the river side. Then the King thought, "If I go back to give my men the alarm, these Galloway men will get through the ford without opposition; and that would be a pity, since it is a place so advantageous to make defence against them." So he looked again at the steep path, and the deep river, and he thought that they gave him so much advantage, that he himself could defend the passage with his own hand, until his men came to assist him. He therefore sent his followers to waken his men, and remained alone by the river.

The noise and trampling of the horses increased, and the moon being bright, Bruce beheld the glancing arms of two hundred men, on the opposite bank. The men of Galloway, on their part, saw but one solitary figure guarding the ford, and the foremost of them plunged into the river without minding him. But as they could only pass the ford one by one, the Bruce, who stood high above them on the bank where they were to land, killed the foremost man with a thrust of his long spear, and with a second thrust stabbed the horse, which fell down, kicking and plunging in his agonies, on the narrow path, and so prevented the others who were following from getting out of the river. Bruce had thus an opportunity of dealing his blows among them, while they could not strike at him. In the confusion, five or six of the enemy were slain, or, having been borne down with the current, were drowned. The rest were terrified, and drew back.

But when the Galloway men looked again, and saw they were opposed by only one man, they themselves being so many, they cried out, that their honour would be lost forever if they did not force their way; and encouraged each other, with loud cries, to plunge through and assault him. But by this time the King's soldiers came up to his assistance, and the Galloway men gave up their enterprise.

About the time when the Bruce was yet at the head of but few men, Sir Aymer de Valence, who was Earl of Pembroke, together with Sir John of Lorn, came into Galloway, each of them being at the head of a large body of men. John of Lorn had a

298

bloodhound with him, which it was said had formerly belonged to Robert Bruce himself; and having been fed by the King with his own hands, it became attached to him, and would follow his footsteps anywhere, as dogs are well known to trace their master's steps, whether they be bloodhounds or not. By means of this hound, John of Lorn thought he should certainly find out Bruce, and take revenge on him for the death of his relation Comyn.

The King saw that he was followed by a large body, and being determined to escape from them, he made all the people who were with him disperse themselves different ways, thinking thus that the enemy must needs lose trace of him. He kept only one man along with him, and that was his own foster-brother, or the son of his nurse. When John of Lorn came to the place where Bruce's companions had dispersed themselves, the bloodhound, after it had snuffed up and down for a little, quitted the footsteps of all the other fugitives, and ran barking upon the track of two men out of the whole number. Then John of Lorn knew that one of these two must needs be King Robert. Accordingly, he commanded five of his men that were speedy of foot to chase after him, and either make him prisoner or slay him. The Highlanders started off accordingly, and ran so fast, that they gained sight of Robert and his foster-brother. The King asked his companion what help he could give him, and his foster-brother answered he was ready to do his best. So these two turned on the five men of John of Lorn, and killed them all.

But by this time Bruce very much fatigued, and yet they dared not sit down to take any rest; for whenever they stopped for an instant, they heard the cry of the bloodhound behind them, and knew by that, that their enemies were coming up fast after them. At length, they came to a wood, through which ran a small river. Then Bruce said to his foster-brother, "Let us wade down this stream for a great way, instead of going straight across, and so this unhappy hound will lose the scent; for if we were once clear of him, I should not be afraid of getting away from the pursuers." Accordingly, the King and his attendant walked a great way down the stream, taking care to keep their feet in the water, which could not retain any scent where they had stepped. Then they came ashore on the further side from the enemy, and went deep into the wood before they stopped to rest themselves. In the meanwhile, the hound led John of Lorn straight to the place where the King went into the water, but there the dog began to be puzzled, not knowing where to go next. So, John of Lorn, seeing the dog had lost track, gave up the chase, and returned to join with Aymer de Valence.

But King Robert's adventures were not yet ended. It was now near night, and he went boldy into a farmhouse, where he found the mistress, an old, true-hearted Scotswoman, sitting alone. Upon seeing a stranger enter she asked him who and what he was. The King answered that he was a traveller, who was journeying through the country.

"All travellers," answered the good woman, "are welcome here, for the sake of one."

"And who is that one," said the King, "for whose sake you make all welcome?"

"It is our rightful King, Robert the Bruce," answered the mistress, "and although he is now pursued and hunted after with hounds and horns, I hope to live to see him King over all Scotland."

"Since you love him so well, dame," said the King, "know that you see him before you. I am Robert the Bruce."

"You!" said the good woman, in great surprise; "and wherefore are you thus alone?—where are all your men?"

"I have none with me at this moment," answered Bruce, "and therefore I must travel alone."

"But that shall not be," said the brave old dame, "for I have two stout sons, gallant and trusty men, who shall be your servants for life and death."

So she brought her two sons, and though she well knew the dangers to which she exposed them, she made them swear fidelity to the King.

Now, the loyal woman was getting everything ready for the King's supper, when suddenly there was a great trampling of horses heard round the house. They thought it must be some of the English, or John of Lorn's men, and the good wife called upon her sons to fight to the last for King Robert. But shortly after, they heard the voice of the good Lord James of Douglas, and of Edward Bruce, the

King's brother, who had come with a hundred and fifty horsemen, according to the instructions that the King had left with them at parting.

Robert the Bruce was right joyful to meet his brother, and his faithful friend Lord James; and had no sooner found himself once more at the head of such a considerable body of followers, than he forgot hunger and weariness. There was nothing but mount and ride; and as the Scots rushed suddenly into the village where the English were quartered, they easily dispersed and cut them to pieces.

The consequence of these successes of King Robert was that soldiers came to join him on all sides, and that he obtained several victories over English commanders; until at length the English were afraid to venture into the open country, as formerly, unless when they could assemble themselves in considerable bodies. They thought it safer to lie still in the towns and castles which they had garrisoned.

Edward I would have entered Scotland at the head of a large army, before he had left Bruce time to conquer back the country. But very fortunately for the Scots, that wise and skilful, though ambitious King, died when he was on the point of marching into Scotland. His son Edward II neglected the Scottish war, and thus lost the opportunity of defeating Bruce, when his force was small. But when Sir Philip Mowbray, the governor of Stirling, came to London, to tell the King, that Stirling, the last Scottish town of importance which remained in possession of the English, was to be surrendered if it were not relieved by force of arms before midsummer, then all the English nobles called out, it would be a sin and shame to permit the fair conquest which Edward I had made, to be forfeited to the Scots for want of fighting.

King Edward II, therefore, assembled one of the greatest armies which a King of England ever commanded. There were troops brought from all his dominions, many brave soldiers from the French provinces, many Irish, many Welsh, and all the great English nobles and barons, with their followers. The number was not less than one hundred thousand men.

King Robert the Bruce summoned all his nobles and barons to join him, when he heard of the great preparations which the King of England was making. They were not so numerous as the English by many thousand men. In fact, his whole army did not very much exceed thirty thousand, and they were much worse armed than the wealthy Englishmen; but then, Robert was one of the most expert generals of the time; and the officers he had under him, were his brother Edward, his faithful follower the Douglas, and other brave and experienced leaders. His men had been accustomed to fight and gain victories under every disadvantage of situation and numbers.

The King, on his part, studied how he might supply, by address and stratagem, what he wanted in numbers and strength. He knew the superiority of the English in their heavy-armed cavalry, and in their archers. Both these advantages he resolved to provide against. With this purpose, he led his army down into a plain near Stirling. The English army must needs pass through a boggy country, broken with water-courses, while the Scots occupied hard dry ground. He then caused all the ground upon the front of his line of battle, to be dug full of holes, about as deep as a man's knee. They were filled with light brushwood, and the turf was laid on the top, so that it appeared a plain field, while in reality it was as full of these pits as a honeycomb is of holes. He also, it is said, caused steel spikes, called calthrops, to be scattered up and down in the plain, where the English cavalry were most likely to advance, trusting in that manner to lame and destroy their horses.

When the Scottish army was drawn up, the line stretched north and south. On the south, it was terminated by the banks of the brook called Bannockburn, which are so rocky, that no troops could attack them there. On the left, the Scottish line extended near to the town of Stirling. Bruce reviewed his troops very carefully. He then spoke to the soldiers, and expressed his determination to gain the victory, or to lose his life on the field of battle. He desired that all those who did not propose to fight to the last, should leave the field before the battle began, and that none should remain except those who were determined to take the issue of victory or death, as God should send it. When the main body of his army was thus placed in order, the King dispatched James of Douglas, and Sir Robert

Keith, the Mareschal of the Scottish army, in order that they might survey the English force. They returned with information, that the approach of that vast host was one of the most beautiful and terrible sights which could be seen—that the whole country seemed covered with men-at-arms on horse and foot.

It was upon the twenty-third of June, 1314, the King of Scotland heard the news, that the English army was approaching Stirling. The van now came in sight, and a number of their bravest knights drew near to see what the Scots were doing. They saw King Robert dressed in his armour, and distinguished by a gold crown, which he wore over his helmet. He was not mounted on his great war-horse, because he did not expect to fight that evening. But he rode on a little pony up and down the ranks of his army, putting his men in order, and carried in his hand a sort of battle-axe made of steel. When the King saw the English horsemen draw near, he advanced a little before his own men, that he might look at them more nearly.

There was a knight among the English, called Sir Henry de Bohun, who thought this would be a good opportunity to gain great fame to himself, and put an end to the war, by killing King Robert. The King being poorly mounted, and having no lance, Bohun galloped on him suddenly and furiously, thinking, with his long spear, and his tall, powerful horse, easily to bear him down to the ground. King Robert saw him, and permitted him to come very near, then suddenly turned his pony a little to one side, so that Sir Henry missed him with the lance-point, and was in the act of being carried past him by the career of his horse. But as he passed, King Robert rose up in his stirrups, and struck Sir Henry on the head with his battle-axe so terrible a blow, that it broke to pieces his iron helmet as if it had been a nut-shell, and hurled him from his saddle. He was dead before he reached the ground. This gallant action was blamed by the Scottish leaders, who thought Bruce ought not to have exposed himself to so much danger, when the safety of the whole army depended on him. The King only kept looking at his weapon, which was injured by the force of the blow, and said, "I have broken my good battle-axe."

The next morning the English King ordered his men to begin the battle. The archers then bent their bows, and began to shoot so closely together, that the arrows fell like flakes of snow on a Christmas day. They killed many of the Scots, and might have decided the victory; but Bruce was prepared for them. A body of men-at-arms, well mounted, rode at full gallop among them, and as the archers had no weapons save their bows and arrows, which they could not use when they were attacked hand to hand, they were cut down in great numbers by the Scottish horsemen, and thrown into total confusion. The fine English cavalry then advanced to support their archers. But coming over the ground which was dug full of pits the horses fell into these holes and the riders lay tumbling about, without any means of defence, and unable to rise, from the weight of their armour.

While the battle was obstinately maintained on both sides, an event happened which decided the victory. The servants and attendants on the Scottish camp had been sent behind the army to a place afterward called the Gillies' hill. But when they saw that their masters were likely to gain the day, they rushed from their place of concealment with such weapons as they could get, that they might have their share in the victory and in the spoil. The English, seeing them come suddenly over the hill, mistook this disorderly rabble for a new army coming up to sustain the Scots, and, losing all heart, began to shift every man for himself. Edward himself left the field as fast as he could ride.

The English, after this great defeat, were no longer in a condition to support their pretensions to be masters of Scotland, or to continue to send armies into that country to overcome it. On the contrary, they became for a time scarce able to defend their own frontiers against King Robert and his soldiers.

Thus did Robert Bruce arise from the condition of an exile, hunted with bloodhounds like a stag or beast of prey, to the rank of an independent sovereign, universally acknowledged to be one of the wisest and bravest Kings who then lived. The nation of Scotland was also raised once more from the situation of a distressed and conquered province to that of a free and independent state, governed by its own laws.

Robert Bruce continued to reign gloriously for several years, and the Scots seemed, during his government, to have acquired a complete superiority over their neighbours. But then we must remember, that Edward II who then reigned in England, was a foolish prince, and listened to bad counsels; so that it is no wonder that he was beaten by so wise and experienced a general as Robert Bruce, who had fought his way to the crown through so many disasters, and acquired in consequence so much renown.

In the last year of Robert the Bruce's reign, he became extremely sickly and infirm, chiefly owing to a disorder called the leprosy, which he had caught during the hardships and misfortunes of his youth, when he was so frequently obliged to hide himself in woods and morasses, without a roof to shelter him. He lived at a castle called Cardross, on the beautiful banks of the river Clyde, near to where it joins the sea; and his chief amusement was to go upon the river, and down to the sea in a ship, which he kept for his pleasure. He was no longer able to sit upon his war-horse, or to lead his army to the field.

While Bruce was in this feeble state, Edward II, King of England, died, and was succeeded by his son Edward III. He turned out afterward to be one of the wisest and bravest Kings whom England ever had; but when he first mounted the throne he was very young. The war between the English and the Scots still lasted at the time.

But finally a peace was concluded with Robert Bruce, on terms highly honourable to Scotland; for the English King renounced all pretensions to the sovereignty of the country.

Good King Robert did not long survive this joyful event. He was not aged more than four-and-fifty years, but his bad health was caused by the hardships which he sustained during his youth, and at length he became very ill. Finding that he could not recover, he assembled round his bedside the nobles and counsellors in whom he most trusted. He told them, that now, being on his death-bed, he sorely repented all his misdeeds, and particularly, that he had, in his passion, killed Comyn with his own hand, in the church and before the altar. He said that if he had lived, he had intended to go to Jerusalem to make war upon the Saracens who held the Holy Land, as some expiation for the evil deeds he had done. But since he was about to die, he requested of his dearest friend and bravest warrior, and that was the good Lord James Douglas, that he should carry his heart to the Holy Land. Douglas wept bitterly as he accepted this office—the last mark of the Bruce's confidence and friendship.

The King soon afterward expired; and his heart was taken out from his body and embalmed, that is, prepared with spices and perfumes, that it might remain a long time fresh and uncorrupted. Then the Douglas caused a case of silver to be made, into which he put the Bruce's heart, and wore it around his neck, by a string of silk and gold. And he set forward for the Holy Land, with a gallant train of the bravest men in Scotland, who, to show their value of and sorrow for their brave King Robert Bruce, resolved to attend his heart to the city of Jerusalem. In going to Palestine Douglas landed in Spain, where the Saracen King, or Sultan of Granada, called Osmyn, was invading the realms of Alphonso, the Spanish King of Castile. King Alphonso received Douglas with great honour and distinction, and easily persuaded the Scottish Earl that he would do good service to the Christian cause, by assisting him to drive back the Saracens of Granada before proceeding on his voyage to Jerusalem. Lord Douglas and his followers went accordingly to a great battle against Osmyn, and had little difficulty in defeating the Saracens. But being ignorant of the mode of fighting among the cavalry of the East, the Scots pursued the chase too far, and the Moors, when they saw them scattered and separated from each other, turned suddenly back, with a loud cry of *Allah illah Allah*, which is their shout of battle, and surrounded such of the Scottish knights and squires as were dispersed from each other.

In this new skirmish, Douglas saw Sir William St. Clair of Roslyn fighting desperately, surrounded by many Moors, who were having at him with their sabres. "Yonder worthy knight will be slain," Douglas said, "unless he have instant help." With that he galloped to his rescue, but presently was himself also surrounded by many Moors. When he found the enemy press so thick round him, as to leave him no chance of escaping, the Earl took from his neck the Bruce's heart, and speaking to it, as he would have done to the King, had he been alive— "Pass first in fight," he said, "as thou wert wont to do, and Douglas will follow thee, or die."

He then threw the King's heart among the enemy, and rushing forward to the place where it fell, was there slain. His body was found lying above the silver case, as if it had been his last object to defend the Bruce's heart.

Such of the Scottish knights as remained alive returned to their own country. They brought back the heart of the Bruce, and the bones of the good Lord James. The Bruce's heart was buried below the high altar in Melrose Abbey. As for his body, it was laid in the sepulchre in the midst of the church of Dunfermline, under a marble stone. The church afterward becoming ruinous, and the roof falling down with age, the monument was broken to pieces, and nobody could tell where it stood. But when they were repairing the church at Dunfermline, and removing the rubbish, lo! they found fragments of the marble tomb of Robert Bruce. Then they began to dig farther, thinking to discover the body of this celebrated monarch; and at length they came to the skeleton of a tall man, and they knew it must be that of King Robert, both as he was known to have been buried in a winding sheet of cloth of gold, of which many fragments were found about this skeleton, and also because the breastbone appeared to have been sawed through, in order to take the heart. A new tomb was prepared into which the bones were laid with profound respect.

# GEORGE WASHINGTON

ON THE 4th of March, 1797, Washington went to the inauguration of his successor as President of the United States. The Federal Government was sitting in Philadelphia at that time and Congress held sessions in the courthouse on the corner of Sixth and Chestnut Streets.

At the appointed hour Washington entered the hall followed by John Adams, who was to take the oath of office. When they were seated Washington arose and introduced Mr. Adams to the audience, and then proceeded to read in a firm clear voice his brief valedictory—not his great "Farewell Address," for that had already been published. A lady who sat on "the front bench," "immediately in front" of Washington describes the scene in these words:

"There was a narrow passage from the door of entrance to the room. General Washington stopped at the end to let Mr. Adams pass to the chair. The latter always wore a full suit of bright drab, with loose cuffs to his coat. General Washington's dress was a full suit of black. His military hat had the black cockade. There stood the

312

'Father of his Country' acknowledged by nations the first in war, first in peace, and first in the hearts of his countrymen. No marshals with gold-coloured scarfs attended him; there was no cheering, no noise; the most profound silence greeted him as if the great assembly desired to hear him breathe. Mr. Adams covered his face with both his hands; the sleeves of his coat and his hands were covered with tears. Every now and then there was a suppressed sob. I cannot describe Washington's appearance as I felt it—perfectly composed and self-possessed till the close of his address. Then when strong, nervous sobs broke loose, when tears covered the faces, then the great man was shaken. I never took my eyes from his face. Large drops came from his eyes. He looked as if his heart was with them, and would be to the end."

On Washington's retirement from the Presidency one of his first employments was to arrange his papers and letters. Then on returning to his home the venerable master found many things to repair. His landed estate comprised eight thousand acres, and was divided into farms, with enclosures and farm-buildings. And now with body and mind alike sound and vigorous, he bent his energies to directing the improvements that marked his last days at Mount Vernon.

In his earlier as well as in later life, his tour of the farms would average from eight to twelve or fourteen miles a day. He rode upon his farms entirely unattended, opening his gates, pulling down and putting up his fences as he passed, visiting his labourers at their work, inspecting all the operations of his extensive establishment with a careful eye, directing useful improvements and superintending them in their progress.

He usually rode at a moderate pace in passing through his fields. But when behind time this most punctual of men would display the horsemanship of his earlier days, and a hard gallop would bring him up to time so that the sound of his horse's hoofs and the first dinner bell would be heard together at a quarter before three.

A story is told that one day an elderly stranger meeting a Revolutionary worthy out hunting, a long-tried and valued friend of the chief, accosted him, and asked whether Washington was to be found at the mansion house, or whether he was off riding over his estate. The friend answered that he was visiting his farms, and directed the stranger the road to take, adding, "You will meet, sir, with an old gentleman riding alone in plain drab clothes, a broad-brimmed white hat, a hickory switch in his hand, and carrying an umbrella with a long staff, which is attached to his saddle-bow—that person, sir, is General Washington."

Precisely at a quarter before three the industrious farmer returned, dressed, and dined at three o'clock. At this meal he ate heartily, but was not particular in his diet with the exception of fish, of which he was excessively fond. Touching his liking for fish, and illustrative of his practical economy and abhorrence of waste and extravagance, an anecdote is told of the time he was President and living in Philadelphia. It happened that a single shad had been caught in the Delaware, and brought to the city market. His steward, Sam Fraunces, pounced upon the fish with the speed of an osprey, delighted that he had secured a delicacy agreeable to the palate of his chief, and careless of the expense, for which the President had often rebuked him.

When the fish was served Washington suspected the steward had forgotten his order about expenditure for the table and said to Fraunces, who stood at his post at the sideboard, "What fish is this?" "A shad, sir, a very fine shad," the steward answered. "I know your excellency is particularly fond of this kind of fish, and was so fortunate as to procure this one—the only one in market, sir, the first of the season." "The price, sir, the price?" asked Washington sternly. "Three—three dollars," stammered the conscience-stricken steward. "Take it away," thundered the chief, "take it away, sir! It shall never be said that my table set such an example of luxury and extravagance." Poor Fraunces tremblingly did as he was told, and the first shad of the season was carried away untouched to be speedily discussed in the servants' dining room.

Although the Farmer of Mount Vernon was much retired from the business world, he was by no means inattentive to the progress of public affairs. When the post bag arrived, he would select his letters and lay them aside for reading in the seclusion of his library. The newspapers he would peruse while taking his single cup of tea (his only supper) and read aloud passages of peculiar interest, remarking the matter as he went along. He read with distinctness and precision. These evenings with his family always ended at precisely nine o'clock, when he bade everyone good night and retired to rest, to rise again at four and renew the same routine of labour and enjoyment.

Washington's last days, like those that preceded them in the course of a long and well-spent life, were devoted to constant and careful employment. His correspondence both at home and abroad was immense. Yet no letter was unanswered. One of the best-bred men of his time, Washington deemed it a grave offence against the rules of good manners and propriety to leave letters unanswered. He wrote with great facility, and it would be a difficult matter to find another who had written so much, who had written so well. General Harry Lee once observed to him, "We are amazed, sir, at the vast amount of work you get through." Washington answered, "Sir, I rise at four o'clock, and a great deal of my work is done while others sleep."

He was the most punctual of men, as we said. To this admirable quality of rising at four and retiring to rest at nine at all seasons, this great man owed his ability to accomplish mighty labours during his long and illustrious life. He was punctual in everything and made everyone about him punctual. So careful a man delighted in always having about him a good timekeeper. In Philadelphia, the first President regularly walked up to his watchmaker's to compare his watch with the regulator. At Mount

Vernon the active yet punctual farmer invariably consulted the dial when returning from his morning ride, and before entering his house.

The affairs of the household took order from the master's accurate and methodical arrangement of time. Even the fisherman on the river watched for the cook's signal when to pull in shore and deliver his catch in time for dinner.

Among the picturesque objects on the Potomac, to be seen from the eastern portion of the mansion house, was the light canoe of the house's fisher. Father Jack was an African, an hundred years of age, and although enfeebled in body by weight of years, his mind possessed uncommon vigour. And he would tell of days long past when, under African suns, he was made captive, and of the terrible battle in which his royal sire was slain, the village burned, and himself sent to the slave ship.

Father Jack had in a considerable degree a leading quality of his race—somnolency. Many an hour could the family of Washington see the canoe fastened to a stake, with the old fisherman bent nearly double enjoying a nap, which was only disturbed by the jerking of the white perch caught on his hook. But, as we just said, the domestic duties of Mount Vernon were governed by clock time, and the slumbers of fisher Jack might occasion inconvenience, for the cook required the fish at a certain hour, so that they might be served smoking hot precisely at three. At times he would go to the river bank and make the accustomed signals, and meet with no response. The old fisherman would be quietly reposing in his canoe, rocked by the gentle undulations of the stream, and dreaming, no doubt, of events "long time ago." The importunate master of the kitchen, grown ferocious by delay, would now rush up and down the water's edge, and, by dint of loud shouting, cause the canoe to turn its prow to the shore. Father Jack, indignant at its being supposed he was asleep at his post, would rate those present on his landing, "What you all meck such a debil of a noise for, hey? I wa'nt sleep, only noddin'."

The establishment of Mount Vernon employed a perfect army of domestics; yet to each one was assigned special duties, and from each one strict performance was required. There was no confusion where there was order, and the affairs of this estate, embracing thousands of acres and hundreds of dependents, were conducted with as much ease, method and regularity as the affairs of a homestead of average size.

Mrs. Washington was an accomplished house-wife of the olden time, and she gave constant attention to all matters of her household, and by her skill and management greatly contributed to the comfort and entertainment of the guests who enjoyed the hospitality of her home.

The best charities of life were gathered round Washington in the last days at Mount Vernon. The love and veneration of a whole people for his illustrious services, his generous and untiring labours in the cause of public utility; his kindly demeanour to his family circle, his friends, and numerous dependents; his courteous and cordial hospitality to his guests, many of them strangers from far distant lands; these charities, all of which sprang from the heart, were the ornament of his declining years and granted the most sublime scene in nature, when human greatness reposes upon human happiness.

On the morning of the 17th of December, 1799, the General was engaged in making some improvements in the front of Mount Vernon. As was usual with him, he carried his own compass, noted his observations, and marked out the ground. The day became rainy, with sleet, and the improver remained so long exposed to the inclemency of the weather as to be considerably wetted before his return to the house. About one o'clock he was seized with chilliness and nausea, but having changed his clothes he sat down to his indoor work. At night, on joining his family circle, he complained of a slight indisposition. Upon the night of the following day, having borne acute suffering with composure and fortitude, he died.

In person Washington was unique. He looked like no one else. To a stature lofty and commanding he united a form of the manliest proportions, and a dignifed, graceful, and imposing carriage. In the prime of life he stood six feet, two inches. From the period of the Revolution there was an evident bending in his frame so passing straight before, but the stoop came from the cares and toils of that arduous contest rather than from years. For his step was firm, his appearance noble and impressive long after the time when the physical properties of men are supposed to wane.

A majestic height was met by corresponding breadth and firmness. His whole person was so cast in nature's finest mould as to resemble an ancient statue, all of whose parts unite to the perfection of the whole. But with all its development of muscular power, Washington's form had no look of bulkiness, and so harmonious were its proportions that he did not appear so tall as his portraits have represented. He was rather spare than full during his whole life.

The strength of Washington's arm was shown on several occasions. He threw a stone from the bed of the stream to the top of the Natural Bridge, Virginia, and another stone across the Rappahannock at Fredericksburg. The stone was said to be a piece of slate about the size of a dollar with which he spanned the bold river, and it took the ground at least thirty yards on the other side. Many have since tried this feat, but none have cleared the water.

In 1772 some young men were contending at Mount Vernon in the exercise of pitching the bar. The Colonel looked on for a time, then grasping the missile in his master hand he whirled the iron through the air and it fell far beyond any of its former limits. "You see, young gentlemen," said the chief with a smile, "that my arm yet retains some portion of my early vigour." He was then in his fortieth year and probably in the fullness of his physical powers. Those powers became rather mellowed than decayed by time, for "his age was like lusty winter, frosty yet kindly," and up to his sixty-eighth year he mounted a horse with surprising agility and rode with ease and grace. Rickets, the celebrated equestrian, used to say, "I delight to see the General ride and make it a point to fall in with him when I hear he is out on horseback—his seat is so firm, his management so easy and graceful that I who am an instructor in horsemanship would go to him and learn to ride."

In his later days, the General, desirous of riding pleasantly, procured from the North two horses of a breed for bearing the saddle. They were well to look at, and pleasantly gaited under the saddle, but also scary and therefore unfitted for the service of one who liked to ride quietly on his farm, occasionally dismounting and walking in his fields to inspect improvements. From one of these horses the General sustained a fall—probably the only fall he ever had from a horse in his life. It was upon a November evening, and he was returning from Alexandria to Mount Vernon with three friends and a groom. Having halted a few moments he dismounted, and upon rising in his stirrup again, the horse, alarmed at the glare from a fire near the road-side, sprang from under his rider who came heavily to the ground. His friends rushed to give him assistance, thinking him hurt. But the vigorous old man was upon his feet again, brushing the dust from his clothes, and after thanking those who came to his aid said that he had had a very complete tumble, and that it was owing to a cause no horseman could well avoid or control—that he was only poised in his stirrup, and had not yet gained his saddle when the scary animal sprang from under him.

Bred in the vigorous school of frontier warfare, "the earth for his bed, his canopy the heavens," Washington excelled the hunter and woodsman in their athletic habits and in those trials of manhood which filled the hardy days of his early life. He was amazingly swift of foot, and could climb steep mountains seemingly without effort. Indeed in all the tests of his great physical powers he appeared to make little effort. When he overthrew the strong man of Virginia in wrestling, upon a day when many of the finest athletes were engaged in the contest, he had retired to the shade of a tree intent upon the reading of a book. It was only after the champion of the games strode through the ring calling for nobler antagonists, and taunting the reader with the fear that he would be thrown, that Washington closed his book. Without taking off his coat he calmly observed that fear did not enter his make-up; then grappling with the champion he hurled him to the ground. "In Washington's lion-like grasp," said the vanquished wrestler, "I became powerless, and went down with a force that seemed to jar the very marrow in my bones." The victor, regardless of shouts at his success, leisurely retired to his shade, and again took up his book.

Washington's powers were chiefly in his limbs. His frame was of equal breadth from the shoulders to the hips. His chest was not prominent but rather hollowed in the centre. He never entirely recovered from a pulmonary affection from which he suffered in early life. His frame showed an extraordinary development of bone and muscle; his joints were large, as were his feet; and could a cast of his hand have been preserved, it would be ascribed to a being of a fabulous age. Lafayette said, "I never saw any human being with so large a hand as the General's."

Of the awe and reverence which the presence of Washington inspired we have many records. "I stood," says one writer, "before the door of the Hall of Congress in Philadelphia when the carriage of the President drew up. It was a white coach, or rather of a light cream colour, painted on the panels with beautiful groups representing the four seasons. As Washington alighted and, ascending the steps, paused on the platform, he was preceded by two gentleman bearing large white wands, who kept back the eager crowd that pressed on every side. At that moment I stood so near I might have touched his clothes; but I should as soon have thought of touching an electric battery. I was penetrated with deepest awe. Nor was this the feeling of the school-boy I then was. It pervaded, I believe, every human being that approached Washington; and I have been told that even in his social hours, this feeling in those who shared them never suffered intermission. I saw him a hundred times afterward but never with any other than the same feeling. The Almighty, who raised up for our hour of need a man so peculiarly prepared for its whole dread responsibility, seems to have put a stamp of sacredness upon his instrument. The first sight of the man struck the eye with involuntary homage and prepared everything around him to obey.

"At the time I speak of he stood in profound silence and had the statue-like air which mental greatness alone can bestow. As he turned to enter the building, and was ascending the staircase to the Congressional hall, I glided along unseen, almost under the cover of the skirts of his dress, and entered into the lobby of the House which was in session to receive him.

"At Washington's entrance there was a most profound silence. House, lobbies, gallery, all were wrapped in deepest attention. And the souls of the entire assemblage seemed peering from their eyes as the noble figure deliberately and unaffectedly advanced up the broad aisle of the hall between ranks of standing senators and members, and slowly ascended the steps leading to the speaker's chair.

"The President having seated himself remained in silence, and the members took their seats, waiting for the speech. No house of worship was ever more profoundly still than that large and crowded chamber.

"Washington was dressed precisely as Stuart has painted him in full-length portrait—in a full suit of the richest black velvet, with diamond knee-buckles and square silver buckles set upon shoes japanned with most scrupulous neatness; black silk stockings, his shirt ruffled at the breast and waist, a light dress sword, his hair profusely powdered, fully dressed, so as to project at the sides, and gathered behind in a silk bag ornamented with a large rose of black ribbon. He held his cocked hat, which had a large black cockade on one side of it, in his hand, as he advanced toward the chair, and when seated, laid it on the table.

"At length thrusting his hand within the side of his coat, he drew forth a roll of manuscript which he opened, and rising read in a rich, deep, full, sonorous voice his opening address to Congress. His enunciation was deliberate, justly emphasised, very distinct, and accompanied with an air of deep solemnity as being the utterance of a mind conscious of the whole responsibility of its position, but not oppressed by it. There was ever about the man something which impressed one with the conviction that he was exactly and fully equal to what he had to do. He was never hurried; never negligent; but seemed ever prepared for the occasion, be it what it might. In his study, in his parlour, at a levee, before Congress, at the head of the army, he seemed ever to be just what the situation required. He possessed, in a degree never equalled by any human being I ever saw, the strongest, most ever-present sense of propriety."

In the early part of Washington's administration, great complaints were made by political opponents of the aristocratic and royal demeanour of the President. Particularly, these complaints were about the manner of his receiving visitors. In a letter Washington gave account of the origin of his levees: "Before the custom was established," he wrote, "which now accommodates foreign characters, strangers and others, who, from motives of curiosity, respect for the chief magistrate, or other cause, are induced to call upon me, I was unable to attend to any business whatever; for gentlemen, consulting their own convenience rather than mine, were calling after the time I rose from breakfast, and often before, until I sat down to dinner. This, as I resolved not to neglect my public duties, reduced me to the choice of one of these alternatives: either to refuse visits altogether, or to appropriate a time for the reception of them. . . . To please everybody was impossible. I therefore, adopted that line of conduct which combined public advantage with private convenience. . . . These visits are optional, they are made without invitation; between the hours of three and four every Tuesday I am prepared to receive them. Gentlemen, often in great numbers, come and go, chat with each other, and act as they please. A porter shows them into the room, and they retire from it when they choose, without ceremony. At their first entrance they salute me, and I them, and as many as I can I talk to."

An English gentleman after visiting President Washington wrote, "There was a commanding air in his appearance which excited respect and forbade too great a freedom toward him, independently of that species of awe which is always felt in the moral influence of a great character. In every movement, too, there was a polite gracefulness equal to any met with in the most polished individuals of Europe, and his smile was extraordinarily attractive. . . . It struck me no man could be better formed for command. A stature of six feet, a robust but well-proportioned frame calculated to stand fatigue, without that heaviness which generally attends great muscular strength and abates active exertion, displayed bodily power of no mean standard. A light eye and full— the very eye of genius and reflection. His nose appeared thick, and though it befitted his other features was too coarsely and strongly formed to be the handsomest of its class. His mouth was like no other I ever saw: the lips firm, and the under-jaw seeming to grasp the upper with force, as if its muscles were in full action when he sat still."

Such Washington appeared to those who saw and knew him. Such he remains to our vision. His memory is held by us in undying honour. Not only his memory alone but also the memory of his associates in the struggle for American Independence. Homage we should have in our hearts for those patriots and heroes and sages who with humble means raised their native land—now our native land—from the depths of dependence, and made it a free nation. And especially for Washington, who presided over the nation's course at the beginning of the great experiment in self-government and, after an unexampled career in the service of freedom and our humankind, with no dimming of august fame, died calmly at Mount Vernon—the Father of his Country.

# ROBERT E. LEE

THE first vivid recollection I have of my father is his arrival in Arlington, after his return from the Mexican War. I can remember some events of which he seemed a part, when we lived at Fort Hamilton, New York, about 1846, but they are more like dreams, very indistinct and disconnected—naturally so, for I was at that time about three years old. But the day of his return to Arlington, after an absence of more than two years, I have always remembered. I had a frock or blouse of some light wash material, probably cotton, a blue ground dotted over with white diamond figures. Of this I was very proud, and wanted to wear it on this important occasion. Eliza, my "mammy," objecting, we had a contest and I won. Clothed in this, my very best, and with my hair freshly curled in long golden ringlets, I went down into the large hall where the whole household was assembled, eagerly greeting my father, who had just arrived on horseback from Washington, having missed in some way the carriage which had been sent for him.

There was visiting us at this time Mrs. Lippitt, a friend of my mother's, with her little boy, Armistead, about my age and size, also with long curls. Whether he wore as handsome a suit as mine I cannot remember, but he and I were left together in the background, feeling rather frightened and awed. After a moment's greeting to those surrounding him, my father pushed through the crowd, exclaiming:

"Where is my little boy?"

He then took up in his arms and kissed—not me his own child, in his best frock with clean face and well-arranged curls—but my little playmate, Armistead. I remember nothing more of any circumstances connected with that time, save that I was shocked and humiliated. I have no doubt that he was at once informed of his mistake and made ample amends to me.

A letter from my father to his brother, Captain S. S. Lee, United States Navy, dated "Arlington, June 30, 1848," tells of his coming home:

"Here I am once again, my dear Smith, perfectly surrounded by Mary and her precious children, who seem to devote themselves to staring at the furrows in my face and the white hairs in my head. It is not surprising that I am hardly recognisable to some of the young eyes around me and perfectly unknown to the youngest. But some of the older ones gaze with astonishment and wonder at me, and seem at a loss to reconcile what they see and what was pictured in their imaginations. I find them, too, much grown, and all well, and I have much cause for thankfulness, and gratitude to that good God who has once more united us."

My next recollection of my father is in Baltimore, while we were on a visit to his sister, Mrs. Marshall, the wife of Judge Marshall. I remember being down on the wharves, where my father had taken me to see the landing of a mustang pony which he had gotten for me in Mexico, and which had been shipped from Vera Cruz to Baltimore in a sailing vessel. I was all eyes for the pony, and a very miserable, sad-looking object he was. From his long voyage, cramped quarters, and unavoidable lack of grooming, he was rather a disappointment to me, but I soon got over all that. As I grew older, and was able to ride and appreciate him, he became the joy and pride of my life. I was taught to ride on him by Jim Connally, the faithful Irish servant of my father, who had been with him in Mexico. Jim used often to tell me, in his quizzical way, that he and "Santa Anna" (the pony's name) were the first men on the walls of Chepultepec. This pony was pure white, five years old, and about fourteen hands high. For his inches, he was as good a horse as I ever have seen. While we lived in Baltimore, he and "Grace Darling," my father's favorite mare, were members of our family.

Grace Darling was a chestnut of fine size and of great power, which he had bought in Texas on his way out to Mexico, her owner having died on the march out. She was with him during the entire campaign, and was shot seven times; at least, as a little fellow I used to brag about that number of bullets being in her, and since I could point out the scars of each one, I presume it was so. My father was very much attached to and proud of her, always petting her and talking to her in a loving way, when he rode her or went to see her in her stall. Of her he wrote on his return home:

"I only arrived yesterday, after a long journey up the Mississippi, which route I was induced to take, for the better accommodation of my horse, as I wished to spare her as much annoyance and fatigue as possible, she already having undergone so much suffering in my service. I landed her at Wheeling and left her to come over with Jim."

Santa Anna was found lying cold and dead in the park of Arlington one morning in the winter of '60-'61. Grace Darling was taken in the spring of '62 from the White House[1] by some Federal quartermaster, when McClellan occupied that place as his base of supplies during his attack on Richmond. When we lived in Baltimore, I was greatly struck one day by hearing two ladies who were visiting us saying:

"Everybody and everything—his family, his friends, his horse, and his dog—loves Colonel Lee."

The dog referred to was a black-and-tan terrier named "Spec," very bright and intelligent and really a member of the family, respected and beloved by ourselves and well known to all who knew us. My father picked up its mother in the "Narrows" while crossing from Fort Hamilton to the fortifications

---

[1] My brother's place on the Pamunkey River, where the mare had been sent for safe keeping.

opposite on Staten Island. She had doubtless fallen overboard from some passing vessel and had drifted out of sight before her absence had been discovered. He rescued her and took her home, where she was welcomed by his children and made much of. She was a handsome little thing, with cropped ears and a short tail. My father named her "Dart." She was a fine ratter, and with the assistance of a Maltese cat, also a member of the family, the many rats which infested the house and stables were driven away or destroyed. She and the cat were fed out of the same plate, but Dart was not allowed to begin the meal until the cat had finished.

Spec was born at Fort Hamilton, and was the joy of us children, our pet and companion. My father would not allow his tail and ears to be cropped. When he grew up, he accompanied us everywhere and was in the habit of going into church with the family. As some of the little ones allowed their devotions to be disturbed by Spec's presence, my father determined to leave him at home on those occasions. So the next Sunday morning he was sent up to the front room of the second story. After the family had left for church he contented himself for a while looking out of the window, which was open, it being summer time. Presently impatience overcame his judgment and he jumped to the ground, landed safely notwithstanding the distance, joined the family just as they reached the church, and went in with them as usual, much to the joy of the children. After that he was allowed to go to church whenever he wished. My father was very fond of him, and loved to talk to him and about him as if he were really one of us. In a letter to my mother, dated Fort Hamilton, January 18, 1846, when she and her children were on a visit to Arlington, he thus speaks of him:

". . . I am very solitary, and my only company is my dog and cats. But Spec has become so jealous now that he will hardly let me look at the cats. He seems to be afraid that I am going off from him, and never lets me stir without him. Lies down in the office from eight to four without moving, and turns himself before the fire as the side from it becomes cold. I catch him sometimes sitting up looking at me so intently that I am for a moment startled. . . ."

In a letter from Mexico written a year later— December 25, 1846, to my mother, he says:

". . . Can't you cure poor Spec? Cheer him up—take him to walk with you and tell the children to cheer him up. . . ."

In another letter from Mexico to his eldest boy, just after the capture of Vera Cruz, he sends this message to Spec:

". . . Tell him I wish he was here with me. He would have been of great service in telling me when I was coming upon the Mexicans. When I was reconnoitering around Vera Cruz, their dogs frequently told me by barking when I was approaching them too nearly. . . ."

When he returned to Arlington from Mexico, Spec was the first to recognise him, and the extravagance of his demonstrations of delight left no doubt that he knew at once his kind master and loving friend, though he had been absent three years. Sometime during our residence in Baltimore, Spec disappeared, and we never knew his fate.

From that early time I began to be impressed with my father's character, as compared with other men. Every member of the household respected, revered, and loved him as a matter of course, but it began to dawn on me that every one else with whom I was thrown held him high in their regard. At forty-five years of age he was active, strong, and as handsome as he had ever been. I never remember his being ill. I presume he was indisposed at times; but no impressions of that kind remain. He was always bright and gay with us little folk—romping, playing, and joking with us. With the older children, he was just as companionable, and I have seen him join my elder brothers and their friends when they would try their powers at a high jump put up in our yard. The two younger children he petted a great deal, and our greatest treat was to get into his bed in the morning and lie close to him, listening while he talked to us in his bright, entertaining way. This custom we kept up until I was ten years old and over. Although he was so joyous and familiar with us, he was very firm on all proper occasions, never indulged us in anything that was not good for us, and exacted the most implicit obedience. I always knew that it was impossible to disobey my father. I felt it in me, I never thought why, but was perfectly sure when he gave an order that it had to be obeyed.

My mother I could sometimes circumvent, and at times took liberties with her orders, construing them to suit myself; but exact obedience to every mandate of my father was a part of my life and being at that time.

In January, 1849, Captain Lee was one of a board of army officers appointed to examine the coasts of Florida and its defences, and to recommend locations for new fortifications. In April he was assigned to the duty of the construction of Fort Carroll, in the Patapsco River, below Baltimore. He was there, I think, for three years, and lived in a house on Madison Street, three doors above Biddle. I used to go down with him to the Fort quite often. We went to the wharf in a "bus," and there we were met by a boat with two oarsmen, who rowed us down to Sollers Point, where I was generally left under the care of the people who lived there, while my father went over to the Fort, a short distance out in the river. These days were very happy ones for me. The wharves, the shipping, the river, the boat and oarsmen, and the country dinner we had at the house at Sollers Point, all made a strong impression on me, but above all I remember my father; his gentle, loving care for me, his bright talk, his stories, his maxims and teachings. I was very proud of him and of the evident respect for and trust in him every one showed. These impressions, obtained at that time, have never left me. He was a great favourite in Baltimore, as he was everywhere, especially with ladies and little children. When he and my mother went out in the evening to some entertainment, we were often allowed to sit up and see them off; my father, as I remember, always in full uniform, always ready and waiting for my mother, who was generally late. He would then chide her gently, in a playful way and with a bright smile. He would then bid us good-bye, and I would go to sleep with this beautiful picture on my mind, the golden epaulets and all— chiefly the epaulets.

In Baltimore, I went to my first school, that of a Mr. Rollins on Mulberry Street, and I remember how interested my father was in my studies, my failures, and my little triumphs. Indeed, he was so always, as long as I was at school and college, and I only wish that all of the kind, sensible, useful letters he wrote me had been preserved.

My memory as to the move from Baltimore, which occurred in 1852, is very dim. I think the family went to Arlington to remain until my father had arranged for our removal to the new home at West Point.

My recollection of my father as Super-intendent of the West Point Military Academy is much more distinct. He lived in the house which is still occupied by the Superintendent. It was built of stone, large and roomy, with gardens, stables, and pasture lots. We, the two youngest children, enjoyed it all. Grace Darling and Santa Anna were with us, and many a fine ride did I have with my father in the afternoons, when, released from his office, he would mount his old mare and, with Santa Anna carrying me by his side, take a five or ten-mile trot. Though the pony cantered delightfully, he would make me keep him in a trot, saying playfully that the hammering I sustained was good for me. We rode the dragoon-seat, no posting, and until I became accustomed to it I used to be very tired by the time I got back.

My father was the most punctual man I ever knew. He was always ready for family prayers, for meals, and met every engagement, social or business, at the moment. He expected all of us to be the same, and taught us the use and necessity of forming such habits for the convenience of all concerned. I never knew him late for Sunday service at the Post Chapel. He used to appear some minutes before the rest of us, in uniform, jokingly rallying my mother for being late, and for forgetting something at the last moment. When he could wait no longer for her, he would say that he was off, and would march along to church by himself or with any of the children who were ready. There he sat very straight—well up the middle aisle— and, as I remember, always became very sleepy, and sometimes even took a little nap during the sermon. At that time, this drowsiness of my father's was something awful to me, inexplicable. I know it was very hard for me to keep awake, and frequently I did not; but why he, who to my mind could do everything that was right without any effort, should sometimes be overcome, I could not understand, and did not try to do so.

It was against the rules that the cadets should go beyond certain limits without permission. Of course they did go sometimes, and when caught were given quite a number of "demerits." My father was riding one afternoon with me, and, while rounding a turn in the mountain road with a deep woody ravine on one side, we came suddenly upon three cadets far beyond the limits. They immediately leaped over a low wall on the side of the road, and disappeared from our view. We rode on for a minute in silence; then my father said: "Did you know those young men? But no; if you did, don't say so. I wish boys would do what is right, it would be so much easier for all parties!"

He knew he would have to report them, but, not being sure of who they were, I presume he wished to give them the benefit of the doubt. At any rate, I never heard any more about it. One of the three asked me next day if my father had recognised them, and I told him what had occurred.

By this time I had become old enough to have a room to myself, and, to encourage me in being useful and practical, my father made me attend to it, just as the cadets had to do with their quarters in barracks and in camp. He at first even went through the form of inspecting it, to see if I had performed my duty properly, and I think I enjoyed this until the novelty wore off. However, I was kept at it, becoming in time very proficient, and the knowledge so accquired has been of great use to me all through life.

My father always encouraged me in every healthy outdoor exercise and sport. He taught me to ride, constantly giving me minute instructions, with the reasons for them. He gave me my first sled, and sometimes used to come out where we boys were coasting to look on. He gave me my first pair of skates, and placed me in the care of a trustworthy person, inquiring regularly how I progressed. It was the same with swimming, which he was very anxious I should learn in a proper manner. Professor Bailey had a son about my age, now himself a professor of Brown University, Providence, Rhode Island, who became my great chum. I took my first lesson in the water with him, under the direction and supervision of his father. My father inquired constantly how I was getting along, and made me describe exactly my method and stroke, explaining to me what he considered the best way to swim, and the reasons therefor.

I went to a day school at West Point, and had always a sympathetic helper in my father. Often he would come into my room where I studied at night, and, sitting down by me, would show me how to overcome a hard sentence in my Latin reader or a difficult sum in arithmetic, not by giving me the translation of the troublesome sentence or the answer to the sum, but by showing me, step by step, the way to the right solutions. He was very patient, very loving, very good to me, and I remember trying my best to please him in my studies. When I was able to bring home a good report from my teacher, he was greatly pleased, and showed it in his eye and voice, but he always insisted that I should get the "maximum," that he would never be perfectly satisfied with less. That I did sometimes win it, deservedly, I know was due to his judicious and wise method of exciting my ambition and perseverance. I have endeavoured to show how fond my father was of his children, and as the best picture I can offer of his loving, tender devotion to us all, I give here a letter from him written about this time to one of his daughters who was staying with our grandmother, Mrs. Custis, at Arlington:

"West Point, February 25, 1853.

"My precious Annie: I take advantage of your gracious permission to write to you, and there is no telling how far my feelings might carry me were I not limited by the conveyance furnished by the Mim's[1] letter, which lies before me, and which must, the Mim says so, go in this morning's mail. But my limited time does not diminish my affection for you, Annie, nor prevent my thinking of you and wishing for you. I long to see you through the dilatory nights. At dawn when I rise, and all day, my thoughts revert to you in expressions that you cannot hear or I repeat. I hope you will always appear to me as you are now painted on my heart, and that you will endeavour to improve and so conduct yourself as to make you happy and me joyful all our lives. Diligent and earnest attention to all your duties can only accomplish this. I am told you are growing very tall, and I hope very straight. I do not know what the cadets will say if the Superintendent's *children* do not

---

[1] His pet name for my mother.

practice what he demands of them. They will naturally say he had better attend to his own before he corrects other people's children, and as he permits his to stoop it is hard he will not allow them. You and Agnes[1] must not, therefore, bring me into discredit with my young friends, or give them reason to think that I require more of them than of my own. I presume your mother has told all about us, our neighbours and our affairs. And indeed she may have done that and not said much either, so far as I know. But we are all well and have much to be grateful for. To-morrow we anticipate the pleasure of your brother's[2] company, which is always a source of pleasure to us. It is the only time we see him, except when the Corps come under my view at some of their exercises, when my eye is sure to distinguish him among his comrades and follow him over the plain. Give much love to your dear grandmother, grandfather, Agnes, Miss Sue, Lucretia, and all friends, including the servants. Write sometimes, and think always of your

"Affectionate father,"
"R. E. LEE."

In a letter to my mother, written many years previous to this, he says:

"I pray God to watch over and direct our efforts in guarding our dear little son. . . . Oh, what pleasure I lose in being separated from my children!

---

[1] His third daughter.
[2] His son, Curtis.

Nothing can compensate me for that. . . ."

In another letter of about the same time:

"You do not know how much I have missed you and the children, my dear Mary. To be alone in a crowd is very solitary. In the woods, I feel sympathy with the trees and birds, in whose company I take delight, but experience no pleasure in a strange crowd. I hope you are all well and will continue so, and, therefore, must again urge you to be very prudent and careful of those dear children. If I could only get a squeeze at that little fellow, turning up his sweet mouth to 'keese baba!' You must not let him run wild in my absence, and will have to exercise firm authority over all of them. This will not require severity or even strictness, but constant attention and an unwavering course. Mildness and forebearance will strengthen their affection for you, while it will maintain your control over them."

In a letter to one of his sons he writes as follows:

"I cannot go to bed, my dear son, without writing you a few lines to thank you for your letter, which gave me great pleasure ... You and Custis must take great care of your kind mother and dear sisters when your father is dead. To do that you must learn to be good. Be true, kind and generous, and pray earnestly to God to enable you to keep His Commandments 'and walk in the same all the days of your life.' I hope to come on soon to see that little baby you have got to show me. You must give her a kiss for me, and one to all the children, to your mother, and grandmother."

The expression of such sentiments as these was common to my father all through his life, and to show that it was all children and not his own little folk alone that charmed and fascinated him, I quote from a letter to my mother:

" . . . I saw a number of little girls all dressed up in their white frocks and pantalets, their hair plaited and tied up with ribbons, running and chasing each other in all directions. I counted twenty-three nearly the same size. As I drew up my horse to admire the spectacle, a man appeared at the door with the twenty-fourth in his arms.

" 'My friend,' said I, 'are all these your children?'

" 'Yes,' he said, 'and there are nine more in the house, and this is the youngest.'

"Upon further inquiry, however, I found that they were only temporarily his, and that they were invited to a party at his house. He said, however, he had been admiring them before I came up, and just wished that he had a million of dollars, and that they were all his in reality. I do not think the eldest exceeded seven or eight years old. It was the prettiest sight I have seen in the west, and, perhaps, in my life. . . ."

As Superintendent of the Military Academy at West Point my father had to entertain a good deal, and I remember well how handsome and grand he looked in uniform, how genial and bright, how considerate of everybody's comfort of mind and body. He was always a great favourite with the ladies, especially the young ones. His fine presence, his gentle, courteous manners and kindly smile put them at once at ease with him.

Among the cadets at this time were my eldest brother, Custis, who graduated first in his class in 1854, and my father's nephew, Fitz Lee, a third classman, besides other relatives and friends. Saturday being a half-holiday for the cadets, it was the custom for all social events in which they were to take part to be placed on that afternoon or evening. Nearly every Saturday a number of these young men were invited to our house to tea, or supper, for it was a good, substantial meal. The misery of some of these lads, owing to embarrassment, possibly from awe of the Superintendent, was pitiable and evident even to me, a boy of ten or twelve years old. But as soon as my father got command, as it were, of the situation, one could see how quickly most of them were put at their ease. He would address himself to the task of making them feel comfortable and at home, and his genial manner and pleasant ways at once succeeded.

In the spring of 1853 my grandmother, Mrs. Custis, died. This was the first death in our immediate family. She was very dear to us, and was admired, esteemed, and loved by all who had ever known her. Bishop Meade, of Virginia, writes of her:

"Mrs. Mary Custis, of Arlington, the wife of

Mr. Washington Custis, grandson of Mrs. General Washington, was the daughter of Mr. William Fitzhugh, of Chatham. Scarcely is there a Christian lady in our land more honoured than she was, and none more loved and esteemed. For good sense, prudence, sincerity, benevolence, unaffected piety, disinterested zeal in every good work, deep humanity and retiring modesty—for all the virtues which adorn the wife, the mother, and the friend—I never knew her superior."

In a letter written to my mother soon after this sad event my father says:

"May God give you strength to enable you to bear and say, 'His will be done.' She has gone from all trouble, care and sorrow to a holy immortality, there to rejoice and praise forever the God and Saviour she so long and truly served. Let that be our comfort and that our consolation. May our death be like hers, and may we meet in happiness in Heaven."

In another letter about the same time he writes:

"She was to me all that a mother could be, and I yield to none in admiration for her character, love for her virtues, and veneration for her memory."

At this time, my father's family and friends persuaded him to allow R. S. Weir, Professor of Painting and Drawing at the Academy, to paint his portrait. As far as I remember, there was only one sitting, and the artist had to finish it from memory or from the glimpses he obtained of his subject in the regular course of their daily lives at "The Point." This picture shows my father in the undress uniform of a Colonel of Engineers,[1] and many think it a very good likeness. To me, the expression of strength peculiar to his face is wanting, and the mouth fails to portray that sweetness of disposition so characteristic of his countenance. Still, it was like him at that time. My father never could bear to have his picture taken, and there are no likenesses of him that really give his sweet expression. Sitting for a picture was such a serious business with him that he never could "look pleasant."

In 1855 my father was appointed to the lieutenant-colonelcy of the Second Cavalry, one of the two regiments just raised. He left West Point to enter upon his new duties, and his family went to Arlington to live. During the fall and winter of 1855 and '56, the Second Cavalry was recruited and organised at Jefferson Barracks, Missouri, under the direction of Colonel Lee, and in the following spring was marched to western Texas, where it was assigned the duty of protecting the settlers in that wild country.

I did not see my father again until he came to my mother at Arlington after the death of her father, G. W. P. Custis, in October, 1857. He took charge of my mother's estate after her father's death, and commenced at once to put it in order—not an easy task, as it consisted of several plantations and many

---

[1] His appointment of Superintendent of the Military Academy carried with it the temporary rank of Colonel of Engineers.

negroes. I was at a boarding-school, after the family returned to Arlington, and saw my father only during the holidays, if he happened to be at home. He was always fond of farming, and took great interest in the improvements he immediately began at Arlington relating to the cultivation of the farm, to the buildings, roads, fences, fields, and stock, so that in a very short time the appearance of everything on the estate was improved. He often said that he longed for the time when he could have a farm of his own, where he could end his days in quiet and peace, interested in the care and improvement of his own land. This idea was always with him. In a letter to his son, written in July, 1865, referring to some proposed indictments of prominent Confederates, he says:

". . . As soon as I can ascertain their intention toward me, if not prevented, I shall endeavour to procure some humble, but quiet abode for your mother and sisters, where I hope they can be happy. As I before said, I want to get in some grass country where the natural product of the land will do much for my subsistence. . . ."

Again in a letter to his son, dated October, 1865, after he had accepted the presidency of Washington College, Lexington, Virginia:

"I should have selected a more quiet life and a more retired abode than Lexington. I should have preferred a small farm, where I could have earned my daily bread."

About this time I was given a gun of my own, and was allowed to go shooting by myself. My father, to give me an incentive, offered a reward for every crow-scalp I could bring him, and, in order that I might get to work at once, advanced a small sum with which to buy powder and shot, this sum to be returned to him out of the first scalps obtained. My industry and zeal were great, my hopes high, and by good luck I did succeed in bagging two crows about the second time I went out. I showed them with great pride to my father, intimating that I should shortly be able to return him his loan, and that he must be prepared to hand over to me very soon further rewards for my skill. His eyes twinkled, and his smile showed that he had strong doubts of my making an income by killing crows, and he was right, for I never killed another, though I tried hard and long.

I saw but little of my father after we left West Point. He went to Texas, as I have stated, in '55 and remained until the fall of '57, the time of my grandfather's death. He was then at Arlington about a year. Returning to his regiment, he remained in Texas until the autumn of '59, when he came again to Arlington, having applied for leave in order to finish the settling of my grandfather's estate. During this visit he was selected by the Secretary of War to suppress the famous "John Brown Raid," and was sent to Harper's Ferry in command of the United States troops.

From his memorandum book the following entries are taken:

"October 17, 1859. Received orders from the Secretary of War, in person, to repair in evening train to Harper's Ferry.

"Reached Harper's Ferry at 11 P. M. . . . Posted marines in the United States Armory. Waited until daylight, as a number of citizens were held as hostages, whose lives were threatened. Tuesday about sunrise, with twelve marines, under Lieutenant Green, broke in the door of the engine-house, secured the insurgents and relieved the prisoners unhurt. All the insurgents killed or mortally wounded, but four, John Brown, Stevens, Coppie, and Shields."

Brown was tried and convicted, and sentenced to be hanged on December 2, 1859. Colonel Lee writes as follows to his wife:

"Harper's Ferry, December 1, 1859.

"I arrived here, dearest Mary, yesterday about noon, with four companies from Fort Monroe, and was busy all the evening and night getting accommodation for the men, etc., and posting sentinels and pickets to insure timely notice of the approach of the enemy. The night has passed off quietly. The feelings of the community seemed to be calmed down, and I have been received with every kindness. Mr. Fry is among the officers from Old Point. There are several young men, former acquaintance of ours, as cadets, Mr. Bingham of Custis's class, Sam Cooper, etc., but the senior officers I never met before, except Captain Howe, the friend of our Cousin Harriet R——.

"I presume we are fixed here till after the 16th. To-morrow will probably be the last of Captain Brown. There will be less interest for the others, but still I think the troops will not be withdrawn till they are similarly disposed of.

"Custis will have informed you that I had to go to Baltimore the evening that I left you, to make arrangements for the transportation for the troops. ... This morning I was introduced to Mrs. Brown, who, with a Mrs. Tyndall and a Mr. and Mrs. McKim, all from Philadelphia, had come on to have a last interview with her husband. As it is a matter over which I have no control I referred them to General Taliaferro.[1]

"You must write to me at this place. I hope you are all well. Give love to everybody. Tell Smith [2] that no charming women have insisted on taking care of me as they are always doing of him—I am left to my own resources. I will write you again soon, and will always be truly and affectionately yours,

"R. E. LEE.

"MRS. M. C. LEE."


In February, 1860, he was ordered to take command of the Department of Texas. There he

[1] General William B. Taliaferro, commanding Virginia troops at Harper's Ferry.
[2] Sidney Smith Lee, of the United States Navy, his brother.

remained a year. The first months after his arrival were spent in the vain pursuit of the famous brigand, Cortinez, who was continually stealing across the Rio Grande, burning the homes, driving off the stock of the ranchmen, and then retreating into Mexico. The summer months he spent in San Antonio, and while there interested himself with the good people of that town in building an Episcopal church, to which he contributed largely.

# THE YOUTH OF LINCOLN

HE WAS long; he was strong; he was wiry. He was never sick, was always good-natured, never a bully, always a friend of the weak, the small and the unprotected. He must have been a funny-looking boy. His skin was sallow, and his hair was black, He wore a linsey-woolsey shirt, buckskin breeches, a coonskin cap, and heavy "clumps" of shoes. He grew so fast that his breeches never came down to the tops of his shoes, and, instead of stockings, you could always see "twelve inches of shinbones," sharp, blue, and narrow. He laughed much, was always ready to give and take jokes and hard knocks, had a squeaky, changing voice, a small head, big ears—and was always what Thackeray called "a gentle-man." Such was Abraham Lincoln at fifteen.

He was never cruel, mean, or unkind. His first composition was on cruelty to animals, written because he had tried to make the other boys stop "teasin' tarrypins"—that is, catching turtles and putting hot coals on their backs just to make them move along lively. He had to work hard at home; for his father would not, and things needed to be attended to if "the place" was to be kept from dropping to pieces.

He became a great reader. He read every book and newspaper he could get hold of, and if he came across anything in his reading that he wished to remember he would copy it on a shingle, because writing paper was scarce, and either learn it by heart or hide the shingle away until he could get some paper to copy it on. His father thought he read too much. "It will spile him for work," he said. "He don't do half enough about the place, as it is, now, and books and papers ain't no good." But Abraham, with all his reading, did more work than his father any day; his stepmother, too, took his side and at last got her husband to let the boy read and study at home. "Abe was a good son to me," she said, many many years after, "and we took particular care when he was reading not to disturb him. We would just let him read on and on till he quit of his own accord."

The boy kept a sort of shingle scrap-book; he kept a paper scrap-book, too. Into these he would put whatever he cared to keep—poetry, history, funny sayings, fine passages. He had a scrap-book for his arithmetic "sums," too, and one of these is still in existence with this boyish rhyme in a boyish scrawl, underneath one of his tables of weights and measures:

> Abraham Lincoln
> his hand and pen
> he will be good but
> god knows when.

God did know when; and that boy, all unconsciously, was working toward the day when his hand and pen were to do more for humanity than any other hand or pen of modern times.

Lamps and candles were almost unknown in his home, and Abraham, flat on his stomach, would often do his reading, writing, and ciphering in the firelight, as it flashed and flickered on the big hearth of his log-cabin home. An older cousin, John Hanks, who lived for a while with the Lincolns, says that when "Abe," as he always called the great President, would come home, as a boy, from his work, he would go to the cupboard, take a piece of corn bread for his supper, sit down on a chair, stretch out his long legs until they were higher than his head—and read, and read, and read. "Abe and I," said John Hanks, "worked barefoot; grubbed it, ploughed it, mowed and cradled it; ploughed corn, gathered corn, and shucked corn, and Abe read constantly whenever he could get a chance."

One day Abraham found that a man for whom he sometimes worked owned a copy of Weems's "Life of Washington." This was a famous book in its day. Abraham borrowed it at once. When he was not reading it, he put it away on a shelf—a clapboard resting on wooden pins. There was a big crack between the logs, behind the shelf, and one rainy day the "Life of Washington" fell into the crack and was soaked almost into pulp. Old Mr. Crawford, from whom Abraham borrowed the book, was a cross, cranky, and sour old fellow, and when the boy told him of the accident he said Abraham must "work the book out."

The boy agreed, and the old farmer kept him so strictly to his promise that he made him "pull fodder" for the cattle three days, as payment for the book! And that is the way that Abraham Lincoln bought his first book. For he dried the copy of Weems's "Life of Washington" and put it in his "library." But what boy or girl of today would like to buy books at such a price?

This was the boy-life of Abraham Lincoln. It was a life of poverty, privation, hard work, little play, and less money. The boy did not love work. But he worked. His father was rough and often harsh and hard to him, and what Abraham learned was by making the most of his spare time. He was inquisitive, active, and hardy, and, in his comfortless boyhood, he was learning lessons of self-denial, independence, pluck, shrewdness, kindness, and persistence.

In the spring of 1830, there was another "moving time" for the Lincolns. The corn and the cattle, the farm and its hogs were all sold at public "vandoo," or auction, at low figures; and with all their household goods on a big "ironed" wagon drawn by four oxen, the three related families of Hanks, Hall and Lincoln, thirteen in all, pushed on through the mud and across rivers, high from the spring freshets, out of Indiana, into Illinois.

Abraham held the "gad" and guided the oxen. He carried with him, also, a little stock of pins, needles, thread, and buttons. These he peddled along the way; and, at last, after fifteen days of slow travel, the emigrants came to the spot picked out for a home. This time it was on a small bluff on the north fork of the Sangamon River, ten miles west of the town of Decatur. The usual log house was built; the boys, with the oxen, "broke up," or cleared, fifteen acres of land, and split enough rails to fence it in. Abraham could swing his broad-axe better than any man or boy in the West; at one stroke he could bury the axe-blade to the haft, in a log, and he was already famous as an expert rail-splitter.

By this time his people were settled in their new home, Abraham Lincoln was twenty-one. He was "of age"—he was a man! By the law of the land he was freed from his father's control; he could shift for himself, and he determined to do so. This did not mean that he disliked his father. It simply meant that he had no intention of following his father's example. Thomas Lincoln had demanded all the work and all the wages his son could earn or do, and Abraham felt that he could not have a fair chance to accomplish anything or get ahead in the world if he continued living with this shiftless, never-satisfied, do-nothing man.

So he struck out for himself. In the summer of 1830, Abraham left home and hired out on his own account, wherever he could get a job in the new country into which he had come. In that region of big farms and no fences, these latter were needed, and Abraham Lincoln's stalwart arm and well-swung axe came well into play, cutting up logs for fences.

He was what was called in that western country a "rail-splitter." Indeed, one of the first things he did when he struck out for himself was to split four hundred rails for every yard of "blue jeans" necessary to make him a pair of trousers. From which it will be seen that work was easier to get than clothes.

He soon became as much of a favourite in Illinois as he had been in Indiana. Other work came to him, and, in 1831, he "hired out" with a man named Offutt to help sail a flat-boat down the Mississippi to New Orleans. Mr. Offutt had heard that "Abe Lincoln" was a good river-hand, strong, steady, honest, reliable, accustomed to boating, and that he had already made one trip down the river. So he engaged young Lincoln at what seemed to the young rail-splitter princely wages—fifty cents a day, and a third share in the sixty dollars which was to be divided among the three boatmen at the end of the trip.

They built the flat-boat at a saw mill near a place called Sangamon town, "Abe" serving as cook of the camp while the boat was being built. Then, loading the craft with barrel-pork, hogs, and corn, they started on their voyage south. At a place called New Salem the flat-boat ran aground; but Lincoln's ingenuity got it off. He rigged up a queer contrivance of his own invention and lifted the boat off and over the obstruction, while all New Salem stood on the bank, first to criticise and then to applaud.

Just what this invention was I cannot explain. But if you ever go into the patent office at Washington, ask to see Abraham Lincoln's patent for transporting river boats over snags and shoals. The wooden model is there; for, so pleased was Lincoln with the success that he thought seriously of becoming an inventor, and his first design was the patent granted to him in 1849, the idea for which grew out of this successful floating of Offutt's flat-boat over the river snags at New Salem nineteen years before.

Once again he visited New Orleans, returning home, as before, by steamboat. That voyage is remarkable, because it first opened young Lincoln's eyes to the enormity of African slavery. Of course, he had seen slaves before; but the sight of a slave sale in the old market place of New Orleans seems to have aroused his anger and given him an intense hatred of slave-holding. He, himself, declared, years after, that it was that visit to New Orleans, that had set him so strongly against slavery.

There is a story told by one of his companions that Lincoln looked for a while upon the dreadful scenes of the slave market and then, turning away, said excitedly, "Come away, boys! If I ever get a chance, some day, to hit that thing"—and he flung his long arm toward the dreadful auction block—"I'll hit it hard."

Soon after he returned from his flat-boat trip to New Orleans he had an opportunity to show that he could not and would not stand what is termed "foul play." The same Mr. Offutt who had hired Lincoln to be one of his flat-boat "boys," gave him another opportunity for work. Offutt was what is called in the West a "hustler"; he had lots of "great ideas" and plans for making money; and, among his numerous enterprises, was one to open a country store and mill at New Salem—the very same village on the Sangamon where, by his "patent invention," Lincoln had lifted the flat-boat off the snags.

Mr. Offutt had taken a great fancy to Lincoln, and offered him a place as clerk in the New Salem store. The young fellow jumped at the chance. It seemed to him quite an improvement on being a farm-hand, a flat-boatman, or a rail-splitter. It was, indeed, a step upward; for it gave him better opportunities for self-instruction and more chances for getting ahead.

Offutt's store was a favourite "loafing place" for the New Salem boys and young men. Among these, were some of the roughest fellows in the settlement. They were known as the "Clary Grove Boys," and they were always ready for a fight, in which they would, sometimes, prove themselves to be bullies and tormentors. When, therefore, Offutt began to brag about his new clerk the Clary Grove Boys made fun at him; whereupon the storekeeper cried: "What's that? You can throw him? Well, I reckon not; Abe Lincoln can out-run, out-walk, out-rassle, knock out, and throw down any man in Sangamon County." This was too much for the Clary Grove Boys. They took up Offutt's challenge, and, against "Abe," set up, as their champion and "best man," one Jack Armstrong.

All this was done without Lincoln's knowledge. He had no desire to get into a row with anyone—least of all with the bullies who made up the Clary Grove Boys.

"I won't do it," he said, when Offutt told him of the proposed wrestling match. "I never tussle and scuffle, and I will not. I don't like this wooling and pulling."

"Don't let them call you a coward, Abe," said Offutt.

Of course, you know what the end would be to such an affair. Nobody likes to be called a coward—especially when he knows he is not one. So, at last, Lincoln consented to "rassle" with Jack Armstrong. They met, with all the boys as spectators. They wrestled, and tugged, and clenched, but without result. Both young fellows were equally matched in strength. "It's no use, Jack," Lincoln at last declared. "Let's quit. You can't throw me, and I can't throw you. That's enough."

With that, all Jack's backers began to cry "coward!" and urged on the champion to another tussle. Jack Armstrong was now determined to win, by fair means or foul. He tried the latter, and, contrary to all rules of wrestling began to kick and trip, while his supporters stood ready to help, if need be, by breaking in with a regular free fight. This "foul play" roused the lion in Lincoln. He hated unfairness, and at once resented it. He suddenly put forth his Samson-like strength, grabbed the champion of the Clary Grove Boys by the throat, and, lifting him from the ground, held him at arm's length and shook him as a dog shakes a rat. Then he flung him to the ground, and, facing the amazed and yelling crowd, he cried: "You cowards! You know I don't want to fight; but if you try any such games, I'll tackle the whole lot of you. I've won the fight."

He had. From that day, no man in all that region dared to "tackle" young Lincoln, or to taunt him with cowardice. And Jack Armstrong was his devoted friend and admirer.

I have told you more, perhaps, of the famous fight than I ought—not because it was a fight, but because it gives you a glimpse of Abraham Lincoln's character. He disliked rows; he was too kind-hearted and good-natured to wish to quarrel with any one; but he hated unfairness, and was enraged at anything like persecution or bullying. If you will look up Shakespeare's play of "Hamlet" you will see that Lincoln was ready to act upon the advice that old Polonius gave to his son Laertes:

> "Beware
> Of entrance to a quarrel; but, being in,
> Bear it that the opposer may beware of thee."

He became quite a man in that little community. As a clerk he was obliging and strictly honest. He was the judge and the settler of all disputes, and none thought of combating his decisions. He was the village peacemaker. He hated profanity, drunkenness, and unkindness to women. He was feared and respected by all, and even the Clary Grove Boys declared, at last, that he was "the cleverest feller that ever broke into the settlement."

All the time, too, he was trying to improve himself. He liked to sit around and talk and tell stories, just the same as ever; but he saw this was not the way to get on in the world. He worked, whenever he had the chance, outside of his store duties; and once, when trade was dull and hands were short in the clearing, he "turned to" and split enough logs into rails to make a pen for a thousand hogs.

When he was not at work he devoted himself to his books. He could "read, write, and cipher"— this was more education than most men about him possessed; but he hoped, some day, to go before the public; to do this, he knew he must speak and write correctly. He talked to the village schoolmaster, who advised him to study English grammar.

"Well, if I had a grammar," said Lincoln, "I'd begin now. Have you got one?"

The schoolmaster had no grammar; but he told "Abe" of a man, six miles off, who owned one. Thereupon, Lincoln started upon the run to borrow that grammar. He brought it back so quickly that the schoolmaster was astonished. Then he set to work to learn the "rules and exceptions." He studied that grammar, stretched full length on the store-counter, or under a tree outside the store, or at night before a blazing fire of shavings in the cooper's shop. And soon, he had mastered it. He borrowed every book in New Salem; he made the schoolmaster give him lessons in the store; he button-holed every stranger that came into the place "who looked as though he knew anything"; until, at last, every one in New Salem was ready to echo Offutt's boast that "Abe Lincoln" knew more than any man "in these United States." One day, in the bottom of an old barrel of trash, he made a splendid "find." It was two old law books. He read and re-read them, got all the sense and argument out of their dry pages, blossomed into a debater, began to dream of being a lawyer, and became so skilled in seeing through and settling knotty questions that, once again, New Salem wondered at this clerk of Offutt's, who was as long of head as of arms and legs, and declared that "Abe Lincoln could out-argue any ten men in the settlement."

In all the history of America there has been no man who started lower and climbed higher than Abraham Lincoln, the backwoods boy. He never "slipped back." He always kept going ahead. He broadened his mind, enlarged his outlook, and led his companions rather than let them lead him. He was jolly company, good-natured, kind-hearted, fond of jokes and stories and a good time generally; but he was the champion of the weak, the friend of the friendless, as true a knight and as full of chivalry as any one of the heroes in armour of whom you read in "Ivanhoe" or "The Talisman." He never cheated, never lied, never took an unfair advantage of anyone;

but he was ambitious, strong-willed, a bold fighter and a tough adversary—a fellow who would never "say die"; and who, therefore, succeeded.

# FATHER DAMIEN

AS WE approached Molokai I found that the slow work of centuries had nearly covered its lava with verdure. At dawn we were opposite Kalaupapa. Two little spired churches, looking precisely alike, caught my eye first, and around them were dotted the white cottages of the lepers. But the sea was too rough for us to land. The waves dashed against the rocks, and the spray rose fifty feet into the air.

We went on to Kalawao, but were again disappointed; it was too dangerous to disembark. Finally it was decided to put off a boat for a rocky point about a mile and a half distant from the town. Climbing down this point we saw about twenty lepers, and "There is Father Damien!" said our purser; and, slowly moving along the hillside, I saw a dark figure with a large straw hat. He came rather painfully down, and sat near the water-side, and we exchanged friendly signals across the waves while my baggage was being got out of the hold—a long business, owing to the violence of the sea. At last all was ready, and we went swinging across the waves, and finally chose a fit moment for leaping on shore. Father Damien caught me by the hand, and a hearty welcome shone from his kindly face as he helped me up the rock. He immediately called me by my name, "Edward," and said it was "like everything else, a providence," that he had met me at that irregular landing-place, for he had expected the ship to stop at Kalaupapa.

He was now forty-nine years old—a thick-set, strongly built man, with black curly hair and short beard, turning gray. His countenance must have been handsome, with a full, well-curved mouth and a short, straight nose; but he was now a good deal disfigured by leprosy, though not so badly as to make it anything but a pleasure to look at his bright, sensible face. His forehead was swollen and rigid, the eyebrows gone, the nose somewhat sunk, and the ears greatly enlarged. His hands and face looked uneven with a sort of incipient boils, and his body also showed many signs of the disease, but he assured me that he had felt little or no pain since he had tried Dr. Goto's system of hot baths and Japanese medicine. The bathrooms that have been provided by the Government are very nice.

A large wooden box of presents from English friends, had been unshipped with the gurjun oil. It was, however, so large that Father Damien said it would be impossible for his lepers either to land it from the boat or to carry it to Kalawao, and that it must be returned to the steamer and landed on some voyage when the sea was quieter. But I could not give up the pleasure of his enjoyment in its contents, so after some delay it was forced open in the boat, and the things were handed out one by one across the waves. The lepers all came round with their poor marred faces, and the presents were carried home by them and our two selves.

As we ascended the hill on which the village is built Father Damien showed me on our left the chicken farm. The lepers are justly proud of it, and before many days I had a fine fowl sent me for dinner, which, after a little natural timidity, I ate with thankfulness.

On arriving at Kalawao we speedily found ourselves inside the half-finished church which was the darling of his heart. How he enjoyed planning the places where the pictures which I had just brought him should be placed! By the side of this church he showed me the palm-tree under which he lived for some weeks when he first arrived at the settlement, in 1873. His own little four-roomed house almost joins the church.

After dinner we went up the little flight of steps which led to Father Damien's balcony. This was shaded by a honeysuckle in blossom. Some of my happiest times at Molokai were spent in this little balcony, sketching him and listening to what he said. The lepers came up to watch my progress, and it was pleasant to see how happy and at home they were. Their poor faces were often swelled and drawn and distorted, with bloodshot goggle eyes.

I offered to give a photograph of the picture to his brother in Belgium, but he said perhaps it would be better not to do so, as it might pain him to see how he was disfigured. He looked mournfully at my work. "What an ugly face!" he said; "I did not know the disease had made such progress." Looking-glasses are not in great request at Molokai!

While I sketched him he often read his breviary. At other times we talked on subjects that interested us both, especially about the work of the Church Army, and sometimes I sang hymns to him—among others, "Brief life is here our portion," "Art thou weary, art thou languid?" and "Safe home in port." At such times the expression of his face was particularly sweet and tender. One day I asked him if he would like to send a message to Cardinal Manning. He said that it was not for such as he to send a message to so great a dignitary, but after a moment's hesitation he added, "I send my humble respects and thanks."

I need scarcely say that he gave himself no airs of martyr, saint, or hero—a humbler man I never saw. He smiled modestly and deprecatingly when I gave him the Bishop of Peterborough's message— "He won't accept the blessing of a heretic bishop, but tell him that he has my prayers, and ask him to give me his." "Does he call himself a heretic bishop?" he asked doubtfully, and I had to explain that the bishop had probably used the term playfully.

One day he told me about his early history. He was born on the 3rd of January, 1841, near Louvain in Belgium. On his nineteenth birthday his father took him to see his brother, who was then preparing for the priesthood, and he left him there to dine, while he himself went on to the neighbouring town. Young Joseph (this was his baptismal name) decided that there was the opportunity for taking the step which he had long been desiring to take, and when his father came back he told him that he wished to return home no more, and that it would be better thus to miss the pain of farewells. His father consented unwillingly, but, as he was obliged to hurry to the conveyance which was to take him home, there was no time for demur, and they parted at the station. Afterward, when all was settled, Joseph revisited his home, and received his mother's approval and blessing.

His brother was bent on going to the South Seas for mission work, and all was arranged accordingly; but at the last he was laid low with fever, and, to his bitter disappointment, forbidden to go. The impetuous Joseph asked if it would be a consolation to his brother if he were to go instead, and, receiving an affirmative answer, he wrote surreptitiously, offering himself, and begging that he might be sent, though his education was not yet finished. The students were not allowed to send out letters till they had been submitted to the Superior, but Joseph ventured to disobey.

One day, as he sat at his studies, the Superior came in, and said, with a tender reproach, "Oh, you impatient boy! you have written this letter, and you are to go."

Joseph jumped up, and ran out, and leaped about like a young colt.

"Is he crazy?" said the other students.

He worked for some years on other islands in the Pacific, but it happened that he was one day in 1873 present at the dedication of a chapel in the island of Maui, when the bishop was lamenting that it was impossible for him to send a missioner to the lepers at Molokai and still less to provide them with a pastor. He had only been able to send them occasional and temporary help. Some young priests had just arrived in Hawaii for mission work, and Father Damien instantly spoke.

"Monseigneur," said he, "here are your new missioners; one of them could take my district, and if you will be kind enough to allow it, I will go to Molokai and labour for the poor lepers whose wretched state of bodily and spiritual misfortune has often made my heart bleed within me."

His offer was accepted, and that very day, without any farewells, he embarked on a boat that was taking some cattle to the leper settlement. When he first put his foot on the island he said to himself, "Now Joseph, my boy, this is your life-work."

I did not find one person in the Sandwich Islands who had the least doubt as to leprosy being contagious, though it is possible to be exposed to the disease for years without contracting it. Father Damien told me that he had always expected that he should sooner or later become a leper, though exactly how he caught it he does not know. But it was not likely that he would escape, as he was constantly living in a polluted atmosphere, dressing the sufferers' sores, washing their bodies, visiting their death-beds, and even digging their graves. In his own words is a report of the state of things at Molokai sixteen years ago, and I think a portion will be interesting:

"By special providence of our Divine Lord, who during His public life showed a particular sympathy for the lepers, my way was traced toward Kalawao in May, 1873. I was then thirty-three years of age, enjoying a robust good health.

"About eighty of the lepers were in the hospital; the others, with a very few Kokuas (helpers), had taken their abode farther up toward the valley. They had cut down the old pandanus groves to build their houses, though a great many had nothing but branches of castor-oil trees with which to construct their small shelters. These frail frames were covered with ki leaves or with sugar-cane leaves, the best ones with pili grass. I, myself, was sheltered during several weeks under the single pandanus-tree which is preserved up to the present in the churchyard. Under such primitive roofs were living without distinction of age or sex, old or new cases, all more or less strangers one to another, those unfortunate outcasts of society. They passed their time with playing cards, hula (native dances), drinking fermented ki-root beer, home-made alcohol, and with the sequels of all this. Their clothes were far from being clean and decent, on account of the scarcity of water, which had to be brought at that time from a great distance. Many a time in fulfilling my priestly duty at their domiciles I have been compelled to run outside to breathe fresh air. To counteract the bad smell I made myself accustomed to the use of tobacco, whereupon the smell of the pipe preserved me somewhat from carrying in my clothes the noxious odour of the lepers. At that time the progress of the disease was fearful, and the rate of mortality very high. The miserable condition of the settlement gave it the name of a living graveyard, which name, I am happy to state, is to-day no longer applicable to our place."

In 1874 a "cona" (south) wind blew down most of the lepers' wretched, rotten abodes, and the poor sufferers lay shivering in the wind and rain, with clothes and blankets wet through. In a few days the grass beneath their sleeping-mats began to emit a "very unpleasant vapour." "I at once," says Father Damien, "called the attention of our sympathising agent to the fact, and very soon there arrived several schooner-loads of scantling to build solid frames with, and all lepers in distress received, on application, the necessary material for the erection of decent houses." Friends sent them rough boards and shingles and flooring. Some of the lepers had a little money, and hired carpenters. For those without means the priest, with his leper boys, did the work of erecting a good many small houses.

"I remember well that when I arrived here," again says Father Damien, "the poor people were without any medicines, with the exception of a few physics and their own native remedies. It was a common sight to see people going round with fearful ulcers, which, for the want of a few rags or a piece of lint and a little salve, were left exposed. Not only were their sores neglected but any one getting a fever, or any of the numerous ailments that lepers are heir to, was carried off for want of some simple medicine.

"Previous to my arrival here it was acknowledged and spoken of in the public papers as well as in private letters that the greatest want at Kalawao was a spiritual leader. It was owing in a great measure to this want that vice as a general rule existed instead of virtue, and degradation of the lowest type went ahead as a leader of the community. . . . When once the disease prostrated them women and children were often cast out, and had to find some other shelter. Sometimes they were laid behind a stone wall, and left there to die, and at other times a hired hand would carry them to the hospital.

"As there were so many dying people, my priestly duty toward them often gave me the opportunity to visit them at their domiciles, and although my exhortations were especially addressed to the prostrated often they would fall upon the ears of public sinners, who little by little became conscious of the consequences of their wicked lives, and began to reform, and thus, with the hope in a merciful Saviour, gave up their bad habits.

"Kindness to all, charity to the needy, a sympathising hand to the sufferers and the dying, in conjunction with a solid religious instruction to my listeners, have been my constant means to introduce moral habits among the lepers. I am happy to say that, assisted by the local administration, my labours here, which seemed to be almost in vain at the beginning, have, thanks to a kind Providence, been greatly crowned with success."

The water supply of Molokai was a pleasant subject with Father Damien. When he first arrived the lepers could only obtain water by carrying it from the gulch on their poor shoulders; they had also to take their clothes to some distance when they required washing, and it was no wonder that they lived in a very dirty state. He was much exercised about the matter, and one day, to his great joy, he was told that at the end of a valley called Waihanau there was a natural reservoir. He set out with two white men and some of his boys, and travelled up the valley till he came with delight to a nearly circular basin of most delicious ice-cold water. Its diameter was seventy-two feet by fifty-five, and not far from the bank they found, on sounding, that it was eighteen feet deep. There it lay at the foot of a high cliff, and he was informed by the natives that there had never been a drought in which this basin had dried up. He did not rest till a supply of waterpipes had been sent them, which he and all the able lepers went to work and laid. Henceforth clear sweet water has been available for all who desire to drink, to wash, or to bathe.

It was after living at the leper settlement for about ten years that Father Damien began to suspect that he was a leper. The doctors assured him that this was not the case. But he once scalded himself in his foot, and to his horror he felt no pain.

Anæsthesia had begun, and soon other fatal signs appeared. One day he asked Dr. Arning, the great German doctor who was then resident in Molokai, to examine him carefully.

"I cannot bear to tell you," said Dr. Arning, "but what you say is true."

"It is no shock to me," said Damien, "for I have felt sure of it."

I may mention here that there are three kinds of leprosy. Father Damien suffered (as is often the case) both from the anæsthetic and the tubercular forms of the disease. "Whenever I preach to my people," he said, "I do not say 'my brethren,' as you do, but 'we lepers.' People pity me and think me unfortunate, but I think myself the happiest of missionaries."

Henceforth he came under the law of segregation, and journeys to the other parts of the islands were forbidden. But he worked on with the same sturdy, cheerful fortitude, accepting the will of God with gladness, undaunted by the continual reminders of his coming fate, which met him in the poor creatures around him.

"I would not be cured," he said to me, "if the price of my cure was that I must leave the island and give up my work."

A lady wrote to him, "You have given up all earthly things to serve God here and to help others, and I believe you must have *now* joy that nothing can take from you and a great reward hereafter."

"Tell her," he said, with a quiet smile, "that it is true. I *do* have that joy now."

He seldom talked of himself except in answer to questions, and he had always about him the simplicity of a great man—"clothed with humility."

My last letter from him is dated:

"KALAWAO, *28th February,* 1889.

"My DEAR EDWARD CLIFFORD—Your sympathising letter of 24th gives me some relief in my rather distressed condition. I try my best to carry, without much complaining and in a practical way, for my poor soul's sanctification, the long-foreseen miseries of the disease, which, after all, is a providential agent to detach the heart from all earthly affection, and prompts much the desire of a Christian soul to be united—the sooner the better—with Him who is her only life.

"During your long travelling road homeward please do not forget the narrow road. We both have to walk carefully, so as to meet together at the home of our common and eternal Father. My kind regards and prayers and good wishes for all sympathising friends. *Bon voyage, mon cher ami, et au revoir au ceil— Votus tuus,*

"J. Damien."

About three weeks after writing this letter he felt sure that his end was near, and on the 28th March he took to his bed.

"You see my hands," he said. "All the wounds are healing and the crust is becoming black. You know that is a sign of death. Look at my eyes too. I have seen so many lepers die that I cannot be mistaken. Death is not far off. I should have liked to see the Bishop again, but *le bon Dieu* is calling me to keep Easter with Himself. God be blessed!

"How good He is to have preserved me long enough to have two priests by my side at my last moments, and also to have the good Sisters of Charity at the *Léproserie*. That has been my *Nunc Dimittis*. The work of the lepers is assured, and I am no longer necessary, and so will go up yonder."

Father Wendolen said, "When you are up above, father, you will not forget those you leave orphans behind you?"

"Oh no! If I have any credit with God, I will intercede for all in the *Léproserie*."

"And will you, like Elijah, leave me your mantle, my father, in order that I may have your great heart?"

"Why, what would you do with it?" said the dying martyr, "it is full of leprosy."

He rallied for a little while after this, and his watchers even had a little hope that his days might be lengthened. Father Conradi, Father Wendolen, and Brother Joseph were much in his company. Brother James was his constant nurse. The Sisters from Kalaupapa visited him often, and it is good to think that the sweet placid face and gentle voice of

377

the Mother were near him in his last days. Everybody admired his wonderful patience. He who had been so ardent, so strong, and so playful, was now powerless on his couch. He lay on the ground on a wretched mattress like the poorest leper. They had the greatest difficulty in getting him to accept a bed. "And how poorly off he was; he who had spent so much money to relieve the lepers had so forgotten himself that he had none of the comforts and scarcely the necessaries of life." Sometimes he suffered intensely; sometimes he was partly unconscious. He said that he was continually conscious of two persons being present with him. One was at the head of his bed and one at his feet. But who they were he did not say. The terrible disease had concentrated itself in his mouth and throat. As he lay there in his tiny domicile, with the roar of the sea getting fainter to his poor diseased ears, and the kind face of Brother James becoming gradually indistinct before his failing eyes, did the thought come to him that after all his work was poor, and his life half a failure? Many whom he had hoped much of had disappointed him. Not much praise had reached him. The tide of affection and sympathy from England had cheered him, but England was so far off that it seemed almost like sympathy and affection from a star. Churches were built, schools and hospitals were in working order, but there was still much to be done. He was only forty-nine, and he was dying.

"Well! God's will be done. He knows best. My work, with all its faults and failures, is in His hands, and before Easter I shall see my Saviour."

The breathing grew more laboured, the leprous eyes were clouded, the once stalwart frame was fast becoming rigid. The sound of the passing bell was heard, and the wail of the wretched lepers pierced the air. ... The last flickering breath was breathed, and the soul of Joseph Damien de Veuster arose like a lark to God.

www.ingramcontent.com/pod-product-compliance
Lightning Source LLC
Chambersburg PA
CBHW032032080426
42733CB00006B/59